9/12

9/12

The Epic Battle of the Ground Zero Responders

WILLIAM H. GRONER
AND TOM TEICHOLZ

Potomac Books / An imprint of the University of Nebraska Press

Manufactured in the United States of America.

Library of Congress Control Number: 2019933374

Set in Lyon Text by Mikala R. Kolander.

For Sue

To the many thousands who
served tirelessly, selflessly,
and at great personal cost in
the aftermath of 9/11

CONTENTS

PHOTOGRAPHS

PREFACE

As one of the attorneys who represented the Ground Zero responders, I had a unique perspective on this story, from our first client in 2003 to the negotiations that led, more than eight years later, to a settlement for more than ten thousand responders. More than once, I said to my colleagues and my family that the story of what the responders endured needed to be told, and that what we were witnessing in the World Trade Center litigation, in all its dimensions, was a unique historical undertaking.

Telling this story was a great responsibility and a great challenge to do justice to what occurred. Tom Teicholz and I quickly realized the impossibility of telling every responder's story. So here the few must represent the many.

There were also hundreds of attorneys, paralegals, associates, assistants, clerks, doctors, nurses, legal experts, medical experts, scientific experts, consultants of all stripes, government officials and their staffs, and journalists who were involved in ways large and small in the events chronicled herein, only a few of whom appear in these pages. We are sorry we can neither include nor mention all of them but are grateful nonetheless for their every contribution. This was more than a legal story; it was also a medical story, a science story, a political story, and a story for which the press reporting on all this played a critical role.

As the story expanded to include these various narratives, my own role became one of many, and so when I appear in this narrative, I do so in the third person. It is my sincere hope that doing so freed me and Tom to tell this complex story more completely.

Bill Groner

ACKNOWLEDGMENTS

There are many very talented and dedicated people to thank for 9/12, a book whose important subject matter led to generous and extensive cooperation from our interview subjects and that has proven to be a magnet for exceptional literary and publishing professionals.

Philip Turner, editorial consultant extraordinaire, who was the project's first champion, helped with its conception. Dan Strone of Trident Media Group, our superagent, became devoted to this project before a proposal was even completed and has been an indefatigable advocate of the book's importance above and beyond the call of duty. A shared cab ride with Laura Yorke turned into an invaluable editorial and publishing resource. We also want to thank Elsye Endick and Lucy Gubernick for research, Ellen Shapiro for fact-checking, and Jason Spira-Bauer for photo research. Tom Swanson of Potomac Books was a more supportive editor than any writer could hope for. We also thank Potomac Books editorial, marketing, and publicity departments for their enthusiasm in promoting our work.

No man is an island. We thank our wives, Sue Groner and Amy Rappeport, and our children, Victoria and Hudson Groner and Natasha Teicholz, for their support, indulgence, and understanding regarding the time away from family that such an undertaking requires. We could not have done it without them.

Finally, we'd like to thank all the first responders we interviewed, all those who appear in the book and the many more who don't. Their sense of duty, their courage and perseverance, and their hard work under difficult and hazardous conditions, at great personal risk, in the face of the most horrific occurrence in our times, was instrumental in New York's recovery in the days and months following the attacks on the World Trade Center.

9/12

DARKNESS

PROLOGUE

As the Godzilla-like cloud engulfed all in its path, what had been a bright sunny day went totally black, covering everything and everyone in thick layers of dust and debris, covering cars, buses, and emergency vehicles.

That morning, September 11, 2001, thousands were staring at the Twin Towers of the World Trade Center. They had been transfixed since the moment when, at 8:46 a.m., a Boeing 767 passenger plane flew into the north side of One World Trade Center (the North Tower). Millions more would watch on TV as another 767 crashed into the South Tower (Two World Trade Center) at 9:03 a.m. Fifty-six minutes after that second unimaginable disaster, they heard a rumbling and watched as an immense bulbous gray cloud swaddled the top floors of the South Tower before bringing down the entire 110-story building. Less than ninety minutes later, the North Tower too collapsed in on itself, pancaking, one floor crushing the one beneath it, as another enormous cloud grew, enveloping the Tower as it disintegrated, spewing dust and debris through most of Lower Manhattan.

The giant cloud, which can be viewed to this day in dozens upon dozens of YouTube videos, spontaneously expanded in height and girth, producing new clouds as big as buildings. The dust shoved its way down streets and between buildings in Lower Manhattan, gathering speed and volume like a tsunami, pushing debris through glass doors and windows, and sending a plume high into space. People tried to outrun the dust storm, but with little success, while many took cover in doorways or under parked vehicles.

The expanse of this smoldering pyre was so great that astronaut Frank L. Culbertson Jr., was able to photograph it from a window on the International Space Station. The cloud was so large that it seemed to linger in place even as it expanded, and like trying to see in a snowstorm, those engulfed by it could only vaguely make out figures and objects. What mattered, they thought, was getting away from the Towers' collapse, the falling steel and concrete and glass. They didn't realize their deadliest attacker was all around them, in the air they breathed.

PART ONE

In 2002 NYPD Detective Candiace Baker, who worked at Internal Affairs, was suffering from a persistent cough. Otherwise she felt fine. She had no other symptoms: no fever or sore throat, no irritated eyes. But Baker kept coughing and coughing. She was trying to treat it with basic over-the-counter cough medicine and by drinking hot tea. A lot of people noticed that she couldn't talk without coughing, but it now seemed normal to her. Since nothing else hurt, it didn't seem important.

Still, when her ears started hurting, she decided to see a doctor. She told him, "I think I have an ear infection. I just need ear drops." While he checked her ears he asked her how long she'd had her cough. Baker wasn't sure but said it had been a while. She just wanted the ear drops. The doctor instead ran a series of tests to see what was going on. Afterward he wanted to know how long she'd had a respiratory condition.

"I don't have any respiratory condition," Baker said.

"Yes, we believe that you do," the doctor replied.

The doctor then administered a cardiogram. Looking at the results prompted him to ask how long she had had a heart condition.

"I don't have a heart condition," Baker said.

The doctor replied, "We believe that you do."

"I can't. I don't have the time. I'm a single mother." Baker was insistent: all she wanted was ear drops. She had to get back to work.

The doctor explained that symptoms she had ignored for months, such as a burning in her stomach, throat, and chest (which she thought was heartburn from something she ate), as well as her unrelenting cough, were potentially serious. He sent her to a series of experts, including a cardiologist and a pulmonologist.

Dr. Sherma Winchester-Penny, the cardiologist, had an office some sixty miles north of New York City. She specialized in treating women with heart disease in a holistic manner and with the care she learned working as a nurse before she went to medical school. After a series of examinations, she sat Baker down to try to figure out why she had become so sick so suddenly.

She began by asking Baker about her job and what exactly she did. "It's just work—office work" was Baker's response. Winchester-Penny asked Baker to walk her through her work history. Baker answered that she worked for the Police Department, for the Internal Affairs Division. She wasn't in the field, and her duties were, for the most part, administrative and deskbound.

Her police career had begun in her mid-twenties, when she went to work for the New York City Transit Police. She started out on patrol. During one incident, she was injured while subduing an assailant. Her back was sprained, and she had ongoing back pain. As a result, she was put on restricted duty, mostly assigned to work a desk job while she healed. She was also assigned as a driver for the chief of her department, Raul Martinez.

After the New York Police Department merged with the Transit Police, Baker made a lateral transfer to the NYPD. She worked various assignments, including in the chief's office, and then was transferred to work in Internal Affairs, where she was again working for Martinez. She started out in the command center, the main hub where people call in to make complaints against officers or to complain about what occurred during the time of the incident or arrest. On the personal front, her son had been born in 1989, and they had moved to Staten Island.

Winchester-Penny explained that it didn't make sense that Baker had had a clean health record at her last full physical, had never suffered more than a cold, and then, all of sudden, was diagnosed with multiple conditions. "It has to be something you were exposed to," the doctor suggested. It was then that Winchester-Penny asked a simple question: "What about when you worked on the Ground Zero cleanup?"

"Honest to God, I had never thought about that," Baker said later. The doctor wanted to know everything that had happened to her on 9/11 and on the days that followed.

On the morning of September 11, 2001, Baker was sitting at her desk at One Police Plaza when she heard a boom. She chalked it up to somebody moving something or something falling. It was just a noise in New York City. When she learned that a plane had flown into the North Tower, Baker joined her fellow detectives in their gym room, which had a panoramic view of the WTC. There she watched as the second plane flew into the South Tower. She didn't understand what was happening, but tears flooded her eyes. Other detectives were crying as well.

Baker was dispatched to several different hospitals to determine the number of injured. When so few showed up, she realized most of the victims were fatalities.

Baker was soon assigned to the missing persons' hotline. She took hundreds of phone calls. To this day, she remembers them vividly: voices full of fear and the desperation of those who didn't know what had become of their loved ones. Baker and her fellow officers sat in a small room answering all those phone calls, taking down names, addresses, phone numbers, and other information. After each call, she would stand, walk to the water cooler, have a drink of water, and wipe away tears. Then she would go back and sit down, waiting for the next phone call to come in.

Mayor Rudolph Giuliani arrived in Downtown just after the second plane hit. He went first to Seven World Trade Center, whose 23rd floor housed the Office of Emergency Management command center that he had built at great expense after the 1993 World Trade Center bombing. The $13 million facility opened in 1999. It was a fifty-thousand-square-foot armored bunker with its own power and advanced communications capabilities, designed to be hurricane- and blast-proof. Those who wondered at the wisdom of housing the command center so close to the site of the 1993 attack may have had a point. On the morning of 9/11, debris from the plane crashes had started fires in Seven World Trade Center, so the building was evacuated. No one, not even the mayor, was allowed in and, as a consequence, the command center was unusable.

The mayor then led a group of city officials, including Deputy Mayor Anthony Coles, along with reporters, through the blizzard of smoke and ash to several locations near where the Twin Towers had stood, looking to set up a makeshift headquarters. (In pictures taken that day Deputy Mayor Anthony Coles, the son of a pulmonologist, was one of the few officials wearing a face mask for protection.) Giuliani told the reporters to tell people, "Keep walking north. Keep walking." He and his entourage went to 75 Barclay Street, where there were working landlines. When the second tower fell, Giuliani and his group evacuated Barclay Street and headed to a vacant fire station on W. Houston Street and Sixth Avenue. From there they decided to head to the Police Academy on 20th Street and use that as their command post.

John Miller, reporting live from the studios of ABC TV, was explaining why New York was one of the best-prepared cities to mount an emergency response. The station's cameras were trained on the fires raging at the top of the South Tower, when, at 9:59 a.m., the building began to implode. Before their eyes and those of viewers all over the world, a giant cloud engulfed the top of the tower, for a few seconds giving the impression that only part of the building had fallen. Miller and the in-studio news people were incredulous as a reporter standing in the street told them that the building was no more.

It was hard to grasp that there was only a void next to the remaining Twin Tower, which was itself on fire. The news reporters on every channel—local, network, and cable—were covering the response and attempted rescue of those remaining in the North Tower. At 10:28 a.m., twenty-nine minutes after the collapse of the South Tower, millions watched, live on TV, as dark smoke poured out of the top of the North Tower.

Suddenly the second tower collapsed in on itself. The giant antenna atop the building tipped back as if it were going to fall off, but then sank straight down as the building disintegrated and even larger clouds metastasized over Lower Manhattan.

"Oh my God. Oh my God," was all the reporter at NBC 4 could say. The collapse of the North Tower shook the ground hard enough to register 2.3 on the Richter scale.

Cameras positioned just north of the World Trade Center complex on West Street showed people rushing north, fleeing the Towers as the giant dust cloud rolled behind and finally overtook them. The speed of the dust storm was so great it could not be outrun. News helicopters flying above the Hudson River captured the cloud on film as it began to engulf all of Lower Manhattan.

The terrorists had treated the airplanes as suicide bombs, turning them against the Twin Towers and making sacrificial victims of all the passengers. The subsequent collapse of the Towers and the attendant loss of life, whether planned or foreseen as a consequence of the attack, added to the enormity of the crime. And although it was right there before everyone's eyes, no one saw the other attacker: the silent killer hidden in the dust cloud.

As the Towers collapsed and dust and debris mushroomed, police, firefighters, and emergency medical services (EMS) volunteers were arriving from all over the city. They would continue to show up throughout the day from the greater metropolitan area, and eventually from all over the country and even Canada. Some were on duty, some were off duty, some had even retired. But they were impelled to be there to do what they could in what everyone understood to be a national emergency.

John Walcott, an NYPD detective with the Narcotics unit, was at home in Rockland County, trying to rest up before that night's midnight shift. As he later recounted to reporters, a friend called to ask what the hell was happening in the city. Walcott had no idea. He turned on the TV and, seeing the Towers burning, jumped into his minivan and started driving toward New York.

Chief Martinez, who was training Internal Affairs investigators, was holding a class at 315 Hudson when the call came in. He was dispatched to the Police Academy on 20th Street, which was becoming emergency headquarters.

Mindy Hersh, an NYPD officer who worked in the District Attorney's Office, was at the dentist's, having snuck away from her office a block away. When she rushed to a window and saw the disaster occurring at the World Trade Center, Hersh's emergency training kicked in, and she ordered everyone in the dentist's office to evacuate the building. Thomas Ryan, a detective in the 106th Precinct in Ozone Park, Queens, had worked the night of September 10, 2001. He was at his home on Long Island, sleeping, on the morning of September 11, when he awoke to learn about the attacks. As he drove to his NYPD station house, he could see the dust cloud over New York City. Once at work he got on a city bus that had been commandeered to take volunteer workers to Lower Manhattan.

Lyndon Harris, an Episcopal priest at St. Paul's Chapel of Trinity Church, had been about to join Rowan Williams (the future archbishop of Canterbury) for a spiritual summit that Trinity was hosting. He rushed out of the chapel to see if he could help.

Suzanne Mattei had recently taken the job as executive of the New York City branch of the Sierra Club. Their offices were at 120 Broadway, facing the World Trade Center. She stood in shock as she looked out her window and saw the fire raging on the upper floors of one of the Towers.

Thousands of people were staggering, running, and walking north, moving as best they could, away from Downtown, away from Ground Zero. They looked like zombies caked with white ash, some with their clothes torn, some bleeding from having been struck by falling debris or showered by human body parts or knocked down or blown through store windows or lobby doors by the sheer force of the impact and its resulting tidal wave of debris.

As so many fled Lower Manhattan, dedicated public servants who would come to be known as Ground Zero responders headed toward the danger to search for survivors. They worked throughout the day, into the night, and on to the next day.

Smoke could be seen rising above the WTC site from all over Manhattan, Brooklyn, Queens, and the Bronx, and even from the rooftops in White Plains some thirty miles away. No one knew if it was from the exploded fuel tanks of the airliners that had crashed in the suicide attacks or combustibles located in the buildings. But the smoke continued to rise—a potent sign of the damage done and the danger still present.

The disaster site covered some sixteen acres, almost 700,000 square feet, about the size of twelve football fields. The tangle of twisted iron and steel wreckage from the collapsed buildings reached seven stories high (and in some places as high as twelve stories). It was soon referred to as "the Pile." It was dangerous even to walk on the Pile. The uneven wreckage was unstable, filled with pockets several stories deep that acted like sinkholes, constituting a danger for workers. And debris was continuing to fall or implode in life-threatening ways.

On September 12 police officers, firefighters, and volunteers from city, state, and federal agencies searched urgently for survivors and began the awful task of confronting what was an active crime scene that—in a matter of minutes—had become New York City's latest mass grave.[1]

The ground at the WTC site still smoldered and fires still burned, and the air in Lower Manhattan was thick with a foul smell. Feathery white-gray dust covered everything and lingered on everyone near Ground Zero. The dust was made up of the jetliners, their tanks of benzene jet fuel, and the entire contents of the buildings: the outside structure, the windows, the interior walls, the ceilings, the insulation, each painted surface, every piece of treated carpet, all the air-conditioning and heating equipment, and all of the office equipment, including monitors, computers, and copy machines. All of these were incinerated by the heat of the explosion, fused by the extreme heat of the subsequent fires, or pulverized by the building's collapse into minuscule particles containing dangerous chemicals and metals, among them cadmium, silica, polycyclic aromatic hydrocarbons (PAHs, a known pollutant), and dozens of other elements in toxic combinations never seen before. The dust containing these particles was carried by the wind and displaced by the Ground Zero responders who were sorting through and removing all the dust-laden material on the Pile, searching for evidence and human remains.

The Ground Zero responders who rushed into Lower Manhattan—Baker, Martinez, Hersh, Ryan, Walcott, Harris, and others—were prepared to rescue the injured and to recover the dead who'd perished in the collapse. They found almost no survivors and very few corpses—only 291 bodies would be recovered from among the 2,753 persons who died that day.

Detective John Walcott knew the attacks on the Twin Towers were the work of terrorists, having actually been in the Towers in 1993 for the first terrorist act. He had joined the NYPD in 1992 and was now a detective assigned to Manhattan North Narcotics. What he saw when he arrived at Ground Zero, he later told reporters, was "chaotic, people running, screaming, debris everywhere. It was total destruction, debris as high as my knee, to my thigh. Cars blown away to nothing, mass destruction." A doctor was handing out paper masks of the type you would get at a home improvement center. Walcott wore one briefly, until it became too clogged to breathe through. On that first day, although he had moments of difficulty breathing and was coughing and gagging, he did not stop working.

Walcott went down to the site every day for the rest of September, often working twelve-hour shifts. He worked on the Pile digging with his hands, filling buckets, and doing security. There were searches of buildings, sometimes with more than fifty floors. After almost three weeks, he and his coworkers were ordered to go to the American Express building, where the commanding officer announced that respirators would be available. But the devices they received were fitted with the wrong filters. Walcott had to remove his respirator whenever he ate, coughed, or could not breathe.

In all his time with the NYPD, Walcott had never taken a sick day. He exercised regularly and coached the ice hockey team at the Fox Lane High School in Westchester, not far from his home in Rockland County. He'd been married for several years and had a baby girl.

Six months before the World Trade Center disaster, in April 2001, Walcott had seen his doctor. A chest exam taken at that time read "normal with an impression of no acute cardiopulmonary disease." Yet as 2002 passed into 2003, Walcott found himself increasingly out of breath and sapped of strength. As he would later tell reporters, this had never happened to him before.

Mindy Hersh was a paramedic with the New York City EMS when she took the police test in 1984. She was called to police service in 1986 as a subway transit cop, working undercover in every part of Manhattan, from Harlem to Greenwich Village. Eventually Hersh was assigned to the District Attorney's Office at 100 Center Street, where she worked in EAP (Expedited Arrest Processing), preparing legal documents for low-level crimes like shoplifting so police officers wouldn't be taken off the streets to do paperwork; the officers just faxed their arrest information to Hersh and her colleagues, and they presented it to the court.

On the morning of 9/11, after ordering everyone at the dentist's office to get their things and leave, Hersh herself had a choice: she could go left, back to her office, or go right and run toward the World Trade Center, which was what her instincts told her to do. Then her cell phone rang. It was one of her coworkers, a born-again Christian who never said so much as a bad word. Which was why Hersh was all the more shocked to hear her cursing, screaming, "GET THE FUCK BACK TO THE OFFICE!"

Hersh now believes, "That was God's way of waking me up, because I would've been in the World Trade Center building getting people out, and I would've been gone. I wouldn't be here today."

I think God put [those curse words] in her to wake me up, because they were words that would've never come out of her mouth. Turning left instead of right changed my life."

Hersh went back to her office and moved some prisoners out of court, after which she was directed to Ground Zero, where she was put on the search-and-rescue mission. For much of the next nine months, she alternated between one day on the Pile and the next at the morgue.

When the Twin Towers of the World Trade Center opened on April 4, 1973, they were the tallest buildings in the world. One World Trade Center was 1,368 feet high, and Two World Trade Center, 1,362 feet high. They were the two centerpieces of the WTC complex, which comprised seven buildings totaling some 13.5 million square feet of office space.[2]

At the time of the attacks there were approximately 430 companies with offices in the Twin Towers, with an average of fifty thousand people working there each day. The North Tower had a public restaurant, Windows on the World, and an observation deck that was a popular tourist destination, averaging as many as 140,000 visitors a day.

Within the walls of both structures was six million square feet of masonry, five million square feet of painted surfaces, seven million square feet of flooring, 600,000 square feet of window glass, two hundred elevators, and countless computers, furniture, office equipment, and fixtures. All of which, on 9/11, turned into one million tons of dust.[3]

At 9:31 a.m. on September 11, President George W. Bush, who was visiting an elementary school in Sarasota, Florida, announced to the nation that there had been an "apparent terrorist attack on our country." At 11:02 a.m. the mayor ordered the evacuation of residents and workers of Lower Manhattan below Canal Street. At 2:30 p.m. Governor George Pataki and Mayor Giuliani held a press conference that included this exchange:

Question: Do we know when you got the composition of that dust that (*offmike*)? Is there any asbestos or any hazardous material in that dust?

Giuliani: I don't know. I don't know the answer to that.[4]

That Tuesday morning, September 11, primary election day voting in New York was canceled. The airports were closed. Trading on Wall Street was suspended. The United Nations building was evacuated. Mayor Giuliani and Governor Pataki declared a state of emergency, the mayor directing "the Police, Fire and Health Commissioners and the Director of Emergency Management to take whatever steps are necessary to preserve the public safety and to render all required and available assistance to protect the security, well-being and health of the residents of the City." The mayor closed Lower Manhattan to all civilian traffic to allow rescue vehicles easier access. Bridges and tunnels into the city were also closed.

The terrorist attacks, coming as they did at the peak of morning rush hour in Manhattan, shut down subway lines, including the PATH train from New Jersey. Cellular phone service was crippled. Regular phone service was overwhelmed, and many callers could not get though. The *New York Times* reported that AT&T shut down its entire phone and communications system in Manhattan.[5]

Beyond the lost value of the demolished and damaged office buildings, which the comptroller of the City of New York would estimate in 2002 as $21.8 billion, the PATH train and its transportation hub and the multiple subways underneath the WTC were rendered inoperable. Verizon and AT&T estimated that 300,000 phone lines were severed and five switching stations affected, while Consolidated Edison, whose electricity powered the city, would need to replace thirty-three miles of cable and repair two WTC substations, at a cost estimated to be $400 million.[6]

The Twin Towers had been built inside a bathtub-shaped foundation, driven down seven stories to bedrock. A massive concrete "slurry wall" prevented the Hudson River from flooding in. The PATH train ran through two sets of tunnels under the Hudson. The danger was that if those tunnels were weakened and the Hudson flooded them, the slurry walls and the foundation could further weaken. If the slurry wall failed, the water could rush through the subway tunnels and flood Downtown Manhattan.

There were also concerns about the freon used to cool the office buildings. It was stored in enormous tanks that were now deep below the rubble of the Pile.[7] At first there was no way to get to those tanks to see if they remained unharmed. If they ruptured and were set aflame, the result would be deadly.

Seven World Trade Center was a trapezoidal building, forty-seven stories tall, sheathed in red granite. An elevated walkway connected the building to the WTC complex. The building was situated above a Con Ed power substation.

Salomon Smith Barney was the building's largest tenant. Among the others were ITT Hartford Insurance, American Express Bank, Standard Chartered Bank, the Securities and Exchange Commission (SEC), a regional office of the IRS, the Department of Defense, the CIA, the Secret Service, Federal Home Loan Bank, Provident Financial, and New York City's Emergency Command Center.

When the North Tower collapsed, Seven World Trade Center was damaged by falling debris. The debris also ignited fires, and by 10:30 a.m. the building itself was on fire. Everyone inside was led to safety; however, the building's internal fire suppression system lacked water pressure to fight the fires, and the building continued to burn throughout the day. At 5:20 p.m., a rooftop penthouse structure began to crumble. Seconds later, a critical internal column buckled and triggered structural failure throughout, causing Seven World Trade Center to collapse. The building became the only steel skyscraper known to have collapsed due to uncontrolled fires.[8]

Fortunately, as the building had been successfully evacuated that morning, there were no casualties. However, one of the falling steel beams cut into a Verizon communications hub that handled some 40 percent of the phone lines in Lower Manhattan and an estimated 20 percent of the lines used at the New York Stock Exchange for voice, data, and internet. The NYSE and Nasdaq had been forced to evacuate earlier in the day and were now closed until further notice.

The national impact of what had occurred at Ground Zero continued to unspool on TV. At 8:30 p.m. President Bush addressed the nation, declaring a "war against terrorism": "Thousands of lives were suddenly ended by evil, despicable acts of terror. The pictures of airplanes flying into buildings, fires burning, huge structures collapsing, have filled us with disbelief, terrible sadness, and a quiet, unyielding anger. These acts of mass murder were intended to frighten our nation into chaos and retreat. But they have failed. Our country is strong."

At 10:00 p.m. Mayor Giuliani held a press conference during which he asked New Yorkers to stay home the next day. In the scrum of press questions afterward, he was asked if there was any concern of an asbestos contamination hazard. "The Health Department has done tests and at this point is not concerned," Giuliani replied. "So far, all the tests we've done do not show an undue amount of asbestos, doesn't show any particular chemical agent that we have to be concerned about. The accumulation of it for people who were down there can become very, very irritating. And there are a lot of people whose eyes have been burned, but I don't think there's any chemical agent that we have to worry about at this point."

Giuliani was correct in saying that asbestos was not of primary concern. However, he was wrong about the lack of any other chemical agents being present. That lack of concern about toxic exposure would have terrible consequences in the days and years to follow.

Gary Acker, a satellite communications expert, was head of AT&T's Network Disaster Recovery Team. He was running a training exercise at a location in New Jersey on the morning of 9/11. His team was readying one of their command vehicles, an emergency communications vehicle (ECV), a trailer full of sophisticated technology, and was loading a satellite dish onto its roof—basically putting a delicate piece of equipment on a moving platform—when Acker received an urgent call from his wife, Alison. "Turn on the radio, turn on a TV," she demanded.

Acker would later say of that morning, "God was with me, because we were on the Bird," meaning they already had the satellite and the ECV ready to go.

The bridges and tunnels had been closed, but Acker's team was able to call ahead and get approval to drive to Ground Zero to help restore phone service to Lower Manhattan. They arrived at the site at midnight on September 11. Amid the tall buildings in Lower Manhattan, they searched for the right spot to put the ECV to connect with the satellite. Acker knew it could take hours to get the setup right, and that reestablishing communications was going to be a nightmare, but he remained overwhelmingly positive and confident. They decided to park the ECV outside police headquarters at One Police Plaza, and in no time they completed their setup.

During the first minutes of September 12 they worked to restore police communications, then worked at manning phone lines across from the Pile. They were able to get a dinner cruise ship from New Jersey to set up ship-to-shore communications for emergency responders and to make humanitarian calls. Acker had about a dozen members of his team going all night, in the ECV and outside of it. It was like being everywhere at once, and Acker had no time to think about anything other than doing the job he knew best.

In those first days, the disorganized mass of police, firefighters, emergency response personnel, construction workers, and volunteers who showed up at the site formed a human chain to remove buckets of debris and allow the search for what they hoped were trapped survivors. The bucket brigade snaked throughout the site, a sea of hardhats of different colors. They wore gloves but little other protection; some had paper masks, and some of the firefighters had breathing masks, but many, many on the bucket brigade did not.

Although at first the Fire Department of the City of New York (FDNY) was in charge, the chief had died on 9/11, as had the first deputy commissioner and the deputy chief of special operations command. So those most qualified and prepared to command were gone, and as a result work at Ground Zero in those first days was disorganized and chaotic. To bring some order to the rescue and recovery efforts, within a week the city's Department of Design and Construction divided the site into four quadrants, each to be managed by a different construction company. However, the Pile was still overrun by non-construction workers wanting to help find survivors.

When Candiace Baker showed up at Ground Zero on September 12, she was assigned to do perimeter security at the site. On that day and those that followed, she sometimes had to stand in place for twelve-hour shifts, answering questions of anyone who asked. She also worked on the bucket brigade. They were using their hands to lift rocks, move them aside, and keep digging because they were still hoping to find survivors in the rubble. She was breathing in dust that made her choke whether she was wearing a paper mask or had taken it off because it had become clogged. Baker's fingers were hurting, blistered, and filthy. Her team hadn't found even one person. She looked at the mass of destruction. Overwhelmed, Baker thought that even with all the people there pitching in, they were having little to no impact. She could move rocks for days and it might make no difference.

On that same September 12, NBC News, the *New York Times, Slate*, and several other news outlets reported that two former U.S. marines, later identified as Jason Thomas and Dave Karnes, had discovered two Port Authority Police officers, John McLoughlin and Will Jimeno, beneath some twenty feet of rubble.[9] Karnes and Thomas were volunteers who had both separately rushed to Ground Zero to help. Dressed in camouflage fatigues, they climbed over the tangled steel of the Pile, Karnes shouting, "If you can hear us, yell or tap!" Then he and Thomas would pause to listen. Carrying flashlights and an infantry shovel, they peered into gaps in the destruction.[10] After about an hour, Karnes heard a reply from deep below the surface. Thomas called out, "Is anyone down there? United States Marines!" McLoughlin and Jimeno hollered back. They were trapped deep inside the debris and had been buried for almost ten hours.

Karnes and Thomas sought more help. Several EMS workers joined them, digging for three hours before they could get to Jimeno. It would take another eight hours to dig him out and even more for McLoughlin, who was buried deeper. Once freed, they were rushed to hospitals for further treatment. Both survived.

That same morning, James Symington, a Canadian police officer, took Trakr, his German Shepherd search-and-rescue dog, to the World Trade Center site. Like thousands of other volunteers, Symington arrived without any official authorization; he simply felt he could help and that he needed to be there. And it was lucky that he was. Trakr found a survivor, Genelle Guzman, in the rubble just below the surface, pinned by heavy concrete and twisted metal. She had worked on the 64th floor of the North Tower, and on 9/11 she was in a stairway on the 13th floor trying to escape the building when it collapsed around her. Miraculously she survived a fall of some 130 feet as the building came crashing down around her; she had been buried for more than a day. After she was found, workers labored for several hours to free her and then took her to a hospital. Guzman would say that while trapped, she prayed and that an angel named Paul appeared to her and told her that she would be rescued. Guzman, who by some counts was the eighteenth (and by others the twentieth) person to be found alive, would be the last.

In the 9/11 World Trade Center disaster more than 2,750 people were killed, including 343 firefighters and 60 New York City and Port Authority officers. Although the formal search would continue until October 6, when the last federal rescue team left the site, no other living person would be found. Still, thousands were assigned, and thousands volunteered, to be of service and work at the site of where the Twin Towers once stood.

The attack on the World Trade Center was intended to devastate the U.S. economy. Wall Street closed on September 11, although President Bush and Mayor Giuliani believed it was imperative to reopen the markets as soon as possible to demonstrate the resilience of the American people and the American economy, and to show that the United States was not and would not be intimidated by terrorism.

Richard Clarke, a White House antiterrorism official at the time, recalled that on the evening of September 11, President Bush told several staff members, including Clarke, "I want the economy back, open for business right away, banks, the stock market, everything tomorrow." Treasury Secretary Paul O'Neill too heard on September 12 from one of his aides that the president wanted to reopen the New York Stock Exchange the next day. The concern was that a prolonged closure of the financial markets could cause the U.S. economy to spiral downward with long-lasting effects on the entire country, and perhaps on the global economy and financial markets. But the NYSE remained shuttered for the rest of the week, the longest closing since 1933.

On September 12, New York senator Hillary Rodham Clinton joined Mayor Giuliani and Governor Pataki at Ground Zero. Wearing paper face masks (Giuliani's remained mostly around his neck rather than covering his nose and mouth), they walked on the Pile. "This attack on New York is an attack on America," Senator Clinton declared. "It's an attack on every American."

On September 13 Christine Todd Whitman, administrator of the Environmental Protection Agency (EPA), told NBC's Ashleigh Banfield that the danger from the air quality was "below any level that is of concern to the general population." In a press release issued that day, Whitman stated that "monitoring and sampling conducted" had been "very reassuring about potential exposure of rescue crews and the public to environmental contaminants." Tina Kreisler, an EPA spokesperson, declared, "The good news for the residents of New York is that the air, while smoky, is not dangerous. . . . It is not something we would classify as toxic."

The morale of rescue workers was boosted on September 14, when President Bush, having declared a national state of emergency, paid a visit to Ground Zero. Standing with retired firefighter Bob Beckwith and not wearing a breathing mask, the president addressed the firefighters and rescue workers with a bullhorn, thanking them. When some workers shouted that they could not hear him, Bush answered, "I can hear you! The rest of the world hears you. And the people who knocked these buildings down will hear all of us soon!"

"I'm shocked at the size of the devastation," Bush later said. "It's hard to describe what it's like to see the gnarled steel and broken glass and twisted buildings silhouetted against the smoke. I said that this was the first act of war on America in the twenty-first century, and I was right, particularly having seen the scene."

Being near Ground Zero those first few nights was eerie. The U.S. government had established a no-fly zone over the area, much of which remained evacuated. So the sky was dark, except for an unreal glow that rose from where the Twin Towers had once stood. This came from special lights that had been installed at the site, allowing work to continue through the night.

The cloud of dust seemed to settle like an unholy fog. You could almost feel the air. And the smell! It wasn't like garbage or something rancid. To Gary Acker, it was the smell of a mixture of metals and burned plastic. He and his team had been given a hotel room nearby to sleep in, but he never went far from the ECV. He was the expert in running and maintaining the equipment, and he worked for thirty-three days straight. Many nights he'd oversee the Police Plaza satellite. Some nights he had to climb up to the satellite to make sure it was working properly.

Throughout the next days more AT&T trailers arrived and more communications lines were established. If not for what Acker and his team were doing, Lower Manhattan's communications would have been down for months. Acker would cook for all these workers, sometimes as many as forty people. That was part of how he built team loyalty and why they continued to work so hard for so many hours.

During the day, he would see people wandering, dazed, sometimes holding pictures of their missing loved ones. Acker felt for them. In the rubble, he found eyeglasses, a random wallet, a shoe, but no people, no dead bodies. It was as if they had been vaporized.

Acker was given a painter's mask that soon became caked with debris. Within days he started coughing so hard he vomited what looked like hardened black sludge. When his wife, Alison, came to visit him, she heard the cough right away. But it was like he had the flu, so he took antibiotics to feel better. He believed Christine Todd Whitman and other officials when they said the air was safe. He was trusting and loyal. Alison said he "believed in the best part of everybody."

Although the president had promised to take care of New York and the victims of 9/11, the mayor took charge of the city's response.

Giuliani, whose post-9/11 approval rating would rise to 79 percent out of admiration for his leadership in the hours and days following the attacks, saw himself as uniquely qualified to make decisions for New York. He chose not to defer to any federal agency or organization or even any international team experienced in environmental disasters, disaster relief, or even building collapses.

In the heat of the crisis, Giuliani took the stance that New York City, like London during the Blitz, would "carry on" and that he was its Churchill. He established an Incident Command Post as part of the FDNY and directed the City Office of Emergency Management to manage operations. And he tasked the New York City Department of Design and Construction with total control over all aspects of safety construction, demolition, and cleanup activities at the site.[11]

Giuliani believed that New York and New Yorkers should return to normal as soon as possible. His hubris would have catastrophic consequences for the Ground Zero responders.

Wall Street reopened on September 17—the phones and the lines carrying data had been given the highest priority and repaired in record time—however, it would be weeks, in some cases months until the rest of Lower Manhattan's other businesses and residences were fully operational. The market that day closed down 684 points, a 7.1 percent decline, setting a then-record for the Dow's largest single day loss. Nevertheless, people cheered because the stock exchange was once again up and running.

The next day, in another press release, EPA Administrator Whitman repeated her earlier reassurances about the air quality at Ground Zero: "Given the scope of the tragedy from last week, I am glad to reassure the people of New York and Washington DC, that their air is safe to breathe and their water is safe to drink." The Occupational Safety and Health Administration (OSHA) gave similar assurances, as did the New York City Department of Health and the New York State Department of Environmental Conservation.

On September 28 Giuliani asserted, "The air quality is safe and acceptable. I know there are people concerned and worried about it, but that's just the reality." Yet there was a persistent odor in the air that couldn't be denied. It was so evident that a few weeks later Giuliani was forced to comment, "You smell it and you feel there must be something wrong, but what I'm told is it's not dangerous to your health."

The next day, more than two weeks after the attacks, the mayor made official what all the workers knew: that no more survivors would be found. What had been a rescue mission was now a mission of recovery—of bodies, body parts, of personal belongings, and of evidence from the largest crime scene ever in New York City. The task was now to clear the World Trade Center site, demolish the remaining structures, remove the thousands of tons of debris, and clean up the site to allow for rebuilding.

Working at Ground Zero would change John Feal's life forever. Feal was the sort of person who was used to things going his way. Popular in high school, he joined the military after graduation, serving for almost three years. Afterward he worked construction, rising to lead a demolition crew. Feal, who had a muscular build and shaved head, was not tall, but he inspired confidence in those who worked with him. On 9/11 he was working as a foreman for a private demolition company on a project about an hour north of New York City. When he heard about the damage to the World Trade Center, he decided to help.

Feal arrived at Ground Zero on 9/12. "I knew my experience as a U.S. Army veteran and demolition supervisor would be of service to my country," he said. He immediately started working, using his talents as a foreman to direct workers who could operate the heavy machinery to move the tons of debris. It was dangerous work, but they were still hopeful they might find survivors trapped beneath the rubble.

Five days later, on September 17, Feal was directing the removal of a large hunk of twisted metal when the chain holding it snapped, sending eight thousand pounds of steel beam crashing down and crushing his left foot. Feal was rushed to the hospital. His luck had run out that day.

Officer Thomas Ryan had grown up on Long Island. After high school, he continued to live at home and attended the New York Institute of Technology, studying architecture. As an athletic young man of nineteen, he had volunteered in his community as a firefighter, taking whatever special training they offered, including medical training and hazardous materials training. Eventually Ryan became a lieutenant on one of the Fire Department rigs.

Ryan discovered that he enjoyed helping people and responding to emergencies more than he was interested in architecture. His uncle was a New York City detective, and Ryan reached out to him for guidance. After taking the police exam he was hired by the Suffolk County Police Department as a "summer cop." It didn't offer full employment or full benefits; you worked for eight months of the year and then went on hiatus. He did that for three years, until the

NYPD finally contacted him. They required that he start all over again and attend the New York Police Academy for nine months—which, given his experience, he found relatively easy to get through. His uncle gave him advice about which precincts to apply for coming out of the academy, which is how he ended up at the 106th in Queens.

The 106th included JFK Airport as well as Ozone Park and Howard Beach and bordered East New York. Ryan would remain at the 106th for his entire career, doing every task a police officer could do: he walked a beat, did bike patrol, went in plainclothes, and did undercover work.

On the morning of 9/11, Ryan rushed to report for duty, glad he had thought to load a duffel bag with a change of clothes in case he needed to remain at work for a while. Because of his EMT training, he volunteered to go into Manhattan. When the commandeered city bus approached Downtown Ryan and his fellow volunteers went silent. They unloaded in Liberty State Park.

Ryan's Aunt Barbara had called to say that his uncle Lou Minervino, an accountant, was in one of the Towers and was missing. She had spoken to him a few minutes before the plane hit. Minervino was a senior vice president at Marsh USA Inc., whose offices were on the 98th floor of One World Trade Center. She wanted Ryan to look for him, and Ryan promised he would.

What Ryan saw when he arrived at the World Trade Center site was utter chaos and disorganization amid the destruction. He had assumed that he would be assigned a specific job, but no one seemed to be in charge. He was frustrated with the lack of leadership. Because most of the injured people and the dead bodies had already been removed he spent the next couple of hours looking for something to do.

At one point that first day, Ryan was sent to the Deutsche Bank Building to make sure there was no looting and to monitor the building's danger of collapsing. He arrived to find out that the place had been set up as a temporary morgue. The police supervisor assigned to the Deutsche Bank Building was a friend of Ryan's and gave him permission to search for his uncle among the recovered bodies. Ryan unzipped each bag and looked inside. It was very difficult to look at the bodies, so many of whom were horribly disfigured. Noticing a giant box containing wallets and purses, he realized that people had probably thrown these out of the buildings to say to their loved ones "I was here."

Eventually Ryan was able to make his way onto the Pile, where he joined the bucket brigade and spent the rest of the day excavating the rubble with no tools and wearing no respirator. Soon his police uniform was covered in white soot. He was not conscious of breathing in the soot, but the air was so pungent that it left a bad taste in his mouth.

It wasn't until Ryan's fourth day working on the Pile that he was given a paper mask. It worked for a while but quickly became caked with dust. About a week later, as Ryan recalled, the officials at Ground Zero were giving out respirators, but only if you were the rank of lieutenant or above; then two weeks later everyone got a respirator and one cartridge to be changed every eight hours. They often ran out of cartridges.

Everyone ate out in the open. No one saw any lasting danger from doing so, or the potential for permanent injury. The Red Cross was serving responders at tables a hundred feet from the Pile. It took a few weeks for that organization to realize they needed to give the responders protection. Ryan was told to take his soot-caked police uniform home with him, but to wash it separately from his family's clothing. A week later, he recalled, rescue personnel were told to dispose of the uniforms and burn them. "No one seemed to have the right answers as far as personal protection equipment, uniforms, or hygiene."

In later years Ryan would recall that on one of his first days working in Downtown, a paper mask his only protection, he saw a bunch of army guys across the street wearing their chemical suits. "What's wrong with this picture?" Ryan asked his partner. "We're out here, we're standing in the street wearing paper masks, and there's a Humvee going by and the army guys are sitting with their chemical suits on." That was when it first dawned on him that "there might be a problem." But he and his crew shrugged it off and continued to do their duty.

Every person working at Ground Zero was well aware of the dust and its smell. However, even when protection was finally provided, using it was problem-filled: wearing a respirator made communicating by walkie-talkie impossible; it also made working in the heat of the fires still burning at Ground Zero more oppressive; and the respirators quickly became clogged with dust. Enforcement of the need to wear the respirators was lax, and as time went on it became laxer still. Yet the responders worked tirelessly, selflessly, compelled to work long hours, with or without respirators, for weeks and then months.

It didn't help that Rudy Giuliani appeared in Lower Manhattan in so many press photos and on TV typically not wearing a respirator. Doing so gave the responders a false sense of safety. They were there out of duty, some out of loyalty to lost comrades, to get the job done. But someone should have been watching out for *them*, for their health.

The Ground Zero dust was like a devil that danced on the graves of the murdered to poison the lives of the living. The longer the responders worked at Ground Zero, the more they inhaled; the harder they worked, the deeper they inhaled. Every action by every person and every machine and vehicle stirred up more dust, animating its toxic dance.

The dust itself was on the move. Beginning on September 12, the debris from the WTC site was transported by truck to barges on the Hudson as the atomized Twin Towers dust continued to swirl about the responders at work. Over the next nine months, more than 108,000 truckloads of debris—1.8 million tons of rubble—would be transported by truck and barge to Fresh Kills, the Staten Island landfill.[12]

Paul J. Lioy looked the part of a brilliant research scientist, with a bulging forehead, a gray fringe of hair, and oversized glasses that sat on a prominent Roman nose. Lioy was New Jersey born and raised, receiving his PhD in environmental science at Rutgers University, where he also taught. He was a pioneer in the field of exposure science and perhaps the world's leading expert on exposure to toxins.

On 9/11 Lioy could see the dark plume rising from the World Trade Center from his home in Cranford, New Jersey. He wondered what was in that dust.

Within the first week after the disaster, Lioy drove down to Ground Zero with a group of colleagues to take air samples. They found the dust so thick that they just scooped it up from the windshields of abandoned cars and secured it in Teflon bags. "It had a weird texture and color to it," he told the *New York Times*, fluffy and whitish gray. They took two samples that first visit, September 16, 2001, and returned the next day to take three more from undisturbed protected locations to the east of the WTC site, at Cortlandt Street, Cherry Street, and Market Street.[13]

In the immediate aftermath of the Towers' collapse much of the concern was focused on possible asbestos exposure. But although Lioy found slightly elevated amounts of asbestos, this did not, in his opinion, pose a significant health risk—a conclusion in line with those of scientists for New York City and the state. However, Lioy was troubled about other elements he uncovered in the dust's composition. When he considered the material present in the buildings, including the concrete, metals, and all the office equipment, as well as the materials from two jumbo jetliners, and given what he already knew regarding building collapses, he was convinced that there was serious reason for health concerns. "It was unprecedented in terms of the complex characteristics of the materials released."[14]

Lioy discovered that the dust was mostly made up of pulverized building and construction materials, including cement, cellulose, and glass fibers. What concerned him most were the airborne aerosol particles—containing toxicants with significant concentrations of asbestos, glass fibers, lead, and PAHs—that the fires produced. As those fires continued to rage, these toxic elements would be present in increasingly smaller particles, making their detection and cleanup more difficult, and more toxins would be absorbed by rivers, plants, and human beings.

It would take until July 2002 for Lioy to publish his analysis of the dust's composition. In that report he argued that continued study was needed to assess the long-term impact of the dust.

What no one was saying in those first few days after 9/11 was that Ground Zero was an unparalleled environmental disaster. If the WTC disaster had been treated like the accident at the Three Mile Island nuclear plant several decades before, or like the 2011 Fukushima Daiichi nuclear disaster, or if the area had been designated a Super-Fund site and put on the National Priority List because it posed a risk to human health and safety, or even if everyone present had been required to wear Hazmat suits like those Ryan saw, the Ground Zero responders would be telling a completely different story today.

The primary organs of the human respiratory system are the lungs, which take in air, absorbing oxygen and expelling carbon dioxide. The air enters through the mouth and nose. The nostrils draw air into the nasal cavity, where long hairs trap large particles, and tiny hairs, called cilia, along with mucus, snare smaller particles. Breathing through your mouth moistens the air going in, but it's much less filtered. The air then enters the throat, larynx, and trachea (the windpipe), which siphons the air into two tubes, called bronchi, that pass into the lungs.

From the very start, those at Ground Zero found that breathing the air caused coughs, sore throats, stinging in the nose. There was a vicious cycle to this: those whose noses became too irritated or mucus-filled increasingly breathed through their mouth, irritating their throat and lungs. Some quickly began to suffer asthma-like symptoms.

Asthma is a medical condition in which the airways become irritated, swell, and narrow in response to certain triggers, such as cold, exercise, irritants, and allergens, making breathing much more difficult. In the most serious cases it can make many regular activities impossible and can lead to life-threatening asthma attacks. There is no cure for asthma, only ways to control the symptoms.

The masks, both the paper ones as well those with cartridge filters, were meant to offer greater respiratory protection by preventing the particulate matter from passing into the airways. Proper protection means wearing the proper respiratory equipment that is fit properly, that is equipped with the proper filter cartridges, and where those cartridges are replaced whenever clogged—allowing for continuous use when the worker is exposed to toxic substances. Failure to take any of these steps results in the inhalation of toxins, which can cause asthma and (depending on the toxins) numerous medical conditions, including cancer.

For NYPD officer Mindy Hersh, being on the Pile in those first few days could only be described as unbelievable. The Pile of debris was blocks long—like a war zone. And high. The first time she saw it, the rubble was so high she didn't know if she could climb to the top. She was grateful for the firefighters who helped her struggle upward. When she looked down from the top, the people at the bottom looked like little peas. Even from up there, she could smell the fires that continued to burn beneath the Pile and the haunting smell of incinerated bodies. The smoldering fires made working at Ground Zero almost intolerably hot. Hersh was up there without a mask or any other respiratory protection. None of the responders thought about the danger. They were there to help.

Hersh climbed underneath fallen rafters to look for survivors. She didn't find any. She had expected to find corpses of the murdered, but once she was told that the fire from the impact of the jetliners and the explosion of their fuel tanks in the Twin Towers had reached nearly 2,000 degrees, she realized how unlikely that was. When she joined the bucket brigade, passing five-gallon buckets of debris hand to hand, she did find fingers and other body parts. Combing through this mass of destruction—what CBS newsman Scott Pelley called a "mountain of misery"—she also found parts of computers and office equipment alongside a single stray shoe. And amid all that, Hersh found a pristine staple remover still in its box, as though it had just been brought from the store. It stood out, untouched, a poignant artifact of what remained after the buildings' collapse.

Another time, Hersh was assigned to enter the area where the Winter Garden atrium once stood, a glass building that was part of the World Trade Center complex, where just a week before the attacks she had listened to part of a Toad the Wet Sprocket concert. When the responders entered the area to look for body parts or evidence, Hersh, a self-described "garage sale freak," went the other way from the group, knowing that at a garage sale that's how you find the treasures.

Beneath a table she found a pilot's wings. Hersh alerted her team and then had to wait as the police and FDNY fought for custody of the object. The Fire Department eventually won; they placed it on the grid they had made to record what was found and where.

Hersh worked for almost a year at Ground Zero, first on the Pile and then at the morgue, where she was charged with vouchering all the personal property that had been recovered; finally, for the last several months, she was assigned to a security detail at Ground Zero. No matter how much time went by, the air still carried that awful smell. Coming in on the Brooklyn-Queens Expressway, she could still smell it. She thought the masks didn't make much of a difference because she was breathing in dust even when she wasn't wearing a mask. For instance, when the construction companies put "the pots of crap" on the back of the trucks to bring them to the pier, they didn't cover the load, so the debris just flew all over. Hersh's office was right in the middle of the cloud of dust they made: "I was breathing that crap forever."

The Fresh Kills Landfill was opened on Staten Island in 1948 to accommodate New York's ever-growing store of garbage. When Fresh Kills exceeded its capacity, the state legislature passed a law requiring it to close by the end of 2001. However, on 9/11 Giuliani asked the governor's permission to reopen the landfill as a site where they could gather the debris, sort through it, and search for evidence and for human remains. By 2:00 a.m. on September 12, the first truckloads of rubble began to arrive at the landfill.

Debris was removed from Ground Zero in sanitation trucks to a transfer station in Manhattan, where it was loaded into barges. Each barge was about half as long as a football field, with open holds fifteen feet deep, and each carried 650 tons of debris. The barges ran day and night. As many as twenty a day sailed back and forth across the Hudson, a trip of some twenty miles each way. The barges docked at Fresh Kills' water access, and the debris was unloaded and trucked to a designated section of the landfill. To hold the debris in place, it was supposed to be wetted and tarped whenever it was moved from truck to barge, from barge to truck, and from truck to landfill. However, enforcement was sporadic, and each transfer caused the dust to swirl into the air. That dust would find its way to the Ground Zero responders, whether on the Pile, at the piers, on the barges, or at Fresh Kills.

Fresh Kills smelled like nowhere else. The air was suffused with methane from the garbage already there, while the debris and dust added their own smells.

Because there was no water or electricity or phone service at Fresh Kills, Congress authorized $125 million in emergency funding for crews to set up office trailers, portable toilets, and a decontamination center. A satellite dish was brought in to improve cell phone reception. Two twelve-thousand-square foot shelters were built so sifting the debris could continue throughout the winter.

Two white trailers were also brought to the landfill, one for the NYPD, the other for the FBI. Various tents were erected. There was a temporary headquarters (eventually there were two); a supply tent where gloves, coats, and other gear were issued; a mustering tent where you went to get your day's assignment; a medical tent; and a cafeteria. At first, all kinds of food appeared, donated by pizza trucks, restaurants, and caterers. And, at first, the Ground Zero responders ate their food right there, among the dust and the debris. At a later

date both OSHA and the Board of Health would realize how dangerous that was.

At first, cranes at the landfill lifted the rubble from the barges and
loaded it onto trucks that carried it to the western section of Fresh
Kills, then workers raked through the debris. At a later stage, sifting
machines with conveyor belts were brought in to speed up the examination. Either way, the dust was always on the move.

All workers at Fresh Kills were supposed to be provided with masks
and respirators with cartridges. The respirators had to fit perfectly
snuggly on the face so there were no spaces between the mask and
the skin where small particles could enter; men with beards had to
shave. Most police officers say they received no special training for
the respirator's use, nor were the devices fit-tested. And few were
told to replace their respirator cartridges regularly.

Officers from the same unit were often assigned in groups to the
same place and task. So, for example, Narcotics detectives from the
same precinct would find themselves working together at Fresh Kills.
They could be working beside a group from Internal Affairs or another
group of detectives from another precinct. Seeing people you knew
added to the feeling of being part of a common cause, even while
working in such a surreal landscape.

This was no traditional crime scene, where detectives, medical
examiners, and forensic investigators examine the location where
a crime took place. Here the evidence had been moved to another
location, where the detectives acted more like archaeologists sifting
through a dig.

An on-site Crime Scene Unit was established. Detectives would
place whatever they found on a plastic table. Everything identified in
the debris—jackets, helmets, shoes, guns, fire equipment, as well as
jet parts and personal office items—was bagged separately and sent
to be further examined for evidence that could lead to identifying
the belongings. An anthropologist would determine whether what
was found was human remains. If so, one detective would take photographs of the discovered body parts while another documented

the evidence. Every day a refrigerated morgue truck would arrive to take the body parts to the City Morgue. There they would attempt to identify the remains by any means possible, including DNA testing from hair, skin, or saliva samples, or fingerprints or dental records when available. If they identified a body part, the family would be notified and the body part could be claimed for burial purposes and, hopefully, to grant the family some measure of closure.

In the first few days and weeks he worked at Ground Zero, Thomas Ryan recalled, air horns would blow whenever they thought another building or part of a building was in danger of collapsing. There was danger in every step among the devastation. The ground was unstable with jagged metals and heavy objects and debris everywhere. Much of the rubble at the Pile was hot—fires were still burning underneath the ground.

Ryan was always looking for ways to get back onto the Pile to keep searching for his uncle's remains. He discovered that a tunnel had been created to go underneath the Pile. To get to it, though, he had to go around the piers on the West Side of Lower Manhattan. It took three or four days until he figured out how to get there, and when he did, he ended up at a dead-end street where he was surprised to see a bunch of 18-wheeler trucks.

Most of the vehicles near Ground Zero were severely damaged and had been abandoned. It was very rare to see a vehicle that could still be driven, but there in front of him were four or five 18-wheeler box trucks in good condition. Ryan walked to the front of the first truck, where a police officer was sitting at a table. Ryan's intention was to walk right by the officer like he knew where he was going, but the man grabbed his arm and turned to him.

"Hey, Tom, how you doing?" he asked.

Ryan recognized the man as a classmate from the Police Academy they'd attended five years earlier. They hugged each other and cried.

Finally, Ryan asked his colleague, "What are you doing here? What's with these trucks?"

"Oh, this is where we're putting the parts—the body parts," the man answered. "I have to log them in." He explained that these were refrigerated trucks that the city had brought in to preserve whatever human remains they found. It was obvious to Ryan that his former classmate took the job he was doing real hard.

Sometimes Ryan would hear "10-13" on his police radio, which is the code for "Officer needs assistance." Then he and hundreds of other cops and firefighters would run to the Pile in hopes that they had found someone alive. Usually it meant only that they had found a body (or a part of one). Like many of the other responders, Ryan worked on pure adrenaline, fueled by the chance that, against all odds, survivors could still be found. "We were all exhausted, but there's something about the human spirit. You could be totally exhausted, hungry, thirsty, but if you have that adrenaline going, you just keep going."[15]

They rotated volunteers in and out. Most often, Ryan worked with a group of some two hundred police officers, and mostly partnered with someone from his precinct. He worked twelve-, sixteen-, and sometimes twenty-hour shifts, during which he was constantly exposed to the Ground Zero dust finding its way into his clothes and on his skin and which he couldn't help but breathe in. Even those with respirators (when they were working) couldn't keep them on the whole time. You still needed to take them off to communicate or when you took a break or ate or when they became clogged. Ryan served approximately twenty-nine shifts at Ground Zero.

As for his uncle, Lou Minervino, Ryan never found him. The general public imagined that survivors must still be trapped under the rubble at Ground Zero. But having been to the World Trade Center site and on the Pile, Ryan knew even that first day that there was no one left alive. Still, he didn't feel he could tell his aunt that her husband was dead until he had looked everywhere possible. Instead he said, "There's a lot of people missing; we're going to do the best we can." He asked her to send him a recent photo, which he put up on a wall at St. Vincent's Hospital among the other photos of the missing.

Work at the site continued twenty-four hours a day seven days a week. There were asbestos workers, boilermakers, carpenters, cement masons, construction managers, electricians, emergency medical technicians, EPA employees, Federal Emergency Management Agency (FEMA) workers, firefighters, heavy equipment operators, insulation workers, ironworkers, laborers, machinists, medical doctors and coroners, National Guard, employees of the National Institute for Occupational Safety and Health (NIOSH), office cleaners, OSHA staff, paramedics, plumbers and pipefitters, police officers, psychologists, Red Cross workers, registered nurses, rescue workers, riggers, safety and health professionals, sheet metal workers, steamfitters, steelworkers, structural engineers, truckers and Teamsters.[16] By the thousands they came to serve the city.

By the end of September, some 135 tons of debris had been removed from the World Trade Center site. Ironworkers and construction workers were dismantling large pieces of the Towers' façade, at first with grappling hooks. When they could go no farther with the hooks, they decided to cut the twisted steel into pieces. Tens of thousands worked at the Pile as the invasive dust particles surrounded them, affixing to their clothing and shoes and becoming part of the already nasty air they breathed.

Over the next month, as Ground Zero was converted to a construction site, many NYPD and firefighters were reassigned to Fresh Kills to sift through the debris there or to work at the morgue or as part of a security detail at the WTC site. However, a substantial number remained at the Pile throughout the entire cleanup operation. They were not leaving until the job was done; they felt they owed that to their brethren who had died there, and to their city and their country.

By mid-December the fires at Ground Zero, already the longest commercial building fire in American history, were deemed extinguished. Still, the site of the World Trade Center remained a gaping abscess in the soul of New York City and the nation, drawing thousands upon thousands of visitors to look upon the void.

The work continued day in, day out. In the first few months after the attack, there was only one holiday that was observed by the city workers: Veterans Day, November 2001.

In March 2002 the city's Municipal Arts Society installed eighty-eight searchlights six blocks south of the Towers to create two vertical columns of light to memorialize the 9/11 terrorist attacks. The idea of the vertical columns of light was independently envisioned by a group of architects and artists shortly after the attack. Two nonprofit arts organizations, the Municipal Arts Society and Creative Time, helped bring their ideas to fruition, hiring a Las Vegas–based light display company to create the installation. The column of lights originally appeared from dusk to dawn from March 11 to April 12, 2002, and has been repeated yearly since then on every September 11. (Until 2012 it was a project of the Municipal Arts Society; since then it has been the responsibility of the 9/11 Memorial & Museum.)

Lyndon Harris and his family had moved to New York City in 1995 so he could pursue a doctoral degree in theology and teach one day. While still a full-time student, Harris worked in a variety of churches in and around New York City. He was particularly adept at working with young adults. Doing so brought him into contact with St. Paul's Chapel in Lower Manhattan, part of the parish of Trinity Episcopal Church, which stood less than a mile from the World Trade Center. Harris was invited to join St. Paul's as a parish priest, to lead what they called the St. Paul's Initiative to reach out to twentysomethings (or Gen-Xers, as they were called then). The demographics of Lower Manhattan were changing as the neighborhood was becoming increasingly residential, home to Wall Street workers and young families.

Harris loved the history of St. Paul's Chapel, the oldest surviving church building in Manhattan, dating from 1766. At the time of its completion, it was the tallest building in New York. George Washington worshipped there. After his inauguration as the first president of the United States, he walked from Federal Hall, a few steps away, to

St. Paul's and prayed for guidance and offered thanks for the opportunity to lead the new nation.

Harris joined St. Paul's officially in April 2001 as an Episcopal priest. He quickly organized a six-week summer pilot program of jazz services, as well as gospel performances that drew big crowds on Monday nights, before taking a mid-August hiatus. The plan was to reconvene on September 17. That was never to occur.

Harris would never forget the morning of September 11. He was in his office at St. Paul's, about to have coffee with the future archbishop of Canterbury, Rowan Williams. The two were scheduled to meet with twenty-five other people that Trinity Church had brought to New York City for a spirituality summit.

Harris did not think it all that unusual when sirens suddenly went off. Then he heard that a plane had hit the World Trade Center. He imagined it must have been a small private plane. The sirens continued, and Harris saw a stream of paper flying by the window. "It was like a ticker tape parade except all the edges of the paper were burned. It looked horrendous."

Harris and John Allen, a Trinity colleague, decided to walk to the World Trade Center site to offer help. They made it to the corner of Liberty and Church Street and were standing right outside the Burger King there when the second plane hit the South Tower. They watched an apocalyptic fireball form, debris falling, and heard the horrible sound of metal tearing at metal. He and Allen thought that perhaps St. Paul's could be used as a triage center. As they ran back toward the chapel hundreds and hundreds of office workers streamed past them in the opposite direction, covered in mud and ashes. Some were injured and bloodied by the falling debris. And all were heading away from the Towers.

Harris and Allen ducked into the New York Stock Exchange, but soon realized that if this was an attack, then the Stock Exchange could be a target, so they left quickly, returning to St. Paul's.

Despite the chaos outside, St. Paul's was following their own emergency protocol. Harris helped evacuate children from their third-floor nursery school to the basement. Shortly afterward, the first tower collapsed, shaking the ground and then filling the building with thick, dark smoke. Harris could barely see, but he and other St. Paul personnel each grabbed a child, and together they ran out the back of the building. As they ran, the second tower collapsed, and they were engulfed in an enormous ash cloud.

There was no time to think, barely time to mouth a silent prayer. They walked the children to safety at the Staten Island Ferry Terminal building, where Harris heard all sorts of rumors: that Boston had been hit, maybe the Sears Tower in Chicago. It seemed as if anything could happen because the unthinkable had just happened before their very eyes.

Eventually the children were reunited with their worried parents and Harris made it home. The next day he put on his work boots, grabbed a bag of water bottles and his Trinity Church ID, and headed downtown, walking down Broadway. He assumed that St Paul's itself would have collapsed, but when he reached City Hall, he could see the steeple of St. Paul's still standing. It took his breath away. He took the fact that the chapel still stood as a sign that they had a mission to do, and that they had to devote St. Paul's resources to the task.

The chapel was opened to any who wanted to take a rest, have a drink of water, or pray, At the corner of Broadway and Fulton, Harris set up a food service offering hamburgers and hot dogs, grilled right there in front of St. Paul's. They called it "the Barbeque on Broadway." By the weekend after the attacks, they had eight grills going and were serving three hundred to four hundred hamburgers a day. It wasn't long before the Health Department came by. Because they didn't know the source of the food and had no idea what was in the air, the health inspectors shut down the operation. But after the inspectors left, Harris fired up the coals again. This continued for several days, with the Health Department shutting them down twice a day, and Harris starting back up each time. After Harris mentioned his problem to the local police command captain, the next time the health inspectors showed up, they were surrounded by brawny police officers who marched them off the premises. One officer told Harris later, "The last time I checked the health department doesn't carry guns, but we do." Nevertheless, eventually the food service was moved inside St. Paul's for the sake of safety.

Harris had no experience in disaster relief or in managing a large and varied group of volunteers and ministering to such a changing population. So what he did first was simply show up. He was there, and he was ready to listen and figure out how to address needs in a reasonable and safe way. They had volunteers serving coffee and food. During the nine months of the cleanup they would serve some 500,000 meals to rescue workers. They offered massage therapy 24/7. They had podiatrists on hand. They had grief counselors and trauma therapists. All working very long days. And Harris continued to show up.

Little by little, over time, the ministries grew. With the support of the Trinity Church hierarchy, Harris accumulated a staff of eight full-time people by June 2002.

Harris had over 240 days of exposure to the dust in the Ground Zero air. He has no complaints about that. "Here's the thing," he says. "If I had been anywhere else in the country, I would have wanted to be right there. I felt that I had been given an opportunity with the capacity to respond in a way that could make a difference, and it was electric. It really was exhilarating to be able to offer support to these men and women doing such difficult work at the site."

Harris, who had never personally known a police officer before, now had scores who were friends. He found it beautiful that the church could actually make a difference. What he was proudest of was that they were able to meet the needs of the individual responders with whatever resources they could offer; there was no proselytizing or attempts to enroll new members in the church. They were there to serve all.

Candiace Baker's boss, Raul Martinez, was born and raised in Manhattan, in what was then called Spanish Harlem. Back then it was a rough, crime-ridden neighborhood. He joined the Department of Corrections in 1983, hoping to qualify for the NYPD. In 1985 he was hired by the New York City Transit Police. When he got promoted to sergeant in 1993, he took charge of the Tactical Patrol Force, whose officers were assigned to ride the trains from 8:00 p.m. to 4:00 in the morning throughout all of New York's five boroughs. As a sergeant supervisor, Martinez had to meet trains at various locations throughout the city, and to do so, he was assigned a car, and Baker became his driver.

A few years later, Martinez was promoted to instructor with the Office of Professional Development, working out of 315 Hudson Street in Lower Manhattan. He was there on 9/11 teaching a group of Internal Affairs investigators from New York City, New Jersey, and as far away as Vancouver, Canada. As soon as the reports came in about the attack on the World Trade Center, everyone there wanted to join the responders.

Martinez was dispatched to the Police Academy on 20th Street and from there to St. Vincent's Hospital on Seventh Avenue and 12th Street, where Candiace Baker had also been dispatched. Much to his surprise, as Baker also observed, very few people were coming in to the hospital; it seemed evident that there were very few survivors. Martinez and other officers recorded interviews with anyone who came there from the Towers. For the next week, he spoke with those who had reported their loved ones missing, taking all their information. He was then assigned to the World Trade Center Missing Persons Taskforce. Although it was soon evident that the missing would not be coming back, the taskforce continued the search and to communicate with the families of the missing.

Martinez next worked on the World Trade Center security detail, first at Ground Zero. He was then assigned to the Fresh Kills Landfill, where he supervised the recovery detail. There he was issued a full-body coverall made out of a nonwoven material that acts as a protection barrier against hazardous dry particles—as well as shoes and a paper mask. He realized the suit was an indication that better protection—full-body and head-covering protection—was needed for all the responders, not just those at Fresh Kills. Moreover, the mask wasn't doing its job because he was still breathing in lots of dust.

However, the other problem was that it was just too hot to be wearing all that gear: the mask, the construction helmet, the protective suit. Martinez recalled many of the workers taking off their equipment, which he realized, in retrospect, wasn't smart. At the time, however, everyone was focused on the work, not their personal safety.

Martinez was assigned to sort through the debris on the conveyor belts. "It was horrible," he said. He worked double shifts of sixteen-hour days: sixteen hours on, eight hours of rest, and then another sixteen-hour shift. The Internal Affairs people all worked together at Fresh Kills on the same shift, and so he worked daily with Baker, among others from IA.

The sign at the entrance to the cafeteria at Fresh Kills read, "World Trade Center Recovery Mission," and carried the seals and insignias of all the agencies and organizations involved in the cleanup effort, including the NYPD, FBI, FDNY, and OSHA.

Thousands of workers, rotated in shifts of twelve hours or more, examined and sorted debris. When identified, metal from the WTC was taken to another area of the landfill, where it was further sorted by type and size. Small debris was put on the conveyor belts to be sorted. The work, day in and day out, was the same, but because you never knew what you might find, the task demanded attention and concentration and, as a result, was exhausting. To avoid distraction or interruption, small talk with visitors or even other workers was discouraged. A sign posted at the debris sorting field reflected the need to concentrate:

Hi, I'm from _____.
Shut up and Pick up a Rake!!!

The focus on the task at hand kept most of the workers from the realization that they were among the dead, that Fresh Kills was, by the very nature of the debris, a mass grave, the ashes of the thousands of murdered men and women of all ages, all races and religions, and all incomes, whose lives were taken because they were present in or near the World Trade Center on the morning of September 11 or had rushed in to help others escape.

By April 1,200 bodies had been identified, along with 54,000 personal items.

No official ever publicly acknowledged Fresh Kills as hallowed ground or consecrated the ground where the ashes of the murdered were gathered. There is no plaque there to memorialize the lives identified there or those remains that never were identified.

There was no logic to what you would find sorting through the debris of Ground Zero. What items survived seemed so random. Candiace Baker recalled, "We found muddy panties with the store antitheft sensors still on them, which were from the Victoria's Secret store in the underground WTC shopping concourse. We found parts of shoes that were probably from DSW, the shoe store, that was also in the underground concourse. There were muddy jeans that we presumed were from the Gap. There were all these metal items— identical—that I kept finding. It looked familiar, but it took me the longest time to figure out what it was. It was actually the lever for a toilet bowl. There were tons of them. No faucets or toilets, but those little levers, they survived."

One day Baker had in her rake what looked like "a wet, rolled up muddy carpet." Suddenly a bone fragment, a piece from an elbow, popped out at her. "It scared the bejeesus out of me. I wanted to cry, throw up, and probably go to the bathroom on myself all at the same time." She realized, "Oh my God. This is a person." Then she realized that she had seen this before, many times.

When a detective came to take the body part away, he told Baker, "This is great. Now a family can have closure." But Baker found it difficult to make peace with what she had uncovered. While working at Fresh Kills, she had nightmares and lost much of her appetite. When she tried to sleep she'd instead think about some of the phone calls she'd answered on September 11 or finding that body at the site. "You don't pick and choose your memories and your thoughts," she learned. Her fiancé at the time was also a police officer who also worked on the cleanup. When they got home after work they would take off their clothes in the garage and put everything in a garbage bag because she didn't want any of the dust to come into her house. She would clean the washing machine both before and after washing their clothes. One day, when her fiancé blew his nose, all this black tar-like mucus came out. "What is that?" she asked. He answered, "I don't know."

The impact on Baker was cumulative. "I was exhausted. I found that I was cranky. I was tired all the time. I was sad all the time. Just the more I was there, the more real it became." She was frustrated that they were never told what they had recovered or even what they were accomplishing by doing the sorting. "There was never a report compiled to my knowledge saying, 'This is what was recovered, this is what you guys found, this is what we were able to do.' . . . They didn't give us a conclusion." There was no way to have closure.

A ceremony was held at the Pile on May 30, 2002, to mark the end of the Ground Zero cleanup. In silence, an empty flag-draped stretcher was carried from the rubble past an honor guard of victims' families, firefighters, and police. Buglers played "Taps," bagpipes performed a funeral march and then "America the Beautiful." A truck carrying the WTC's last steel beam, draped in black cloth and an American flag, followed. The steel girder, from the South Tower, had been cut down in a separate ceremony for the cleanup workers two days before and was decorated with tributes and remembrances of rescue and recovery workers. (It is now housed and can be seen at the 9/11 Memorial & Museum.)

All the heroic first responders, the thousands who worked at Ground Zero and at Fresh Kills, believed this chapter was closed. In less than a year up to ninety thousand persons had worked on the cleanup at varying times, at varying lengths, in various locations, and in a wide variety of capacities.[17] They returned to their families and careers and imagined better days ahead.

In April 2002, Raul Martinez started getting rashes on his body. He'd never had anything like them before. He went to his doctor, who couldn't say what caused the rashes but believed it was some kind of infection or exposure. Martinez had a chest x-ray at his doctor's insistence. The following week, while he was on vacation, he got a call from his doctor, who said, "You need to come in immediately because we found some abnormalities in your chest X-rays."

Martinez had a lung biopsy that revealed he had active sarcoidosis. He had never heard of sarcoidosis. He could barely say it, much less understand what it meant. His doctor explained that sarcoidosis is an inflammatory disease that creates abnormal cells (granulomas), most often in the lungs (but also in other organs). There is no cure. Sometimes the condition goes away, and some treatments may help, but chronic cases can last a lifetime. In the worst cases, organ damage occurs.

In a physical Martinez had had just the year before, everything looked fine. That this condition manifested so quickly, so seriously did not make sense. His doctor wondered if the sarcoidosis could have been activated by an exposure at his workplace.

Nonetheless Martinez continued to work at the World Trade Center site as NYPD security, even after the end of the cleanup. He was then promoted to lieutenant and later assigned to a housing division command. His skin condition did not improve. He started having symptoms of other diseases, such as gastroesophageal reflux disease (GERD), which included feelings of severe heartburn and acid reflux every night. He couldn't sleep. "It was horrible. It felt like it was stuck in my throat, the acid, like it was burning my throat."

Martinez was taking a lot of medication for the sarcoidosis, as well as a lot of breathing medications. His breathing "totally was out of whack," he realized. "I wasn't the same person, I can tell you, that I was before I started working at the landfill."

He felt that he could no longer do the police work the way he used to, so he filed for a three-quarters disability pension, which required showing that his injuries were from workplace exposures. Although he was convinced that the dust he inhaled and the debris he worked with at Ground Zero and at Fresh Kills over the course of hundreds of hours was toxic and had made him sick, the disability board turned him down, several times, refusing to believe his many injuries were from the dust. And he was not alone; he knew many other police officers who were told their illnesses were unrelated to the Ground Zero cleanup. He retired on a service retirement, what the Police Department calls a non-work-related disability. He never fought it.

Candiace Baker, Gary Acker, Raul Martinez, Mindy Hersh, Lyndon Harris, and John Walcott were just a few of the many, many thousands of individuals who worked on the cleanup of Ground Zero beginning on September 12. They were construction workers, city workers, utility workers, police, firefighters, and emergency personnel responding in a time of crisis and staying to do the task before them, the cleanup of the World Trade Center site and the search for (and investigation of) evidence and remains there.

They arrived at Ground Zero healthy, in the prime of their careers, in jobs they loved. They worked long hours, for long days, doing the job that needed to be done. They became sick. At first, many experienced a bad cough. Others developed flu-like symptoms. Some had stomach problems. Some found themselves short of breath, their lung capacity decreased. They went to doctors all over the Tri-State area, not realizing that their colleagues were suffering too.

The doctors diagnosed hundreds of different conditions afflicting these first responders: asthma, interstitial lung disease, chronic rhinosinusitis, GERD, sarcoidosis, as well as heart conditions. Some had cancer—leukemia, lung cancer, breast cancer, and even brain cancer.

The illnesses were real. The patients were sick. But even those doctors who believed the conditions resulted from some sort of toxic exposure at Ground Zero could not say so definitively. There were no medical or scientific studies that linked such illnesses to Ground Zero dust or debris—and there was no consistency as to who developed what illness based on what they did or where they worked or for how long at Ground Zero. Many of the illnesses, such as cancers, were not known to appear so soon after exposure to a toxic event; the latency period should have been years longer. The doctors were stumped.

When the Ground Zero responders sought to get medical disability or to retire because of a medical disability, the union disability boards turned them down. As far as the City of New York and many members of the medical and scientific community were concerned, there was no connection and no proof between exposure to and inhalation of Ground Zero dust and the illnesses they were experiencing.

David J. Prezant was a professor of pulmonary medicine at Albert Einstein College of Medicine in the Bronx who also worked for the FDNY as a lung specialist. At first, Prezant had the standard FDNY physician responsibilities, such as going to fires and emergencies. Over time his responsibilities expanded to include other health issues, such as infection control. In 1996 he was promoted to deputy chief medical officer to develop a state-of-the-art medical monitoring program for firefighters and work on general leadership issues. That same year FDNY merged with EMS, which expanded the range of potential health risks and injuries among members.

On September 11 Prezant arrived at the World Trade Center just after the second plane hit. "I was 15 feet from the south tower and had turned to take some stuff out of an ambulance when there was this roar," he told the *New York Times*. The explosion as the South Tower fell blew him to the edge of the south pedestrian bridge, which collapsed. As the *Times* reported, after he dug himself out of the rubble, he was blown across West Street. The air was so thick with debris that it felt as if he were "breathing soup."

That same day, Prezant and Dr. Kerry J. Kelly, the FDNY's chief medical officer, set up a triage center that saw patients until late that night. Prezant continued to treat patients in those first few weeks, dealing with respiratory and other issues, including posttraumatic stress disorder (PTSD). He observed that many of the Ground Zero responders were having a severe and unrelenting cough that produced a thick phlegm, which he would name World Trade Center cough syndrome in a 2002 study published in the *New England Journal of Medicine*.

For a doctor to name a new diagnosis is rare and noteworthy. It speaks to how singular the physiological response to dust exposure was for Ground Zero responders. Prezant's naming this condition helped to affirm that the victims were not inventing their condition—and it went a long way toward others accepting that there were harmful health effects from Ground Zero exposure.

The Fire Department started offering a monitoring exam for firefighters the first week of October because of the various issues doctors were observing in treatment. At that time they also met with other organizations setting up their own monitoring and treatment programs, including a group of Mount Sinai Hospital physicians and the Department of Health in New York City, to share what they were seeing and to coordinate their activities.

Acknowledging these Ground Zero–related health issues caused the city to adopt a Jekyll-and-Hyde posture. On the one hand, as an employer and municipal government, they wanted to inform firefighters, police, and emergency personnel of health hazards they may suffer. On the other, despite being obligated to provide benefits to its sick employees, the city would go to great lengths over the ensuing years to minimize these illnesses and their relation to Ground Zero dust and debris exposure. For the responders, this failure to validate the cause of their illnesses and deny them their disability benefits was disheartening; some considered it a shocking and appalling insult to their selfless service.

In January 2003, Detective John Walcott was examined as part of the World Trade Center Worker and Volunteer Medical Screening Program at Mount Sinai Hospital. The exam detected significant abnormalities, including elevated liver enzymes. Walcott thought this strange as his lab reports from the previous February were normal. As reported in *New York Magazine*, he felt "his energy deserting him." At first, he blamed it on having a new baby and working long shifts in Narcotics. But he wasn't a complainer, and he wasn't, as he often said, a "run-to-the-doctor kind of guy." He figured it would pass, and he would just soldier on.

One Sunday, as Walcott recounted in *New York Magazine* and several other media outlets, he stopped to pick up groceries on his way home from coaching high school hockey practice. At home in his driveway, he turned off the car, got out and opened his trunk, grabbed a bag of groceries in each arm, and started to walk to his door. He didn't take more than a few steps before he passed out.

He was taken to a hospital, where doctors ran a series of tests. Two weeks later he had a bone marrow biopsy and a verdict: he had leukemia. Walcott was initially treated with chemotherapy. However, his condition suggested that he needed a stem cell transplant; no matching donor was immediately found.[18]

Walcott was convinced his leukemia came from the toxins at Ground Zero. His sister, who worked for an airline, was the one who told him that exposure to jet fuel could cause cancer. But the Police Department would not give him a line-of-duty disability. He couldn't understand why working at Ground Zero didn't make him eligible for the fund set up by Congress, the September 11 Victim Compensation Fund.

Walcott was a dogged investigator. It's what made him a good detective. He was the kind of person who kept knocking on doors until he got the answer he needed. He never stopped. He turned to a lawyer friend of his who recommended he find a personal injury attorney. He spoke to several, including one attorney who asked that Walcott give his house as collateral for the case's expenses. Walcott's reply was "No way."

When he discussed his situation with one of the parents whose son he coached on the hockey team, the parent offered one piece of advice: "You need to talk to David Worby."

PART TWO

David Worby was, by general consensus, the best-known personal injury attorney in Westchester County. His father was a car salesman and, according to Worby, "an unhappy guy." Worby's escape was going to Cornell and then to Villanova Law School, where he made *Law Review*, won the moot court competition, and graduated near the top of his class. All of which led him to believe he might make a decent trial lawyer.

After law school, although he had offers from big law firms, Worby was eager to try cases, and so he joined a small White Plains firm that specialized in personal injury cases (also known as tort litigation). After four years of doing defense work for insurance companies, he wanted to do commercial and contract cases. "I didn't want to be known as someone who was just a personal injury lawyer. I wanted to be known for more than that." So in 1981, at the age of thirty, he started his own firm, "against everyone's advice."

Over the next fifteen years, Worby built one of the largest firms in Westchester County, with thirty lawyers: Worby DelBello Donnellan and Weingarten. Alfred B. DelBello was a former county executive who also served as lieutenant governor under Mario Cuomo. Their firm had a litigation, corporate, real estate, zoning, and personal injury practice. In 1989 Worby won an $18 million judgment for a construction worker in a car accident.[1]

As Worby recalled, "I was all over the place. I was always going to breakfasts, dinners, black-tie events. I chaired Governor Cuomo's campaign for this region." He was married and had three young children, and it all became too much. In 1995 he decided he needed to change his life. He didn't want to have to get up early for United Jewish Appeal breakfasts or to go to Westchester Council for the Arts dinners; he no longer needed to be at the helm of a large law firm, particularly one whose clients demanded his appearance at every meeting and for him to personally handle every litigation. He decided to get a friendly divorce—from his wife. Separating from the law firm wasn't as easy. "I said goodbye to everything except the plaintiffs' personal injury. I gave up a huge amount of dollars and money to the other partners who took over the business, and it wasn't the nicest breakup, either."

After taking over the personal injury practice, Worby realized that if he wasn't going to work full time, he would need another partner who would. He called a top-flight trial lawyer, Howard Borowick, and asked him to consider becoming his law partner. As Worby tells it, Borowick said, "David, I'll do anything to work with you, but you've got to meet my partner, Bill Groner, who's the brains of the operation. I'm the trial lawyer. Bill's the inside guy. Bill knows everything about computers and using data for litigation."

Worby wasn't sure that was what he was looking for. He was utterly unschooled about computers at the time and didn't appreciate what they could do for his legal practice. Borowick and Groner invited Worby to see their operation. He found the pair so upbeat and energetic that he couldn't understand why nobody in Westchester knew who they were.

Worby found Groner a great fit. Whereas Worby's personality was a magnet for new business—he was someone whose name alone brought in business—Groner was a dot-the-i, cross-the-t guy. "He's anal and he's obsessive-compulsive." They made a team that worked well together, and their law firm prospered. (In 1999 they bought out Borowick, who passed away in 2013.)

Groner had attended Binghamton University in New York and graduated from Boston University School of Law as class president and student commencement speaker. Those honors, however, didn't translate into a job at a New York City law firm. One day he saw an ad in the *New York Law Journal* from Richard Shandell, an attorney who would soon become president of the New York State Trial Lawyers Association, an important lobbying and bar association organization for personal injury attorneys with around five thousand members at the time. Shandell was looking for a trial assistant, commonly known as a "bag man," who would carry his trial bags and more. Groner applied and was offered the job at a salary of $15,000 a year. He complained that the secretaries made more than he did. "They're more valuable to us than you," Shandell responded. That put Groner in his place.

For the first year Groner carried Shandell's bags to court for all of Shandell's trials. During his first week he followed Shandell into the courtroom of Judge Louis Kaplan on a million-dollar labor law case. Back then, you picked juries for a week or two. The system allowed you to really work jurors and find those most receptive to your client's case. Groner would be present for every moment of jury selection. At the end of this case Shandell told Groner, "Okay, write the jury instructions."

Groner asked, "What are jury instructions?"

"Find out," Shandell answered. Groner was doing menial work and at the same time writing jury charges for a million-dollar case. It was a great start to a career as a trial lawyer.

Groner worked next for a personal injury attorney, Philip Damashek (now deceased), who was a legendary figure in New York courts. In a simple case, if the insurance companies were offering much less than what he thought the case was worth, say, $2,500 (in the mid-1980s), Damashek would authorize Groner to spend $10,000 on medical experts and trial expenses. This would signal to the insurance companies that they were willing to take the case all the way to a jury verdict. More often than not, the insurance companies would settle at Damashek and Groner's higher number rather than have the expense and risk of a jury trial. Damashek provided Groner with great training—not only in terms of trial strategy, preparation, and in-court experience but also in negotiating against larger and better-financed opponents.

Damashek, who with his partners would go on to successful litigation against the tobacco companies in New York State, became president of the New York State Trial Lawyers Association. He was revered by his fellow attorneys and was an incredible mentor to Groner, who ended up preparing some fifty trials for Damashek's firm over a three-year period (many of which settled before going to verdict). Groner started winning cases, even though he looked like a kid and it was a struggle to get taken seriously by the other attorneys, judges, and, most critically, the juries—no matter how skilled a litigator he was becoming.

After three years of that, Groner went out on his own, partnering with a Binghamton classmate, Larry Hollander. Well on his way to becoming a highly regarded construction attorney, Hollander did hourly billing while Groner was building a personal injury department that was contingency-fee based, which seemed like a formula for keeping them afloat in the short term.

In anticipation of raising a family, Groner decided that he wanted to move to Westchester. He put an ad in the *New York Law Journal* saying, "New York City personal injury attorney looking to partner with Westchester County attorney with large client base." The ad produced hardly any takers and nothing that panned out. So Groner reached out to Howard Borowick, his college karate-sparring partner, who was rapidly developing a reputation as an outstanding trial lawyer. They set up a practice in Westchester. And it was through Borowick that he met Worby.

With Worby's name and Groner's energy, and partnering with Michael R. Edelman, a well-known personal injury attorney in Westchester County, they built a powerful firm, Worby Groner Edelman. Groner, who likes to start organizations, approached the New York State Trial Lawyers Association, where he was already on the board, about starting a Westchester chapter, for which he became its first president. He got involved in the Westchester County Bar Association on the Executive Committee and was chair of the Trial Committee. As time went by, he found that his organizational talents made him gravitate to the administration of cases as well as high-end mediations, arbitrations, settlements, and the business of the law firm. He became the firm's "inside man."

What Groner loved about personal injury cases was the ability to help significantly injured clients receive compensation that allowed them to lead their best possible lives. Often he found himself getting emotionally involved in his cases and with his clients. One case continued to resonate for many years: a motorcyclist who was going the speed limit on the Brooklyn-Queens Expressway, a road that is continuously under repair, hit a pothole, fell, and then was hit by a car. As a result, the man became blind and a quadriplegic. The man's dream was to receive enough money to get off public assistance and marry his girlfriend, who had stood by him throughout his ordeal.

Groner fought for the man in a multiyear litigation, urged on by the thought of being able to change his client's life. And the client continued to be an inspiration to Groner. He was one of the first to develop and use "sip and puff" technology, which enables a paralyzed person to communicate with others by breathing Morse code into a computer-attached straw that decodes the speech. It took years and years to make the case, but Groner eventually won the man millions, enough for him to marry his girlfriend and move with her into a country house that was customized to accommodate his needs. To this day Groner cites that case as "one of the highlights of my life," and he remains in regular contact with his favorite client.

Paul Barrese had worked as a claims investigator for the Hartford Insurance Company out of their Mt. Kisco office, which brought him into contact with Worby. At Worby's suggestion, he decided to establish his own investigation firm with Worby and then Groner as his main client.

Gina Barrese, Paul's wife, had also worked at Hartford Insurance in the claims department. Worby was impressed with the multitude of her talents, and when there was an opening in his office, she came to work for him.

In the spring of 2004 Worby got a call from one of the parents at Fox Lane High School, where his eldest son had been a student. The call was on behalf of John Walcott, an NYPD detective and a hockey coach at Fox Lane. Walcott had leukemia and believed he got it from working on the Ground Zero cleanup.

Worby asked Paul Barrese to drive to Rockland County to meet with Walcott. Barrese's impression was that Walcott was "a pretty sharp guy, if a little rough around the edges."

In the meantime, Worby looked into the September 11 Victim Compensation Fund. The VCF was created by an Act of Congress as part of the Air Transportation Safety and System Stabilization Act (ATSSSA) shortly after 9/11 to provide compensation for individuals (and any deceased individuals' beneficiary) who "was physically injured or killed as a result of the terrorist-related aircraft crashes of September 11, 2001." To qualify for the VCF one had to agree not to sue the airlines involved, the airport security companies, the Port Authority, or WTC leaseholder Larry Silverstein.

As an alternative to the fund, ATSSSA also provided that one could sue for damages in federal court in Brooklyn. However, the conditions under which you could file a claim were strict: there were a number of very specific requirements as to when the person was injured and treated, and all claims had to be filed by December 22, 2003.[2] Unfortunately Walcott didn't qualify under any of those regulations.

Having met with Walcott and seen the condition he was in, Paul was convinced that Worby needed to find a way to help Walcott. "This guy's a hero," Paul said. "He was there in 1993 when the first attack on the World Trade Center happened, and when 9/11 happened, he worked there day and night for months."

Paul had also told Gina all about Walcott's case. She too urged Worby to help him. "H's so weak he can barely hold his baby girl," Gina said. "He deserves better. All he wants is to get his disability payment because he can't work."

"And the Police Department is not giving it to him because they're saying it's not line-of-duty-related," Paul added.

"This is outside of our wheelhouse," was Worby's first reaction. "We do personal injury, not police pension applications."

"Come on, boss," Gina pleaded. "It's one letter." She put an already drafted letter in front of him, and he signed it. Then she sent it to the Police Department to approve Walcott's disability payment. A few weeks later, they heard that the application was denied.

Worby decided the wisest thing would be to file a notice of claim (a warning that you are going to file a lawsuit) against New York City. Doing so would protect Walcott's rights to sue the city for his illnesses, if indeed they decided that was worth pursuing. Soon Worby and Groner were receiving inquiries from other NYPD officers who'd become ill after working on the cleanup of Ground Zero.

Each day when Candiace Baker arrived at Fresh Kills Landfill, she boarded a bus that took her to the top of a hill. From there she entered a tent, where she received her equipment for the day's work and suited up, putting on and zipping up her protective suit, donning her gloves, and slipping booties over her shoes. Then she and the other workers would head to the pile of debris to sift its contents.

At first, Baker was given a paper breathing mask. A few days later, she was directed to a box of respirators and told to take one. They weren't fitted to her. She was given a filter to put in the respirator. She doesn't recall being told that she needed to change the filters. No attention was given to being vigilant about keeping the dust out; as far as Baker was concerned, the supervisors were treating the dust as more of a nuisance and an irritant than a danger.

The job itself was surreal, Baker later said. It was difficult to grasp that this was all that remained of almost three thousand lives.

The smell was putrid, nauseating. She could smell it from the bottom of the hill, before she even boarded the bus. She had never smelled anything like that before. When she first started working there, she had asked another officer, "What is that smell?"

"Death," he had answered.

The days blurred one into another, but Baker remembered having Thanksgiving dinner there, provided by the Red Cross. She appreciated the humanity of the gesture. Doing the same work day after day, it was hard to feel like you were accomplishing anything and that anyone appreciated what you were doing. That's why the Red Cross's gesture meant so much to her.

Baker would spend more than four hundred hours working the Ground Zero cleanup. Because she lived only minutes away on Staten Island, she was always willing to take the shifts of other officers who lived farther away. She worked day in, day out, for months among the dust and debris, the thick air and its putrid smell. At times she felt sick to her stomach. The more she recalled of her time at Fresh Kills, the more she thought her doctor could be right about why she had developed so many health complications.

Juan Gonzalez had been a *New York Daily News* columnist since 1987. Born in Ponce, Puerto Rico, he grew up in East Harlem and Brooklyn and attended Columbia University during the 1960s, where he was a student leader and a member of Students for a Democratic Society (SDS) as well as the New York chapter of the Puerto Rican activist group the Young Lords.

Gonzalez did not lose his passion for social justice when he became a journalist. He just had a louder bullhorn. And he was an excellent reporter. He won a George Polk Award in 1998 for his committed advocacy journalism.

Within days of 9/11, Gonzalez was hearing stories about officers developing hacking coughs and spitting up dark phlegm. Fellow *Daily News* reporters who lived in Lower Manhattan, such as George Rush and Joanna Molloy, told him their concerns about the air and dust. He'd been in the Financial District himself and knew the air at Ground Zero didn't smell healthy—and he certainly didn't believe the government officials' claims that the air was safe. Wanting to learn more, he spoke with Joel Kupferman of the New York Environmental Law and Justice Project.

In his column on September 28, 2001, "Health Hazards in Air Worry Trade Center Workers," Gonzalez reported that Kupferman had independent labs test the dust around Ground Zero and that they found greater-than-normal asbestos contamination. The EPA and city officials explained away these concerns as temporary spikes and that any irritation or respiration issues were not serious and would subside with time.

Kupferman, undeterred, had filed a Freedom of Information Act request for the EPA to release its own test results on the air, dust, and debris at Ground Zero. He shared more than eight hundred pages of the released EPA documents with Gonzalez, which formed the basis of his October 26, 2001, column, featured on the newspaper's front page with the headline "A Toxic Nightmare at Disaster Site." Gonzalez's reporting forced the EPA to confirm that they had found elevated levels of toxic substances such as benzene, PCBs, lead, and chromium in the air and water at Ground Zero.

This was a major revelation, given that it was the EPA that had produced the reports. It suggested that the toxic dangers in the air at Ground Zero should have been known to EPA Administrator Whitman at the federal level and Mayor Giuliani at the city level. Regardless, Gonzalez and Kupferman were convinced: the air was not safe.

Giuliani didn't see it that way. He held a press conference to challenge the *Daily News* story, insisting that any side effects from inhaling Ground Zero dust were temporary and did not pose any actual threat. Despite the eight hundred pages of EPA information to the contrary, the mayor professed to know better, and New York's political and business establishments chose to take his word on the dangers in the dust from Ground Zero.

The backlash to Gonzalez's columns was strong. Whitman called the publisher of the *Daily News* to complain and later published an op-ed in the paper defending herself. Leaders of New York City civic organizations also protested. Gonzalez's editor, Richard T. Pienciak on the Metropolitan desk, who had worked on the Three Mile Island nuclear accident story for the Associated Press, was removed without explanation soon after the piece ran, and the Ground Zero investigative team Pienciak had assembled, which Gonzalez was part of, was disbanded. Coincidence? Gonzalez thought probably not.

Greg Fried was a former New York police surgeon who'd been injured on 9/11. When he heard that Worby, whom he'd known for years, was representing police officers who had become ill after working on the Ground Zero cleanup, he called him and asked, "David, are you really taking these cases?"

Worby said he was. Fried told him, "You have no idea how many cops are coming to me. They are sick. The Department is not covering their illnesses and they want to know what to do. The NYPD's lawyer is also getting a lot of these calls. They all want to know who to call to take their case." Worby was amazed. Fried was sending him cases?

In 1980 Fried was working at Cabrini Hospital in Manhattan, near the Police Academy on East 20th Street, when he was hired by the Police Department; within a year he became a police surgeon. Whenever police officers took sick time, they needed to see the police surgeon to confirm they were ill and to determine what their illness was. In the years that followed, Fried was promoted and trained police surgeons all over the city. When a police officer was injured, it was Fried who would interact with the hospital to make sure he was satisfied with the officer's care.

Over the years Fried became friendly with New York City's mayors, including Rudy Giuliani, who conferred with him when police were injured. The mayors relied on Fried for such information.

On the morning of September 11, Fried was in a police car when he heard the call on the police radio, and he rushed downtown. Having been a first responder at the World Trade Center in 1993, he knew what to do. At the scene he found a firefighter who was bleeding to death, having been injured by falling debris. Fried bent down to treat him, just as the second Tower collapsed, crushing them both in debris. As he recounted to *Newsday,* "In that instant you think you're dead and the entire building is coming down on top of you, so I rolled into a ball. I got hit in the back and could feel numbness in my leg and I realized I'm not dead. I had pain all over the place and I was buried in rubble up to my shoulder, in pitch black. I had never experienced blackness like midnight in a coal mine."

He managed to crawl out of the rubble and make his way to the harbor. The firefighter he was treating remained among the missing. From the harbor Fried was thrown on a boat that took him to New Jersey, where he received much-needed medical care. He had suffered "a bunch of busted ribs and [his] back was broken."

Two months later he had recovered enough to return to work. However, he quickly discovered he could no longer stand long enough to perform surgery. "My back was killing me. If I stand for an hour, my back bothers me. You really don't want a surgeon operating on you who can't concentrate and can't stand still." In 2003 he put in for his pension.

In recognition of Fried's extraordinary service on 9/11, he was given a three-quarters permanent disability pension, which is both rare and remarkable. He believes he is the only police surgeon to ever receive a service-related pension. In addition, he was the only surgeon ever awarded the NYPD's Medal of Valor.

Despite having retired, Fried continued to follow what happened to the Ground Zero responders. It was clear that the toxic mess down there was going to cause all kinds of significant illnesses. But at the time the city and the federal government took the position that there was no evidence Ground Zero was making people sick. Fried thought that was ridiculous. "I was there," Fried recalled at a later date,. "I know damn well how bad it was and I know what these guys went through and that's crazy. I know quite a few people who have very serious injuries."

Fried showed Worby photos that first responders had given him of the dust cloud and of the first responders working there without respirators. He wanted to light a fire under Worby, convinced there were fifty more potential cases out there.

On February 9, 2002, the *St. Louis Post-Dispatch* published "Caustic Dust Blankets World Trade Center Area" and a follow-up the next day, "Public Was Never Told That Dust from Ruins Is Dangerously Caustic," both by Andrew Schneider, their Pulitzer Prize–winning environmental journalist. Schneider had uncovered that the U.S. Geological Survey found pH levels in the dust at the WTC site that were "as corrosive as drain cleaner." When Schneider confronted the EPA about these results, the agency claimed that they had been released to the public. Schneider was not one to take the EPA's word for it, so he reviewed all the statements the agency had made since 9/11 and discovered that, in fact, they had never released to the public any information about the danger present in Ground Zero dust.

The *St. Louis Post-Dispatch* was not alone in covering this news. On March 17, 2003, Chris Bowman and Edie Lau wrote an article for the *Sacramento Bee* titled "Air Today . . . Gone Tomorrow" with this declaration: "The U.S. Environmental Protection Agency's pollution tests in the smoke-filled days following the World Trade Center collapse did not support the agency's pronouncements that air around ground zero was safe to breathe, an independent federal investigation has found. Further, the EPA reached its conclusion using a cancer risk level 100 times greater than what it traditionally deems 'acceptable' for public exposure to toxic air contaminants according to the EPA's Office of Inspector General." In other words, the EPA and the mayor's office were wrong to tell the Ground Zero responders and the citizens of New York that the air at the site was safe. Neither Giuliani nor Whitman acknowledged the truth in these articles.

On August 26, 2003, Senator Hillary Rodham Clinton, having learned about the dangerous nature of the air at Ground Zero, held a press conference on the steps of New York's City Hall to express her indignation. "I don't think any of us expected that our government would knowingly deceive us about something as sacred as the air we breathe," she said, anger coloring her voice. "The air that our children breathe in schools, that our valiant first responders were facing on the pile."

"I am outraged," she continued. "In the immediate aftermath, the first couple of days, nobody could know. But a week later? Two weeks later? Two months later? Six months later? Give me a break!"

The following week, Thomas Cahill, who led a study by scientists at UC Davis, told Ellen Wulfhorst of Reuters for a September 3 article, "The debris pile acted like a chemical factor. It cooked together the components and the buildings and their contents, including enormous numbers of computers, and gave off gases of toxic metals, acids and organics for at least six weeks."

It was striking to see these stories breaking in newspapers outside of New York. Some felt the New York press was too dependent on New York advertisers or too beholden to New York's financial and political establishment to accept that police, firefighters, EMS personnel, and volunteers at Ground Zero were the victims of toxic exposure that the city and the EPA denied was present.

The more Baker heard about the health hazards of working on the Ground Zero cleanup, the more she realized that many other people were becoming sick. They had breathing problems, severe coughs, sinus problems, gastrointestinal problems, skin problems, cancers. There was no clear pattern as to who got sick. They were separate people living separate lives, yet they shared the connection of having worked at Ground Zero.

Baker had been sifting debris on the conveyor belt one day, trying to separate out and make sense of the contents moving by, when she suddenly felt nauseated. She was sent to the medical tent, where she was given a standard breathing test, blowing into a tube to raise the ball inside. A rating between 4 and 5 is considered normal. Baker could manage only between a 2 and a 3 because she was having trouble breathing. She was told to sit outside and wait until she felt better, and then go back to sorting at the landfill.

She was sitting outside, still feeling nauseated, when a young woman walked over and asked if she was okay. Baker told her that her breathing wasn't good and that she was feeling nauseated. Sandra Adrian, an NYPD detective who also worked in Internal Affairs, introduced herself as "Sandy" and asked Baker if she could sit with her. They just sat there, sharing water and crackers, and talked, becoming closer. Baker found Adrian a very compassionate person, very sweet. From that time on, Baker considered Sandy a friend. They would say "Hi" or wave to each other whenever their paths crossed.

In March 2004 Worby and Groner asked Dr. William Sawyer, of Toxicology Consultants & Assessments Specialists, a medical expert on toxic exposure, to review the available information concerning Ground Zero exposure and any connection between the dust and cancer. Proving toxic exposure in a court of law required finding ways to quantify the exposure. One of the problems was that the events at the World Trade Center site knocked out or destroyed the air monitors that had been in place. In the weeks that followed, various individual and government labs had tested the air and water quality in or around Ground Zero and tested samples of the dust, tests that would be crucial to proving the case for toxic exposure.

On March 29, writing to Richard Vecchio, an attorney at Worby Groner, Dr. Sawyer reported that the total destruction of the Twin Towers and several other buildings at the World Trade Center, as well as the buildings' collapse and the smoldering fires at the Pile, released "a dust and vapor that hovered over the area" and that the burning building materials released a "toxic mixture of chemicals" into the air that was hazardous to human health. Among the toxic elements were "organic and inorganic compounds from air conditioners, broken gas lines, jet fuel, plastics, vinyl chloride wire insulation, computers, light ballasts, carpeting, and other sources that produced toxic pyrolysis emissions from the smoldering rubble pile into the air." In other words, toxic substances were present in the air and in the dust that Ground Zero responders had inhaled.

Sawyer noted that the earliest testing for volatile organic compounds at the site, including toluene and benzene, was conducted at the request of the EPA's Office of Emergency and Remedial Response. Air analyses had been conducted from October 3 through 23, 2001. According to Sawyer, "the analyses revealed high levels of benzene and toluene in excess of guidelines protective of human health. . . .

The average benzene exposure levels at the North Tower Center site were approximately 7.2 to 580 times in excess of the NIOSH benzene exposure limit designed for an 8-hour work week, 5-days per week." That was just for the North Tower site. When Sawyer looked at the average benzene level reported based upon the seventeen analyses done at Ground Zero, it was "168 times in excess of the NIOSH standard. Factoring in an 84-hour work week increased the exposures to 352.8 times in excess of the NIOSH recommended exposure level."

Sawyer concluded, "I am certain to within a very high degree of toxicological certainty that . . . exposures to volatile benzene at levels far in excess of any public health or occupational standards substantially contributed to . . . AML [acute myeloid leukemia], a [classic] benzene-induced malignancy." He also found extraordinarily high levels of polynuclear aromatic hydrocarbon (PAH) molecules, which have been found to persist in the environment, are notably toxic, and can be cancer-causing. Noting that "an increased incidence rate of acute myelogenous leukemia has been measured and reported among PAH exposed workers," Sawyer added, "I am also certain to within a high degree of toxicological certainty that . . . extended daily ingestion of PAH containing dust at the [Ground Zero] site and Freshkill Landfill [would substantially contribute to or induce] . . . AML."

Sawyer's determination was critical. The overwhelming majority of physicians were saying that the standard latency period for blood cancers caused by toxin exposure was a minimum of ten years. The city, the insurance companies, and the doctors working for the NYPD and FDNY would continue to deny any link between Ground Zero dust and the illnesses responders were experiencing. More alarming still, Sawyer reported that not only could Ground Zero dust cause cancer but that, in all probability, as time went on there would be many, many more victims.

In the weeks that followed 9/11 Thomas Ryan's Aunt Barbara came to accept her husband's death. The family arranged to hold a memorial for Ryan's uncle in Middletown, New Jersey. At that point, they had a tombstone but no grave. But at least the memorial would help his family start to heal.

Almost a year later there was a knock at his aunt's door. The family priest and two New Jersey state troopers were there with a little black box. "We're sorry to inform you," they said, "that we identified your husband." In the box was a one-centimeter piece of bone they had identified in a DNA lab as belonging to Lou Minervino.

Ryan felt it was wrong for them to show up out of the blue one year later. Whatever closure his aunt had managed to achieve was undone. It basically ripped her heart open again. They buried the piece of bone at her husband's gravesite.

Worby believed the Ground Zero responder cases had big potential—getting vindication for these heroes was a worthy objective and given that there could be as many as fifty plaintiffs, it could be a significant case for the firm. But this was just Worby's instinct. He turned to Groner to discuss whether they wanted to handle John Walcott's case and seek out others.

Groner saw clear challenges in taking on these cases. First, you needed to prove that someone is at fault and that you could sue them. In this case, the injuries arose, directly or indirectly, out of a terrorist act. It was an act of war, but not by another country—it was an act committed by an international terrorist network. There was no person or company with discernible assets to sue.[3]

Another option was to consider whether the city or contractors could be at fault for failing to protect the responders from the toxic dust. But there had been an environmental catastrophe and an emergency in the greatest sense of the word. Who could have prepared for such an eventuality? It would be hard to hold the leaseholders of the Twin Towers or the Port Authority or New York State responsible. Or to hold the city or the construction companies doing the cleanup responsible for accomplishing this task, given the circumstances. And the defense would be sure to argue that the police, firefighters, EMS, construction workers, and volunteers who rushed in to Ground Zero and who failed to wear respirators were the cause of their own injuries.

Second, how do you prove causation? A giant dust cloud had permeated all of Lower Manhattan and traveled over New Jersey and Brooklyn for months, yet many people did not get sick. Some did, but how could you prove that it was only because of working at Ground Zero? And how do you show the amount of toxins that each person inhaled, which was required by New York law to file a claim? The defense was sure to argue that the responders were exposed to dust whenever they were anywhere in Lower Manhattan or Brooklyn, not just when they were working.

Third, there were no bad guys here. Were you really going to say that on 9/11 the City of New York or the Port Authority had done something wrong? Are you going to accuse Mayors Giuliani and Bloomberg of being villains?

Fourth and last, such a case would take enormous time and effort, not to mention lots of experts, and the expense could bankrupt the law firm long before any settlement was reached or judgment was delivered.

Despite all this, and after talking to Dr. Fried, who had a number of potential cases to refer, Groner thought they should take on the Ground Zero responders' cases. The victims were police, firefighters, and other emergency responders who came to the defense of the nation and the city at its greatest time of peril. These were the heroes who ran toward the buildings when everyone else was running away, who undertook the hard and dangerous work of the rescue and recovery missions, and stayed to complete the cleanup. They knew they were exposed to a dust that could have grave consequences, but they fearlessly performed their duties for the betterment of society. What they had done, what they had endured, and what they were suffering was heartbreaking. Taking this kind of case was why Groner became a lawyer.

He also thought the cases made good business sense. They were, in his opinion, cases that would eventually be settled—with the city or the Port Authority, the real estate owners or leaseholders, or the construction companies who worked on the cleanup. This was a decision he came to, he now admits, out of a combination of arrogance and ignorance. The arrogance was that he believed these were cases that one could win in front of a jury—despite the overwhelming number of legal and medical proof problems. A New York City detective in all respects healthy before working on the Pile, where he had prolonged exposure to the WTC dust and who became sick with cancer, seemed like a case that a jury would be sympathetic to and find for—and one that would, as a consequence, be settled. Groner couldn't imagine the city would fight the Ground Zero responders on that.

The ignorance was that he had no idea what he was getting into.

"All of a sudden, we started getting calls," said Paul Barrese. "We didn't even know what to do with them." Worby's response: "Sign them up."

There was no question that those first clients who came into the office were sick. They weren't exaggerating or looking for an easy payday. What the law firm could offer them, then, was something valuable, in Gina Barrese's opinion: someone who believed them. Sometimes she thought they just wanted someone to listen, to hear them. In a way, she said, that was how the whole case started. The Ground Zero responders just wanted someone to believe them, to validate their story. "And then the word spread."

Worby was determined to find a scientific or medical basis for the illnesses the Ground Zero responders were experiencing. "What happened is that I couldn't find experts, so I became the expert," he now says. "What I uncovered is that if you're a cigarette smoker you can get asbestosis if you're exposed to asbestos about seven years quicker, because the cigarette smoke and the asbestos co-accelerate each other. That's what happened here: people who were exposed to the lead and the mercury and asbestos. I can't explain it scientifically other than to tell you there was a cross-accelerant behavioral toxic stew here that reduced people's latency periods to get these illnesses. The other thing that did it is that 80 percent of all the people down there were construction workers, firemen, and cops, and guess what they've been breathing in for their professional careers? Smoke and dust!"

Worby realized that the latency period of the Ground Zero firefighters, police officers, and emergency personnel didn't start on September 11, 2001; they had all been breathing smoke and dust since they started working. That's why the cancers were showing up so soon. At least, that was his theory. Much to his frustration, nobody bought it.

In early 2004 Worby and Groner were considering how best to proceed on behalf of their first Ground Zero injury cases. Based on their conversations with Fried about injured firefighters as well as with an attorney who represented NYPD officers, Groner thought they could soon be representing as many as two hundred clients—and if they had two hundred, there were probably a thousand potential clients out there.

A thousand cases was more than the firm could logistically handle. Worby was essentially retired and working only part time. Moreover, if they went to trial, the litigation expenses could financially break them before they ever saw a dime. The Ground Zero responders were not clients who would pay by the hour; they were going to be contingency-based fee cases. (If they won, the attorneys would collect a percentage, usually 33 percent.) Groner decided they needed to find a partner, a law firm that was experienced in mass torts and who would be able to underwrite the cost of the case.

Groner contacted the preeminent mass tort law firm, Weitz & Luxenberg, headquartered in New York, that had won large settlements for their clients in cases. (DES was a pregnancy-related drug that caused health problems for the women who took it as well as their children.) But they never called him back. Groner also reached out to Marc Bern of Napoli Bern, who did call him back. His firm had recently won more than $100 million for clients who had used the diet supplement fen-phen. Groner explained that he and Worby (whom Bern knew) wanted to discuss a case that had to do with the World Trade Center Ground Zero responders. Bern said, "Sure. Come on in."

Napoli Bern's offices were at 115 Broadway, a twenty-two-story Neo-Gothic tower that stood next to Trinity Church and its cemetery, less than a mile from the World Trade Center. The offices were on the twelfth floor, and Paul Napoli's corner office had a view straight up Broadway, as if the whole city lay before him. On 9/11 the dust had engulfed the building.

After they met with Groner and Worby, Napoli and Bern asked for time to discuss the case. There were several reasons, in Bern's opinion, not to take them on. First of all, he was concerned about the political aspects of the case, which he deemed "pretty hot." Second, there was no certainty that they would ever get paid. Third, he wondered, "How do you sue someone for an act of war?"

Within days of 9/11, Dr. Robin Herbert, Dr. Stephen Levin, Dr. Philip Landrigan, and other Mount Sinai Hospital doctors met at a home in Westchester County to organize a response to the events at Ground Zero. Workers and volunteers who were coughing or experiencing other ailments were being sent for evaluation to Mount Sinai's Irving J. Selikoff Center for Occupational and Environmental Medicine (named after a pioneering asbestos researcher who died in 1992). The Center had been examining workers exposed to pollutants such as PCBs, lead, and silica since 1987.

By the end of November 2001, Dr. Levin was seeing cases of early-onset asthma and RADS (reactive airways dysfunction syndrome) in Ground Zero workers. He was concerned that these symptoms could plague the victims for the rest of their lives. Levin and Landrigan feared that the workers at Ground Zero were not being sufficiently protected against the respiratory and medical hazards posed there. In press interviews, including with *Mother Jones* magazine, Levin and other doctors argued for the necessity of comprehensive testing and screening of Ground Zero responders. They warned that the workers needed training and protective equipment and urged the use of masks with special filters.

In April 2002, thanks in no small part to the efforts of Senator Clinton, FEMA awarded Mount Sinai $12 million to establish the WTC Worker and Volunteer Medical Screening Program, and by July examinations of nine thousand workers had begun. The group also began to collect data. They learned that first responders who suffered from asthma and breathing conditions were also exhibiting severe psychological strain. Some could not stop crying. Some were depressed because of what they had seen; others were depressed because their illnesses no longer allowed them to do the work they loved. Others had anger issues.

Mount Sinai recognized the importance of treating the responders' mental health issues and developed programs to do so. Over the next several years, the hospital would see and follow up with thousands of Ground Zero responders as they became increasingly ill, developing an important database for ongoing clinical study.

Landrigan was part of a research workgroup named Health and Environmental Consequences of the World Trade Center Disaster. Their report, posted online on February 18, 2004, begins, "The attack on the World Trade Center (WTC) created an acute environmental disaster of enormous magnitude." This was a significant determination. For the most part, the events of 9/11 had been treated as a national tragedy, an emergency crisis, and a terrorist attack. It was a political matter, a rescue and recovery matter, even a logistical and construction challenge for the cleanup that followed. Landrigan's workgroup was among the first to discern in what occurred on 9/11 at Ground Zero and on 9/12 and the days that followed a never-before-seen environmental disaster that would have far-reaching health consequences.

The workgroup's report spelled out the danger present in the Ground Zero dust: "WTC dust was found to consist predominantly (95%) of coarse particles and contained pulverized cement, glass fibers, asbestos, lead, polycyclic aromatic hydrocarbons (PAHs), poly-

chlorinated biphenyls (PCBs), and polychlorinated furans and dioxins. . . . Dust pH was highly alkaline (pH 9.0–11.0)."

Each of the individual elements of the dust cited above had known
dangers; inhaling either glass fibers or asbestos or pulverized cement
was hazardous in itself. Here the toxic elements were combined in
ways never seen before. Because this combination of toxins was new,
the Mount Sinai doctors could turn to no scientific or medical studies about their effects. Still, even at this early stage, it was clear that
Ground Zero dust was extremely caustic, equal to the pH of drain
cleaner or ammonia, and the dust particles were likely to remain
irritants once inhaled. The question remained: What would be the
long-term health effects of inhaling Ground Zero dust?

Given that almost a quarter of all Ground Zero responders were
from Long Island, Dr. Benjamin Luft, chairman of the Department of
Medicine at Stony Brook University Medical Center, had established a
major program for the monitoring and treatment of responders shortly
after the attacks. Dr. Luft found that over 70 percent of responders
were affected by the toxic dust and suffered from respiratory and
gastrointestinal diseases. Many were found to also be suffering from
depression and PTSD. The program received a $9 million grant from
NIOSH, an arm of the Centers for Disease Control and Prevention, to
fund patient monitoring and treatment. "This project, which is truly
unique, can be one way our society may extract something positive
from this great disaster," Luft asserted.

On May 24, 2004, the front page of the *New York Daily News* blared,
"Ill Winds of 9/11." In a special report Michele McPhee, the newspaper's Police Bureau chief, outlined "escalating health problems."
The article took up two full pages and featured Walcott with Worby at
his side. Walcott told McPhee, "I've never been sick a day in my life,
except for a sore throat or a common cold." Now he was living with
acute ALM, a form of cancer, that his doctors believed was caused by
exposure to toxins at Ground Zero and the Fresh Kills Landfill. Walcott's concern was not for himself alone: "I've had friends of mine

who were stationed with me [at the landfill] visit me in the hospital and panic, asking me, 'Am I next?'"

After meeting with Groner and Worby, Paul Napoli had begun looking into the toxic nature of the dust at Ground Zero and found reasons for concern about the responders' exposure. He came to believe they could make a case against the city and its contractors.

Marc Bern also came around to joining Worby and Groner in the responder suits, reasoning that, that at its core, the city sent the responders to Ground Zero and so they were entitled to the protections of New York labor law. Napoli and Bern called Worby and Groner and said, "Okay. Let's go for it!"

On June 23, 2004, the four attorneys met to outline how a joint venture would make use of each of their strengths. Worby would be the lead person in dealing with the press, and he and Groner would focus on the marketing effort—getting the word out to as many first responders who were exposed and injured as possible. Napoli and Bern would run the case out of their offices and advance the costs. The four shook hands and set out to strategize how best to make their case.

Dr. Greg Fried wrote Worby and Groner the following frightening, yet prescient, email on July 15, 2004:

As I see it, there are 4 groups of people involved with 9/11:
1. People who were seriously injured or who developed cancer or other clearly incapacitating illnesses. . . .
2. People who have significant illnesses, coughs, sinusitis, lung impairment, hearing loss, exercise intolerance, sarcoid (although this might fit in category 1), reflux esophagitis, skin rashes, and other recognizable illness which have been either not attributed to 9/11 or are not so disabling as to cause retirement.
3. People who are ticking time bombs which haven't gone off yet . . . those who will be getting sick or sicker in the next

few to many years with renal failure from toxic exposures, liver cancer, mesothelioma, lung cancer, sterility, small birth weight children, and thousands of other potential illnesses not as yet diagnosed but highly likely as we accumulate more patients with more findings and symptoms. . . .

4. People who are well. . . .

As we go forward, group 4 will diminish and they will become members, unfortunately, of the other groups.

On September 10, Worby Groner Edelman Napoli Bern (WGENB, as the joint venture between the law firms was called) filed suit against Silverstein Properties, the World Trade Center's leaseholder and the company responsible for the Twin Towers, as well as the major construction companies who worked on the Ground Zero cleanup, on behalf of some six hundred clients. Worby told the press that the cases were worth more than $1 billion in damages.

In response to the lawsuit, Silverstein spokesman Howard J. Rubenstein said, "The rescue, recovery and cleanup of the World Trade Center site was conducted completely under the auspices and control of the Federal Emergency Management Agency (FEMA) and the City of New York. We had no control over that operation and no ability to supervise what safety precautions were taken." WGENB countered that further claims were planned against New York City, the Port Authority of New York and New Jersey, the U.S. Environmental Protection Agency, and the federal Occupational Safety and Health Administration.

On the third anniversary of 9/11, in 2004, New York University Law School held a conference on Ground Zero illnesses and their legal consequences. Among the attorneys attending was Andrew Carboy, who was himself an NYU Law graduate. His firm, Sullivan Papain Block McGrath & Cannavo, represented the Uniformed Firefighters Association. While the Victim Compensation Fund was in operation the firm actively helped firefighters and their families file claims—and did so pro bono until the Fund closed on December 22, 2003. Right about that time Carboy started seeing the first firefighters with acute respiratory problems, one after another. Then they started having asthma, sinusitis, and then cancers. As Carboy recalls, the firm called up the Fund and said, "We've got some more guys. Can you take them?" The VCF, having closed, could not.

In the spring of 2004 Sullivan Papain filed a number of claims on behalf of affected firefighters who were ineligible for the VCF. They had decided to "sue the City of New York for its failure to provide respiratory equipment to the firefighters." OSHA regulations, if violated, can form the basis of a special type of lawsuit that firefighters can bring, unique to New York State.[4] "If there's a statutory violation, whoever violated that statute is responsible for direct- or indirect-cause injuries," Carboy said. "The OSHA code mandated respiratory protection that was appropriate. It wasn't provided, and these guys got sick. That was the lawsuit."

Napoli and Groner also attended the NYU conference. Carboy recalled that Napoli was telling everyone he met that they were representing the Ground Zero responders and that attorneys who had clients affected by their service at Ground Zero could refer them to him. "I'll never forget," Carboy said. "Bill and Paul were there. . . . Paul stands up and tells me, 'We have thousands of firefighters, thousands of responders and construction workers and day laborers. We're going to be lead liaison counsel.'" Carboy represented many affected firefighters, and he wasn't going to just turn them over to Napoli. Despite what Napoli said, liaison counsel would be decided by the judge in the case, and Carboy intended that judge to include him and Sullivan Papain among the attorneys litigating the case.

At this early stage, WGENB had found no scientific studies published in reputable journals to affirm their contention that responders' illnesses were caused by exposure to toxins while working on the cleanup. They had no oncologist who could *prove* causation of cancer. What they had was their gut instinct that these heroes, who were healthy before 9/11, became ill because of their exposure to toxins beginning on 9/12. So they did what they could to put the city on the defensive, particularly in the court of public opinion.

On September 13, 2004, WGENB held a press conference at the New York Marriott Financial Center Hotel at 85 West Street, a block from Ground Zero. Worby stood surrounded by a dozen persons who had worked on the recovery and become ill, including John Walcott. Speaking for the legal joint venture representing the responders, Worby addressed the assembled press: "The tragic reality is that so many of the brave heroes who worked so tirelessly and unselfishly are becoming a second wave of casualties of this horrific attack. . . . More people, unfortunately, will probably die from post-9/11 toxic problems than died on 9/11. These [people] are our new class of World Trade Center victims that need our new rescue and recovery efforts. . . . There was only one important thing to do after there was no more rescue of human lives at that site, and that was [to protect] the lives of everyone else, the health, safety and general welfare of our police, our firemen. We let them down."

Worby charged that most rescue and cleanup workers at Ground Zero were not given protective gear or were given gear of dubious or defective quality, and that the EPA "should've known from Day One what they were looking at [at Ground Zero]." Instead agency officials approved "this rush to clean up the worst toxic site in our history— with no one having proper protection."

Toxicologist William R. Sawyer also spoke at the press conference. Working on behalf of the plaintiffs, he had conducted assessments of contaminant levels in numerous WTC rescue and cleanup workers. He described Ground Zero in the weeks after the attacks as "a giant toxic waste site containing all of the necessary ingredients that, when heated, or 'pyrolized,' made a smoldering, hundred-foot-plus pile of toxic material which generated unprecedented concentrations of carcinogens."

Walcott told the reporters that as a result of working at the Trade Center site and Staten Island's Fresh Kills Landfill, he had developed leukemia and was now living "by the hour." Maggie Haberman, reporting for the *Daily News*, wrote, "Detective John Walcott, who has terminal cancer . . . claimed the city didn't protect them from the chemical plume at Ground Zero and the fumes at Staten Island landfill where tons of debris from the Sept. 11, 2001 terror attack were taken."

"We want to avoid this happening to anyone else," Walcott said.

Concern about the effects of Ground Zero dust became widespread and much more urgent with the publication of *New York Magazine*'s cover story on September 20, 2004. "Fallout" by Jennifer Senior, about a potential WTC "cancer cluster," began, "Three years after the World Trade Center attacks, thousands of cops, firefighters, and people who worked and lived near ground zero are sick with respiratory problems. Some have cancer. Is 9/11 to blame? And how safe are the rest of us?"

Senior reported that Mount Sinai Hospital had just released a study of Ground Zero responders showing that nearly 75 percent of its 1,138 subjects had experienced new or exacerbated respiratory problems. The Fire Department reported that its firefighters who worked at the Pile that first week after 9/11 had lost, on average, 300 milliliters of breathing capacity. If first responders were becoming ill, what about all the residents of Lower Manhattan? Were their illnesses on the horizon?

Senior enumerated the toxins and dangers present in the dust and air at Ground Zero: "It contained glass shards, pulverized concrete, and many carcinogens, including hundreds of thousands of pounds of asbestos, tens of thousands of pounds of lead, mercury, cadmium, dioxins, PCBs, and polycyclic aromatic hydrocarbons, or PAHs." It also contained benzene. Senior cited diseases caused by Agent Orange as an example of results that took decades to manifest.

The victims of 9/12, however, were developing cancers faster—in a matter of years, not decades. Could exposure be a cancer accelerant? It was a possibility. "But here's the reality," Senior wrote. "No one knows for certain what the fallout from the World Trade Center is or will be. . . . Not for anyone."

Worby tried to explain why Ground Zero responders were developing cancers, such as leukemia, whose latency period was normally eight to eleven years, in only three. "There's these fireman cancer presumption studies whereby [when] a firefighter gets a certain cancer in a certain period of time, it's presumed he's got it from exposure to smoke. There are firefighter cancer presumption studies of leukemias, blood cell cancers, lung cancers, even some testicular cancers, despite the fact that they have protective gear." Worby argued that if firefighters developed cancers from working to put out fires at old wooden buildings, and even modern buildings, then it should also apply to what occurred at Ground Zero.

Senior noted Worby's belief that an equitable resolution would include both a fund for victims' treatment as well as setting up a medical monitoring program. She reported the city's and other defendants' strong aversion to any settlement, and concluded with the words of Greg Fried: "You got a cause, you got an effect, and if you're not going to link them, shame on you."

Just reading the *New York Magazine* article caused many Ground Zero responders to panic about their future: Would their illnesses only get worse? What other sicknesses could they expect? Groner began to fear that the scope of the injuries was so unprecedented that the city was never going to admit to all its liability, much less settle.

PART THREE

The WGENB offices began fielding daily calls from more and more Ground Zero responders, whose conditions included not only suffering from breathing and digestive or gastric ailments but also sinus problems, skin rashes, and neurological issues.

Worby told Groner, "Let's get involved. Let's get to the unions. Let's find out what's going on. There are people out there who are getting sick." Worby instructed Paul Barrese to investigate and reach out to the organizations of Ground Zero workers.

The firm learned that the responders were exposed to Ground Zero dust not only at the World Trade Center site but also from the trucks and barges that transported the debris from the crash site to Fresh Kills and at the landfill itself.

The cases were also beginning to draw press attention. On February 15, 2005, Carl Campanile in the *New York Post* reported, "A major city law firm filed 600 cases in Manhattan Federal Court," and quoted Bern as saying, "Total damages could be in the 'billions of dollars.'"

The attorneys at WGENB were actively looking for leads that would support—legally, medically, or scientifically—their contention that the dust at Ground Zero caused the responders' injuries. The press provided several potential leads. For example, on June 28, 2004, the *Philadelphia Inquirer* reported that after 9/11, about one hundred search dogs from across the country and Canada who participated in the search and rescue were contacted for a study by word of mouth and through local veterinarians and dog handler groups. The study looked at blood samples, x-rays, and general physical attributes to judge the health of the dogs. They were found to have an unusually high incidence of cancer, leading to a high number of deaths. Could this be tied to Ground Zero exposure? The study made the case that it could, but a connection to the first responders' illnesses was still speculative.[1]

An article in the *New York Daily News* on June 22, 2004, by Juan Gonzalez, "Sick Lungs, Strong Proof: Post-9/11 Air Wasn't Safe," profiled Julio Roig, a project manager for an engineering firm who was caught in the dust cloud of the Towers' collapse. Three years later he was suffering from granulomatous pulmonary disease, a scarring of the lung so severe that his doctor thought he might eventually need a lung transplant. Was that just a coincidence? According to Gonzalez, what was significant about Roig was that his doctor, Benjamin Safirstein, "concluded in a peer-reviewed scientific article published in Chest Journal in January 2003 that 'exposure to dust at the WTC accounted for his illness.'" Here was a scientifically proven, medically established direct link between Roig's illness and exposure to Ground Zero dust. Safirstein had conducted an electron microscope examination of Roig's biopsied lung and discovered "large quantities of silicates" that were also present in Ground Zero dust. Roig applied to the VCF and was offered only $50,000.

Groner felt Roig's medical studies held huge potential for their pulmonary cases. But it was only one study, and the defense was sure to have many more that found no provable connection.

WGENB undertook a serious and costly marketing effort to advise potential victims of the lawsuit and their rights. As part of this effort, a great amount of time and effort was spent arranging for and securing specially named URLs, websites, and 800-numbers. They also spent time staffing and training a call center and creating and placing ads in newspapers and on radio about joining the lawsuit. They held meetings with associations of police officers, firefighters, labor unions, and other groups.

The infrastructure Napoli had to build to accommodate the tremendous number of documents and medical records was enormously complex. Each new client needed to sign a retainer agreement. They had to fill out form after form with dozens of data fields about their

Ground Zero experience and exposure and their medical complaints and treatments, submit medical records, or be examined by physicians and then submit those records and those of each follow-up visit and new physician they saw. Napoli used optical character recognition technology to scan and convert these millions of pages of different kinds of documents, such as scanned and PDF files, into searchable databases. It was a mountain of paperwork and information that grew and grew.

For this mass tort case, WGENB established three databases that the law firm employees could access: the Legal Database, the Medical Database, and the Discovery Database. The Legal Database tracked the specifics of each client's work at Ground Zero and work history, including client injuries and locations of work. The database recorded the progress of each client's case from intake and the various litigation stages and events, such as filing of the notice of claim, filing of the complaint, deposition, and/or hearing. In addition, the Legal Database tracked all correspondence with clients, medical providers, defense counsel, and the court. The Medical Database contained all the medical records of each client, including records of physician visits, test results, doctor's reports, prescriptions, medications, and treatments and medical procedures. Though highly specialized and technical, the WGENB attorneys considered it the litany of the tragedies their clients were enduring. The Discovery Database contained the information provided by clients to a series of lengthy questionnaires, supplemental questionnaires, and follow-up questionnaires. This information was required for preparation of a number of responses and requests from the defense and the court, some of which would be submitted to the court's database. It also contained relevant information on the client's injuries, medical provider information, core discovery responses, and prescription medication history. All databases were created and designed specifically for the plaintiffs by Larry Casey, WGENB's information technology expert.

With each passing month, more and more persons who'd been present at Ground Zero for the cleanup and had inhaled the dust there were becoming sicker. By the end of the cleanup, Lyndon Harris, the parish priest at St. Paul's, needed an inhaler to get through the day. That went on for several years as his respiratory sickness got worse. This was made all the more difficult because he saw so many of the responders suffering as well, many worse than he.

It affected Harris deeply. After the cleanup ended, his marriage failed, in part due to the difficulties and the tremendous time commitment of running the operation at St. Paul's. All he will say about this today is that he lost his way.

Harris had imagined that after his work at St. Paul's, he would go back to school and complete his PhD, but he never did. He couldn't get anything done. He lost his house in a foreclosure. "I just went to a really dark place," he admitted. He was bitter, angry, and full of resentments.

Judge Alvin Hellerstein was a lifelong New Yorker with a deep connection to the city. He had attended Columbia College and Columbia Law School and practiced law at Strook (formerly Strook & Strook & Lavan) for thirty-eight years, becoming co-head of the litigation department. In 1998 President Bill Clinton appointed him a federal judge for the U.S. District Court for the Southern District of New York.

Initially Judge Hellerstein did not believe that all of the WTC responder cases belonged in his courtroom, as he made clear in 2003 in the case of Thomas Hickey.[2] Hickey claimed that he had developed his respiratory illnesses while working at the WTC site beginning on September 13, 2001. He claimed that the City of New York and its contractors had failed to protect him against the "dangerous and hazardous toxic conditions" at the site. Hellerstein noted that New York State had provided for the safety of workers at their workplaces for almost one hundred years, and therefore it made sense for Hickey to want to be tried in state court. However, he continued, the city and state believed the case should be tried in federal court under the Air

Transportation Safety and System Stabilization Act, a federal statute applied in all lawsuits "for damages arising out of the hijacking and subsequent crashes." More simply, if the Ground Zero responders' claims were ATSSSA claims, then by statute they belonged in federal court; if not, then they should be heard in state court.

Hellerstein therefore made a distinction between those workers who, following 9/11, were part of the attempt to rescue survivors and those who, once it was determined on September 29 that no more survivors would be found, remained to work on the cleanup for the next eight months. His Solomonic decision found those in the first group were under federal law, and those in the second were under New York State labor laws.

The plaintiffs appealed Hellerstein's decision to the Second Circuit Court of Appeals, and Hellerstein agreed to wait for that court's determination before transferring the cases to state court. However, shortly thereafter, in a 2005 case, *McNally v. Port Authority of New York & New Jersey*, the Second Circuit Court of Appeals asserted that the federal ATSSSA applied to all tort claims arising from the terrorist crashes without time limitations (such as Hellerstein had made), and they asked Hellerstein to reconsider his judgment. Hellerstein did, and, as a result, Hickey and all 9/11-related cases to follow would be federal cases.

This was one of those small decisions with a tremendous impact: all injury claims arising out of 9/11 were now Hellerstein's.

At this early stage, Hellerstein was not treating these cases as a class action because the circumstances of each Ground Zero responder's exposure and injuries were so different. Certifying this as a class action would have made many facets of the case easier going forward, but Hellerstein could see, even at this stage, that no two victims were the same.

On February 2, 2005, Hellerstein entered an order consolidating all the 9/11-related claims involving workers or volunteers on the Pile as Master Complaint (MC) 100. Although in a mass tort each case is separate, they are often argued by the same attorneys, and they are suing defendants who also are most often represented by the same attorneys. This allows for the cases to be gathered in one Master Complaint. Hellerstein could then issue orders, requests, regulations, and decisions for all related cases in one docket.[3] By mid-July claims arising out of 9/11 would be concentrated in Hellerstein's federal courtroom at 500 Pearl Street in the Daniel P. Moynihan U.S. Federal Courthouse, across from Foley Square.

In gathering all these related cases in one courtroom under the heading *In re: World Trade Center Disaster Site Litigation*, Judge Hellerstein did not want to deal with numerous individual attorneys. As Worby Groner Edelman Napoli Bern had the greatest mass tort experience and represented the greatest number of plaintiffs, they were chosen as lead liaison counsel for the plaintiffs, with Paul Napoli appearing for them. Co-leads were Sullivan Papain, who represented the firefighters union and many individual firefighters; Nick Papain and Andrew Carboy would appear for them. Similarly Hellerstein appointed the city and its contractors' attorney as lead defense liaison counsel.

Judge Hellerstein did not take on these 9/11-related cases lightly. Ground Zero was less than a mile from his courtroom. He knew people who had worked in the Trade Center and had died on 9/11. He felt a personal responsibility to these cases, to see justice done.

Late one night in 2004, as the initial cases were being filed and preliminary research was being done, Groner was at home searching the internet for anything he could find related to the case or claims against the city. It was early enough in Google's history (they went public in August 2004) that he still marveled at the wealth of information one could find just by typing in certain keywords. In minutes you could find something that only a few years earlier would have taken untold time in the library—or that you might never find. Groner came across an article reporting that Governor George Pataki had approved a law creating a single-purpose captive insurance fund related to 9/11 injuries. That led Groner to search further.

When the 9/11 disaster occurred, municipal agencies and private contractors had responded immediately to the crisis. None of them waited to negotiate and sign contracts with the city. The city neither searched for contractors with insurance in place nor required them to have adequate insurance coverage or to obtain indemnity for their work—which would normally be required for debris removal. The four main contactors (Amec, Bovis, Tully, and Turner) in turn hired over 150 subcontractors.[4] To their credit, the contractors and subcontractors took on the job despite the uncertainties and possible dangers at the site.

New York City was able to obtain $500 million in marine insurance from Lloyds of London and $79 million in general liability insurance from Liberty Mutual and London Market insurers for itself and its contractors. In order to further protect itself and the contractors, the city sought the support of the White House and Congress. For most of 2002, the city and its contractors met with White House staff and congressional representatives to decide the best way to provide the city and the contractors with the necessary coverage, finally deciding upon having FEMA fund a captive insurance company. This type of company is generally created to obtain coverage for risks that others might not cover, and usually at a lower cost than commercial insurance companies. In February 2003, Congress passed and the president signed Public Law 108-7, which directed FEMA to use "up to $1,000,000,000 to establish a captive insurance company or other appropriate insurance mechanism for claims arising from debris removal, which may include claims made by city employees." The World Trade Center Captive Insurance Company, Inc. (the Captive), was incorporated in July 2004, with all agreements officially signed by December 2004. After spending $100,000 to hire insurance industry consultants to provide expertise on how captive insurance companies work, FEMA granted $999,900,000 to New York State, which transferred the funds to the city, which transferred the funds to the Captive so it could start operating as a single-purpose insurer for the benefit of New York City and its contractors that participated in 9/11 recovery work and debris removal.[5]

Groner couldn't believe his eyes. The Captive was set up specifically for claims arising out of 9/11 activities, including debris removal—could it be more on point? A billion dollars set aside for Ground Zero claims? Was he reading this right? He quickly emailed Napoli and some of the other attorneys to dive deeper and get more information. The existence of these funds could provide a solution for the responders—it could even mean game over before the cases had really begun.

"Double Triple Bingo!" was Napoli's reaction to the discovery. It was incredible that they had not known, and the city had not informed them, of the existence of the Captive.

The Captive began operations with Christine LaSala as CEO. LaSala was a prominent and highly respected figure in the insurance industry, the first and only female director of the insurance brokerage Johnson & Higgins. When that firm was acquired by Marsh & McLennan Companies she became a managing director. David Biester, who was appointed general counsel, was a 1993 graduate of Columbia Law School who had clerked for a district court judge in Philadelphia before joining Hughes Hubbard & Reed as a commercial litigator. As their outside counsel they engaged Margaret Warner of McDermott Will & Emery. Warner had received her law degree from the University of Notre Dame in 1981 and, at McDermott Will & Emery, was known for her hard-nosed ability to litigate complex corporate issues, often involving public policy issues such as Superfund litigation for such controversial sites as Love Canal and the Hudson River.

The Captive was prepared to outsource to private firms such tasks as claims administration and processing, financial and investment management, and media relations. With regard to the claims WGENB had filed, the Captive had put out a "request for proposal" (RFP) for law firms wanting to bid on representing the City of New York, its contractors, and the Captive.

The WGENB attorneys were ecstatic. As they read the legislative history, the Captive was specifically funded to pay out claims such as theirs. Although WGENB believed their clients' claims were worth more, in total, than $1 billion, knowing that those funds were there was a very good start.

Although 9/11 was unquestionably a national emergency, it was also a unique event, and how the courts or a jury would treat the injuries arising out of the Ground Zero cleanup was unknown. Beyond that, the claims involved exposure to a mix of toxins of a complexity never before seen. The city felt it was imperative to dismiss these claims to prevent further legal and financial exposure for its contractors and itself. For that, they needed an attorney practiced in major toxic exposure defense backed by a law firm with the resources to mount an aggressive challenge to any and all suits.

That person was James Tyrrell Jr., known as the "Master of Disaster." Tyrrell had a stolid bearing, a broad open face, the build of a brick wall, and looked the part of a well-heeled establishment corporate attorney. He'd had a long and successful legal career in toxic exposure defense, product liability, and multi-plaintiff litigation. New Jersey born and raised, he had attended the Foreign Service School at Georgetown University and Harvard Law and was a former lieutenant in the U.S. Navy's Judge Advocate General Corps. He had clerked for Judge Leonard I. Garth of the Third Circuit before beginning his career at the prestigious white shoe Wall Street law firm of Sullivan & Cromwell.

Tyrrell had become a partner in the Newark, New Jersey, office of Pitney Hardin, a law firm that dated back to 1902 and whose partners included William J. Brennan Jr. before he became a Supreme Court justice. According to the *New York Times*, "over the past decades he ha[d] become to the go-to attorney for any major entity contemplating litigation over pollution, an area of law known as 'toxic torts.'" He got his break in 1982 representing the Monsanto chemical company against claims by Vietnam veterans who had been exposed to Agent Orange. He settled the case on the eve of trial for $180 million—a large sum, but a pittance considering Monsanto's potential exposure.

The company, pleased with the outcome, retained Tyrrell to continue defending them in toxic liability cases. He also represented General Electric in the 1990s, defending the corporate giant, a producer of silicone, in cases related to faulty breast implants.

New York Times journalist Anthony DePalma wrote that Tyrrell was "honored by some and considered a scoundrel by others." Clients "love him and pay mightily for his services," while opponents "accuse him of being rapacious and underhanded." Tyrrell told one business journal that the key to succeeding for a client was "all in the 'C's.' Command of the facts, command of the law, command of the science, command of the courtroom and credibility." He added, "You have to be the person that the judge and jury looks to when they want the truth." To his law partners, Tyrrell was a rainmaker: he handled large product liability and mass tort defense work that could prove extremely lucrative.

In June 1997, Tyrrell moved to Latham & Watkins's Newark office, where his partners included Michael Chertoff (who would serve as Homeland Security director and help to write the Patriot Act). He brought with him several talented litigators, including Joseph Hopkins and Chris DiMuro.

In late 2004, according to DiMuro, Christine LaSala, who sat on the same charity board as Tyrrell, told him, "They're going to put me in as the president of the World Trade Center Captive Insurance Company. I understand you do mass torts work." He was invited to bid on the RFP for the case.

Joseph Hopkins had worked as a summer associate at Pitney Hardin during law school. Upon graduation, he became a ligation associate working closely with Tyrrell, who took him along to the New Jersey office of Latham & Watkins. Tyrrell and Hopkins spent a weekend in the Newark office putting together their RFP bid. Hopkins recalled that his five-year-old daughter was playing on his office floor as he typed out their proposal. He held out little hope that a New Jersey firm would be chosen to represent the city, assuming the prize would go to some white shoe New York firm.

So Hopkins was surprised to learn that they had made it to the second round. Tyrrell went with another partner from the New York office for the in-person interviews. Shortly thereafter Tyrrell informed Hopkins they'd gotten the case.

Chris DiMuro was born in Brooklyn and spent his first four years looking out at the Verrazano Bridge. He went to Rutgers on a four-year ROTC scholarship, graduating in 1985, after which he went to Boston University School of Law from 1985 to 1988. His first job out of law school was at Pitney Hardin, where he became a litigator handling mostly product liability cases. DiMuro represented medical device companies, drug companies, chemical companies, children's products companies, and some landlords of big malls in run-of-the-mill "slip and fall"-type cases. He also started working on cases for Monsanto on the defense of chemicals they had made starting back in the 1930s. It was while working on the Monsanto cases that he got to know Tyrrell, who had come to Pitney the year before him. DiMuro would develop an expertise in medical and scientific experts and evidence that made him a valued partner in tort litigation defense.

Managing the defense was somewhat chaotic at first, Joe Hopkins recalled. The city had its own in-house attorneys, the Office of the Corporation Counsel, and most of the 150+ contractors and subcontractors had their own attorneys. Tensions abounded from the first, as the city and the contractors did not have the same level of insurance or protection from liability. Some of the contractors' attorneys wanted to play a greater role in the litigation (and thus earn more). They resented that Latham & Watkins's New Jersey office was handling a case for New York City.

Tyrrell and Hopkins would hold large meetings for the associated defense attorneys. Amid discussion and dissension, Tyrrell was quick to point out that they needed to present a unified front, Hopkins recalled. Tyrrell made clear to the various other client attorneys that after twenty-five years of product liability work for clients such as Monsanto, he knew what he was doing. The other attorneys and law firms could monitor him, but they needed to know that he was in charge and that he had a deep bench at Latham & Watkins to do whatever needed to be done. He told them that his primary objective was that none of the clients he was representing would have to go into their own pockets regarding this litigation. He believed the $1 billion Captive insurance funds were meant to be used in the defense of the city and its contractors, not to pay the claims of the Ground Zero responders.

As far as Hopkins was concerned, this was a fascinating and tremendously complex case. As he saw it, there were several challenges. One, you had firefighters and police officers and other Ground Zero responders claiming to have been injured from working at the World Trade Center site and the landfill, and that was certain to be very emotionally charged, especially in New York. Two, there was the complexity of the numerous injuries and conditions people were alleging, and how they might relate to the multitude of substances present at the site. They would have to investigate whether there was anything to connect any of that scientifically. Three, unlike most of the cases he and Tyrrell took on, they were not just representing an insurance company on behalf of a policyholder. They were representing the City of New York and a group of contractors—and the relationship between the two was not always harmonious. The contractors believed that the city had promised to protect them from any liability, but the city didn't fully accept that responsibility.[6] The city contended that the federal government should bear that responsibility.[7]

Hopkins thought that, as with any major complex tort action, it would take several years for them to get their arms around what the basic issues were, who the major players were, and what the possible paths to resolution might be. In fact, given the political and public dimensions of this case, and the way it was being played in the press, he doubted it would ever go to trial. But there was no way to know that for sure, and so they approached it as they would any major litigation.

Concern for the Ground Zero responders was growing. Not confined to the lawsuit or the courtroom, it was a political issue as well.

On June 28, 2005, Senator Hillary Rodham Clinton and Representative Carolyn Maloney hosted a screening in the Russell Senate Office Building of *Never the Same: The 9/11 Responders' Health Crisis*, a twenty-seven-minute documentary produced and directed by Jonathan Levin. It contained footage of the devastation at Ground Zero that many had never seen: smashed subway cars, crushed automobiles, a yellow gas cloud that one first responder said enveloped him, after which he was "never the same." The film featured Dr. Stephen Levin and Dr. Robin Herbert of Mount Sinai Hospital, as well as social workers and psychologists, all of whom had treated and continued to treat Ground Zero responders.

The screening was followed by a speech by Dr. Levin, who spoke movingly of the fact that the responders, who had been initially hailed as heroes, now felt abandoned. He recounted that some had been accused of faking or exaggerating their illnesses in order to qualify for early retirement and to receive a disability pension. Levin underlined that these heroes were suffering both physically and mentally.

Having consolidated his position among the defendants, Tyrrell now set about deploying his considerable team of Latham & Watkins litigators. Hopkins was in charge of the legal aspect, DiMuro in charge of the injuries and damages aspect of the case, handling almost all of the medical and science issues. Lisa Glasband managed the liability experts. Lisa Ruggiero was in charge of the document review and also handled most of the budgeting for the case, in conjunction with Tyrrell. Knowing that there would be thousands, if not millions, of pages of medical records, construction and subcontractor contracts, municipal laws and federal ordinances and their legislative histories, and countless depositions, Tyrrell also established a document review and discovery center in the city, whose necessity other attorneys would later question but which, over time, would become a source of great earnings.

In 2005, shortly after the litigation commenced, Judge Hellerstein called for an off-the-record meeting of the attorneys in his chambers.[8] Groner saw this as a tremendous opportunity early in the litigation to sit down with their adversaries, look them in the eye, and take their measure. It was a chance to hear them as well as the judge express their opinions and attitudes about the case before embarking on what was sure to be years of warfare. In Groner's experience, this was critical. A trial lawyer's job is to read everything possible about the people in the room (your adversaries, the judge, and eventually the jury) from what they say (and what they don't), how they say it, and, critically, their mannerisms and body language.

Tyrrell's initial gambit had been to use the very ATSSSA law that had landed the cases in Judge Hellerstein's courtroom to neutralize the case before it began, claiming that the City of New York was immune from suit because both state and federal law provided immunity when responding to a civil defense emergency. Hellerstein, an experienced litigator himself, wanted the parties to conduct limited discovery—tailored to what each side needed to know in order to argue the immunity defense. If the lawsuits survived the immunity challenge, then Hellerstein wanted to move to settlement discussions. Actual trials were a last resort; however, the judge made clear that, absent good faith progress on a settlement, he would schedule a series of first trials.

Tyrrell maintained that the Captive was meant as a defense fund for the city and its contractors to allow them to dismiss all claims such as those by WGENB because there had been an emergency. Groner was outraged. Yes, it was Tyrrell's job to protect the defendants, but it seemed just plain absurd that they were going to use the $1 billion FEMA had given them to dismiss the cases.

Hellerstein then asked the attorneys for the city a simple question: Even if the cases were dismissed because of immunity, didn't the victims deserve some compensation?

Everyone in the room was stunned. To Hopkins this was a clear indication that Hellerstein viewed the Captive as a fund for the benefit of the responders. Groner heard the question as compassionate and empathetic to the plight of the responders—but worried that the city would now move for Hellerstein to recuse himself from the case because of a lack of impartiality. However, the defense never asked for a recusal.

It was about a year after Candiace Baker had returned to work at Internal Affairs following her Ground Zero service that she heard her friend from the cleanup, Sandra Adrian, was out sick. Nobody knew the details of what was wrong with her. Then someone told Baker that Adrian had died.

"What do you mean?" Baker asked. "What'd she die from? What happened?"

"Oh, she had cancer."

Baker was shocked. "Oh my God. That's horrible. Was it in the family?"

No, Baker was told. It seemed impossible: Sandra Adrian was just forty-five when she died from brain cancer on January 11, 2006.[9]

Suddenly it hit Baker that Adrian had sat with her, had been exposed to Ground Zero dust just like her. Baker listed in her mind all the ways that dust could have gotten to them: first they didn't have masks, then the masks they got were made of paper; then they got respirators, but no one taught them how to fit them properly; they weren't told about changing the filters, or even that the filters needed to be regularly checked and replaced.

What Baker couldn't get out of her head was that Christine Todd Whitman had assured them the air was safe to breathe. But Baker and the other responders knew that wasn't true; they could see the air was dirty. Even back at the command center on Hudson Street, the computer screens were filthy. When you tried to wipe them clean, whatever cloth you used would be black from what looked like soot. The windows were filthy too, and because they were cracked open the soot drifted into the building. "It seemed insignificant at the time,"

Baker said, "but looking at it as an overall picture, we had little signs that there was something wrong."

Despite Judge Hellerstein's plan for limited discovery, the WGENB attorneys were flooded with thousands of documents. Under Napoli's infrastructure management, those documents would be scanned, stored, reviewed, and digested, and those with potential significance were singled out. Many of the documents were unimportant or irrelevant, yet each needed to be assessed.

On March 2, 2005, Napoli (whose enthusiasm often led to hyperbole) was excited about a lengthy document they had uncovered, the WTC Emergency Project Partnership Agreement, put in place for worker safety as part of the project plans for the Ground Zero cleanup. The parties to the plan included the four main construction companies, the city, OSHA, and various worker trade associations.

Secretary of Labor Elaine Chao had led the signing of the formal partnership of companies working on the Ground Zero cleanup. Speaking at the signing ceremony in New York City on November 20, 2001, Chao had declared, "American workers—from city, state, and federal government agencies, trade associations, contractors, and labor organizations—formed a partnership to reclaim this site and recover our fellow citizens. They've done this with pride, dignity, talent, hard work, and dogged determination."

The Partnership Agreement was a critically important document because two of the questions implicit in the lawsuit were *What were the safety protocols at Ground Zero?* and *Who was in charge?* This document established that after the initial chaos following the terrorist attacks, New York City had a planned response, negotiated and agreed to by the city and its contractors. WGENB could now make the argument that although granting immunity was understandable for the immediate emergency, once the rescue operation ended, there were no grounds for immunity as the safety plan had been ignored.

For Napoli, the implication was clear: the city was at fault for the injuries suffered by the first responders. He emailed Groner: "This

Is the Holy Grail for This Case. Unbelievable Great Stuff to Defeat the [Immunity] Motion."

What made Napoli so excited was not only that there was a detailed emergency plan—but that the city didn't follow it. Instead Giuliani had directed the city's resources not to the safety of the workers at Ground Zero but to returning New York as quickly as possible to "normal." Working in full protective gear and having proper breathing equipment would certainly have slowed down the workers in their tasks. But if Ground Zero had been treated as an environmental disaster and a potentially toxic site, and there had been vigilant oversight in the proper use of personal protection equipment, many lives would have been saved. In this instance, safety had been sacrificed for speed. Proving that, however, would take many more years of study and work.

Mayor Giuliani's leadership in the months immediately following 9/11 won him many plaudits: Queen Elizabeth II gave him an honorary knighthood, and *Time* magazine named him "Person of the Year." Despite President Bush's offers and the resources of the EPA and OSHA, as well as those of New York State and its agencies, Giuliani was resolute that New York City be in command of the Ground Zero rescue, recovery, and cleanup.

On its face, the mayor's public posture of taking control to save the city seemed at odds with Tyrrell's defense argument that the city should be entitled to federal immunity under the Stafford Act.[10] However, the mayor's pronouncements, on TV for the press, were not determinative evidence in court. WGENB needed to find those documents that would demonstrate New York City's control of the WTC site and the cleanup.

Andrew Carboy contributed the following important discovery: "We have an e-mail from Ben Mojica, an official of New York's Health and Hospitals Corporation, saying that as of October 2001, there was an actual plan not being enforced: 'New York City Department of Health (NYCDOH) is responsible for health and safety of workers on site,' the memo said, 'and coordinating the implementation of the health and safety plan at the site. . . . We need to enforce this plan as no other agency is responsible or able to do so.'"

Groner responded, "It does not get much better than that."

At the time Officer Mindy Hersh finished her service at Ground Zero, she felt fine. Nonetheless, at the suggestion of the Patrolmen's Benevolent Association she registered to be part of the Mount Sinai World Trade Center Monitoring Program, for which she was examined yearly.

Soon thereafter she retired from the force. It was only in 2005, while in the shower, that she detected a lump in her breast. It was the size of a golf ball and was found to be cancerous. She was treated with both chemo and radiation but eventually needed to have a mastectomy. She also discovered she had thyroid cancer, for which she was treated.

Despite all this, the NYPD would not give Hersh a line-of-duty disability. There was no proof, they said, that her cancer was caused by exposure at Ground Zero.

No other explanation made sense to Hersh, however. There was no history of cancer in her family. Her father was in his nineties and her mother in her eighties, and both were healthy. Nor did she have any genetic or hormonal markers for the disease. She was forced to go to her own doctor, who saw a clear connection between her exposure and the cancer she developed. Moreover Hersh knew that she was not alone. Quite a few of her colleagues, her same age, were seriously ill, some with cancer. She was convinced all these illnesses were related to exposure to Ground Zero dust. What she found so terrible was that the cancer struck so unexpectedly: "You feel good and, BAM, it hits you."

Hersh, who joined the lawsuit against the city soon after it began, thought it hypocritical that the city was opposing the sick responders. "[After 9/11,] everybody loved us." But once they got sick, the city and politicians like Christine Todd Whitman abandoned them. "And it was bullshit. It was just unbelievable."

In a 9/11-related lawsuit, the families of Ground Zero responders who died in the Twin Towers claimed their loved ones were denied even the most basic of courtesies: a respectful burial.

A group of WTC families, known as the World Trade Center Families for Proper Burial, sued the city in August 2005 to force it to release at least 360,000 tons of materials from Ground Zero that had been taken to Fresh Kills Landfill and sifted for evidence. These materials contained remnants of human lives lost in the Towers, and the families wanted to create a formal burial place for those remains.

Judge Hellerstein, assigned to the case, announced, in what the *New York Times* called "an unorthodox approach," that instead of litigating he would convene a public hearing for the families and the city to resolve the issue of the victims' remains. Hellerstein seemed to want to make the point that trial was not always the best remedy for conflicts as personal and emotional as those related to 9/11. He was attempting to use his judicial power in a nontraditional manner to allow the plaintiffs to voice their concerns, and perhaps resolve this issue. This approach, more of a "truth and reconciliation," mediated approach than a traditional legal process, was one that had been favored in other mass tort situations, most notably in the settlement of Agent Orange claims by Judge Jack Weinstein in the Eastern District of New York.

At the hearing on January 13 Judge Hellerstein began by saying that both sides' interests would be better served by resolving the issue than pursuing a long, drawn-out fight. He stated the city's position as wanting to turn what had been a garbage dump into a beautiful park. At this point, Laura Walker stood up from her seat in the gallery and shouted, "Are you crazy?" She was the wife of Benjamin J. Walker, an insurance broker at Marsh & McLennan, whose offices were at the Trade Center, where he perished. The lawsuit was necessary, she said, "so my children don't have to think that their father is buried in a garbage pile." She walked out, as did Rose Foti, another victim's relative.

Judge Hellerstein apologized. "I'm trying to deal with this as a human problem," he said, confiding, "I only lost friends and associates at the World Trade Center. I did not lose family." If the suit had to be handled as formal litigation, he explained, he would be bound by cold statutes and technicalities, and the outcome could be worse for the families. He appealed for a little slack and then showed two videos. One, made by the Army Corps of Engineers, demonstrated the efforts made to recover human remains; the other showed the city's plans for a park on the site.

Although this hearing was for the families of those who died on 9/11 (and not the Ground Zero responders who became ill after working on the cleanup), it was indicative of Judge Hellerstein's interest in finding compassionate and nontraditional (some would say extra-legal) ways of achieving justice for victims, and how he wanted to incorporate the thoughts, opinions, even the feelings of the victims' families as part of the resolution process. He would bring this same sensibility to bear in attempting to resolve the Ground Zero responders' claims for their illnesses.

Norman Siegel, the civil rights lawyer representing the WTC families, said he was encouraged by Hellerstein's response: "Having a federal judge demonstrate that he cares and is willing to listen is positive and needed more in federal court." However, as the families would insist, the city's plan for a park was no solution for their present pain.[11]

John Feal had thought he was Bo Jackson, that he was John Wayne. As he would later recount, he was the hardest worker and the world's greatest weekend athlete. That ended when his left foot was crushed at Ground Zero, only some 120 hours after he'd started working there on 9/12.

Feal spent eleven weeks in the hospital, having several surgeries on his foot, part of which had to be amputated when it developed gangrene. Becoming handicapped was a humbling experience. Following the amputation, he didn't speak for four days. It was a slap in the face that demanded he bow to his injury. In the months following his release from the hospital, he became depressed and his weight dropped from 185 to 120 pounds.

At that time, the injury was the worst thing that had ever happened to him. Now he freely admits that he felt sorry for himself and spent a great deal of time thinking "Poor me, what am I going to do?" He continued to need medical care, undergoing a half-dozen follow-up surgeries.

He knew that he was damaged—and not only physically. He sought counseling, and was diagnosed with PTSD. He tried a variety of therapies, including more than two years of eye movement desensitization and reprocessing (EMDR), which uses triggers for rapid-eye movement to desensitize patients' trauma. He started attending various support groups set up for 9/11 responders by the Red Cross, the Salvation Army, and Catholic Charities. As often occurs in such support groups, Feal discovered that there were a lot of people who had it worse than he did, whose injuries were life-threatening, whose financial situation was more precarious, whose mental state was more challenged. Still he remained discouraged and sorry for himself, complaining to whoever would listen.

Feal's epiphany occurred in 2003. As he routinely did after his therapy sessions, he went to McDonald's for a #2 combo (two cheeseburgers, fries, and a Diet Coke). As he was sitting there, mulling over what he was going to do with his life, a father and his two daughters, ages about eight and ten, sat down next to him. In Feal's account, one daughter was "normal as day" and the other was severely handicapped. Feal watched the father bring them each a Happy Meal and treat them the same. The handicapped girl had to struggle to even get the straw in her mouth, yet she was clearly loving life.

And that's when it hit Feal that happiness was a choice. Being productive with his life was a choice. He decided he would no longer feel sorry for himself or complain.

In a January 6, 2005, decision Judge Michael D. Stallman, having consolidated the cases of twenty-six demolition workers at Ground

Zero (among them John Feal's), read New York's State Defense Emergency Act (SDEA) to grant immunity during the rescue operation until September 29, 2001, and not afterward.[12] Feal's injury had occurred after the time allowed for a VCF injury award, but during the time that Stallman determined the law granted the city immunity. Although Feal had suffered a great injury, the court was dismissing his claim.

This was just one of the many no's Feal received in trying to recover for his injuries and that would motivate him to keep fighting and become an advocate for other Ground Zero responders.

By claiming that the city was entitled to immunity from the victims' claims, James Tyrrell was delaying further discovery and any momentum Judge Hellerstein was trying to foster in arriving at a trial date. Despite this, Tyrrell himself was not slowing down. In 2006 he left Latham & Watkins for the New Jersey office of Patton Boggs, and the Captive approved Tyrrell's moving his representation of the city and its contractors and the Captive to Patton.

Tyrrell was also able to bring along his team of more than a dozen attorneys, including Hopkins, DiMuro, Ruggiero, and Glasband, and a dozen paralegals and secretaries (not all of whom were working on the Ground Zero litigation). It was believed that the move to Patton Boggs was very lucrative for Tyrrell, that he would now receive a direct percentage of the billings he brought in, including from the Ground Zero litigation.

Hopkins had charge of a lot of the day-to-day management of the case. Tyrrell's discovery and document review center in New York was very labor-intensive and produced many, many billable hours. Soon it seemed to Hopkins as if almost everyone in the Patton Boggs Newark office was working on the case. At its peak, he estimated, somewhere between twenty-five and thirty lawyers were working on some aspect of the case, as well as countless paralegals, consultants, experts, and office support staff. Their job was to use all their talents and resources to protect the city and its contractors as vigorously and thoroughly as they could from any liability claimed by Ground Zero responders.

Raul Martinez had tried three times to get a work-related disability and was denied each time. The city's unwillingness to recognize the harmful effects of Ground Zero dust pervaded almost every official interaction with sick responders, from their appearances for annual physicals to their applications for medical leaves, retiring due to a disability, and applications for pensions.

Not having the money to hire an attorney to fight it, Martinez let the matter drop. By that time he was an army reservist. He tried to get disability from the army too, which even put him in front of a medical board because of his diminished lung capability. The army was trying to discharge Martinez because he didn't have the breathing capacity to do what he was supposed to do, which kept him from being deployed to a war zone. But Martinez wanted to do more for his country, which led to his being mobilized to a state-side mission to train medics in San Antonio, Texas.

Martinez remained in San Antonio for three years, training medics who were going overseas. His sarcoidosis and his breathing got worse. He had severe arthritis in one hip and in his shoulders, and his knees started failing. He had been treated with prednisone, a powerful medical-grade steroid. By the age of forty-nine he had to get both of his knees replaced. In the end, neither Martinez nor the doctors he saw knew why he was experiencing so many health issues, or what their true cause was. Eventually he retired at an early age.

It was Candiace Baker who got Martinez involved in the lawsuit. To Martinez, Baker was not only his friend; she was also his advocate. He was reluctant to spend any effort on the lawsuit because he doubted it would be successful. Beyond that, he didn't want to revisit 9/11. Its aftermath was something he was trying to forget. But Baker told him, "You need to get involved, because you're the only one who's going to help you. If something happens to you, you need to protect yourself and protect your family."

Because Baker was still working at Internal Affairs, she was able to obtain for Martinez most of his police paperwork, as well as the medical records he needed to file his claim. He was able to show that after exposure to Ground Zero dust, his health had gotten progressively worse. Martinez felt a deep debt of gratitude to Baker for all the ways she helped him. He understood that it would be an uphill battle to prove causation, but with Baker's support he was ready.

In all his years of practice, Groner had never had a case like this, where the press and the scientific community were doing his research for him. The Centers for Disease Control and Prevention (CDC), as well as the doctors at Mount Sinai, Stony Brook, and universities all around the country were either compiling or doing original research that could provide breakthroughs for WGENB's scientific and medical evidence.

Each day Groner would check his Google alerts, and then read the relevant newspaper articles, and if there was an alert regarding the CDC, he'd go to their website to see what had been uncovered or discovered or what medical studies or reports had been published that were relevant to their case. At the same time, WGENB was collecting a tremendous amount of medical data from their clients and generating reports and analysis. They were looking for patterns: What kinds of injuries? Were there similarities or differences based on where you worked, what you did, and for how long? They were reaching out to experts and doctors.

Scientists and medical researchers were applying for grants and conducting their own studies, looking at injuries among different categories of workers (for example, ironworkers), different types of injuries (such as respiratory or gastrointestinal), analyzing different aspects of the dust and what it contained. The press was looking to doctors and scientists for comment and reaching out to the Ground Zero responders themselves to tell the stories of their illnesses.

Despite all this, the question remained: Why were the responders getting sick?

The Sierra Club, an environmental rights organization, had asked Suzanne Mattei, their New York City executive and a public interest environmental attorney, to investigate and prepare a report on the environmental hazards posed by 9/11. What Mattei originally thought would be a short assignment turned out to be a year's investigation. And the deeper she dug, the more outraged she became.

Mattei discovered that Rudy Giuliani and Christine Todd Whitman had no basis for reassuring New Yorkers the air was safe to breathe in the hours, days, and first weeks after 9/11. She had uncovered an August 2003 report by the EPA's inspector general which revealed that when Whitman declared the air safe in 2001, the EPA had not yet completed testing for cadmium, mercury, dioxin, or other toxins. So how could she claim the air was safe when she didn't even have the most basic information?

Moreover, Mattei had learned that the EPA inspector general had issued a 165-page report which revealed that the White House itself had been involved in whitewashing public pronouncements about air safety in Lower Manhattan following the Towers' collapse. National Security Adviser Condoleezza Rice sat on the White House Council on Environmental Quality, which vetted all EPA statements, including Whitman's. The *New York Post* reported that Rice's office had edited the EPA's press releases to give the impression that the air was safer than it was. Contrary to what Whitman and others claimed, the U.S. Geological Survey had concluded that Ground Zero dust was as caustic as liquid drain cleaner.[13]

"There was never a proper investigation of what happened," Mattei said. "It seems to me that it is a national imperative that if our country is attacked, one of the jobs of our government is to minimize the harm from that attack . . . from the health effects [unleashed] during the attack. We know this now."

Mattei was indignant: "This was definitely deception. It was economically motivated. You can claim that it was politically motivated, but it was really economically motivated. They would not have had anywhere near as much concern if this had happened someplace other than Wall Street. This all had to do with opening Wall Street."

Mattei was also critical of the local press coverage: "How did we find out that the pollution levels were worse than the oil fires in

Kuwait? We found that out from the *Sacramento Bee.* How did we find out that the dust was as caustic as drain cleaner? We found that out from the *St. Louis Post-Dispatch.*"

Mattei released her 185-page Sierra Club report, "Pollution and Deception at Ground Zero: How the Bush Administration's Reckless Disregard of 9/11 Toxic Hazards Poses Long-Term Threats for New York City and the Nation," in 2004.

James Zadroga was a twenty-nine-year-old NYPD officer who rushed to Ground Zero on 9/11. Michael J. Palladino, president of the Detectives' Endowment Association, told the *New York Times* that Zadroga had been in Seven World Trade Center when it collapsed and narrowly escaped death. He worked more than 450 hours on the Ground Zero cleanup. He had a winning smile and was one of those guys who lit up any room. A healthy nonsmoker, he had never had asthma or any other respiratory ailments before working at Ground Zero. As reported in several news outlets, including the *New Yorker*, he developed "World Trade Center cough," shortness of breath, as well as flu-like symptoms. Within months he couldn't walk more than a hundred yards without gasping for air.

In 2004 Zadroga retired from active duty with a disability pension as a result of pulmonary illness related to his 9/11 service. A *New York Times* article reported, "With 31 medals for excellence and seven others for meritorious duty, Detective Zadroga was considered an exceptional officer." Over the next few years his health failed as his lung disease became progressively worse. He and his family, a wife and infant daughter, moved to Florida for his health. Unfortunately his young wife died unexpectedly in 2005. Zadroga moved back to his parents' home in New Jersey and spent much of 2005 needing a personal oxygen tank. On January 5, 2006, he died, age thirty-four.

The *New York Times* reported Zadroga's death on January 8 in an article by Kareem Fahim and quoted Palladino as saying that although other detectives had retired from the department because of "disabilities resulting from the terrorist attacks of Sept. 11, 2001," Zadroga was "the first emergency responder to die of a related illness."

In a sense, all the responders and their families feared that this day would come. They hoped and prayed it wouldn't, but they knew that, too soon, there would be other deaths resulting from inhaling Ground Zero dust. At the same time, in the face of this fear and concern, the City of New York and its medical examiner, Charles Hirsch, were adamant in claiming that no medical cause or provable connection existed between fatalities such as Zadroga's and any other serious illnesses that struck persons who had worked on the Ground Zero cleanup. Hirsch was a man of science, rigorous and thorough. As far as he was concerned, the evidence just wasn't there.

This was a critical determination with far-reaching political and legal ramifications, affecting the many Ground Zero responders who were sick and getting sicker. They needed the city to acknowledge that inhaling Ground Zero dust played a role in Zadroga's death.

Gerard Breton, a pathologist in the Medical Examiner's Office in Ocean County, New Jersey, conducted an autopsy of Zadroga in April 2006 at his parents' request and found talc, plastic, and cellulose in his lungs. Breton concluded with a reasonable degree of certainty that Zadroga's death was from respiratory illness related to Ground Zero exposure. The *Daily News* front page cried, "9/11 Air Doomed Cop," and the *New York Post* proclaimed, "POISON Proof: Ground Zero Killed Cop," striking fear into the hearts of all Ground Zero responders, those who were ill and those who feared they would become ill.

At the end of April 2005, Napoli and Groner invited Tyrrell to lunch. Like the meeting in chambers, this was an opportunity for them to take the measure of their adversary. They planned to keep things light and friendly, but both sides were deadly serious.

They met at the Yale Club, a storied clubhouse in an imposing limestone building just across from Grand Central Station. Tyrrell joined them in the dining room, with its high ceiling and arched leaded windows that led out to a terrace overlooking Midtown Manhattan.

The club was very establishment, but Groner saw himself as being in the business of taking on the establishment and relished doing so. He saw this lunch with Tyrrell as an opportunity to see if settlement was a possibility.

"The VCF awarded $7 billion dollars to the families of three thousand victims," Napoli reminded Tyrrell. "The potential plaintiffs in this case are more than twice that number. This could easily be a $14 billion case." Napoli wasn't wrong. WGENB represented many plaintiffs whose injuries could trigger verdicts of $1 million or more.

Groner suggested Tyrrell could begin by transferring the $1 billion from the Captive to their plaintiffs, since their damages were clearly greater than that. And if the city was worried about future cases, they could just go back to Congress and ask for more money.

Tyrrell said that would never happen. (Groner wondered if Tyrrell knew something about the funds that they didn't.) Besides, Tyrrell told them, it was a little too early to discuss settlement.

Tyrrell was playing his cards close to his vest. As was true in any toxic injury case, time was on the defense's side. Time and expenses. The plaintiffs' attorneys would spend significant amounts of their own money to pay for the costs and overhead of the litigation, while Tyrrell was paid regularly by the client. He thanked them for lunch.

In late November 2006, the *Village Voice* published "Death by Dust" by Kristen Lombardi. The article opened in October 2004, with a Ground Zero responder "trembling, racked by a pain like nothing he had experienced in his 40 years of sound health." The article told the ominous story of his cancer diagnosis and how it was his wife who said to his oncology nurse, "What about 9/11? What about all that smoke and dust?"

If Jennifer Senior's article had raised fears of cancer striking Ground Zero responders, Lombardi's article made plain that cancer cases were increasingly becoming a reality for them. Lombardi wrote that among the thousands of victims filing suit against the city, some seventy-five had blood cell cancers "that a half-dozen top doctors and epidemiologists have confirmed as having been likely caused by that exposure." Four hundred victims had developed cancer.

David Worby was quoted in the article saying, "In the end, our officials might be responsible for more deaths than Osama bin Laden on 9/11." Worby propounded the theory that there was a "synergistic" effect, whereby compounds never before combined were potentiating and amplifying the toxic effects of other compounds. He predicted, "There is going to be a cancer catastrophe the likes of which we've never seen in this country. The numbers are going to be staggering." Lombardi found several medical and environmental exposure experts, such as Richard Clapp, the director of the Massachusetts Cancer Registry from 1980 to 1989, who agreed: "We'll be seeing a cancer explosion from 9/11, and we're starting to see it today."

Nonetheless the article pointed to a "lack of definitive data" linking the cancers to Ground Zero dust or exposure there. Lombardi stated that although the cancers afflicting responders were real, linking their cancers to toxins present at Ground Zero was not yet possible. Robin Herbert, the director of the Mount Sinai screening program, told the *Voice* there was "no full epidemiological proof linking the two." Charles Hesdorffer, associate professor of oncology at Johns Hopkins School of Medicine, observed, "We're in this period where no one wants to accept the link." This was devastating to the Ground Zero responders who were legitimately sick and suffering and who desperately wanted validation that their illnesses stemmed from their Ground Zero exposure.

At the time of 9/11, Dr. John Howard directed California's Division of Occupational Safety and Health, where he had been administering a staff of nearly a thousand for more than a decade. In 2002 he was appointed director of the National Institute for Occupational Safety and Health. Among Dr. Howard's first tasks was to administer funding issued through NIOSH to New York to take care of Ground Zero responders, primarily firefighters. As director, Howard had oversight of the government research contracts with the FDNY and with the Mount Sinai WTC program and its doctors.

In April 2006, in response to requests from the New York delegations in the House and the Senate for a singular administration coordinator to handle medical issues affecting the Ground Zero responders, Dr. Howard was named special coordinator. He traveled to New York to listen to and collaborate with the various stakeholders. He met with the FDNY and the physicians at the Mount Sinai monitoring program, and the Mayor's Office.

At that time, scientists and medical researchers had a limited pool of Ground Zero responders to study because each victim went to his or her own doctor and often to different hospitals and treatment centers. The FDNY saw a good number of responders, as did the Mount Sinai program. However, there was no coordination, pooling, or correlation of their information. None had as big a technical data resource as WGENB, which had the records of doctors' visits, test results, diagnoses, injuries and their progression over time of an increasing number of ill responders.

Dr. Howard traveled to Worby and Groner's office in White Plains to learn what their data showed. They detailed the illnesses their clients were suffering from and the correlation they saw in the exposure to Ground Zero dust and debris. They singled out the great number who had developed cancer, although there were still no studies that explored the relationship between exposure to Ground Zero dust and the development of cancer. The oncologists WGENB consulted for the case put the latency period for blood cancers at around ten years, and much longer for solid tumor cancers. As Howard pointed out at a later date, "Cancer doesn't happen overnight. There usually is a latency period associated between the exposure that causes cancer and the appearance of clinical symptoms. That latency period for some cancers can be very, very lengthy. For others, it can be relatively short. I think in 2006, we were at five years on, and I think we were beginning to wonder about whether or not cancer would appear in this population disproportionate to what would be expected."

Howard likened Ground Zero to Chernobyl, to the extent it was a unique event with exposure. He admitted that at present cancer causation was still "behind science." And he warned that they may never know the answer.

Here was the nation's top environmental doctor, sent to them by the government, saying that proving cancer causation did not seem likely. Causation may have been scientifically unknown at that point, yet WGENB believed their clients were increasingly suffering from cancers that had to have been catalyzed by their exposure to Ground Zero dust: they were healthy before exposure and increasingly sick after it. There were too many responders developing cancers for it to be an anomaly or even a coincidence. Groner was determined to find scientific or medical evidence that would prove it so.

Over the first years of the WTC litigation, the WGENB joint venture team had grown significantly. Depending on how many medical records and discovery documents they were reviewing, and the number of motions filed by the defense and the number of depositions occurring, total staff (including paralegals and assistants) sometimes grew to as many as seventy-five people working on the case at any given moment.

Napoli was directing, managing, and overseeing the massive infrastructure of the complex litigation. Bern and Worby were working on lobbying, public relations, and various science issues. Groner was immersing himself in countless Ground Zero responder records regarding exposure and the resulting medical circumstances. Although each story was unique, certain damning factors were the same.

Over and over again, Groner learned how the city and its contractors failed to properly warn the responders of the toxic dangers of working at Ground Zero. Those who were provided with respirators were often given the wrong ones or were not provided with replacement filters once the masks became clogged. The city had a detailed safety program and emergency plan that was not followed.

It was disgraceful and shocking. So many illnesses could have been prevented; so many lives could have been saved.

Groner was struck by the totality of the deception, the mismanagement, and the evil it caused: the city and the EPA misrepresenting the air quality, or worse, burying the information on the toxicity of the dust and the debris at Ground Zero and the Fresh Kills Landfill; not offering the proper protection and not enforcing the standards of protection; and, what affronted Groner most, the city's denying the dust caused the injuries and sometimes denying that certain responders were even injured. It was not just shameful; it was outrageous.

For the victims, the delays and denials were torture—they didn't know how they would pay for their medical expenses or even their living expenses, given their compromised health. No one could tell them how long this case would take, or how it would end. The city appeared willing to go to any length to dismiss the case and not pay them at all.

Depositions were ongoing and time-consuming. Napoli was deposing Port Authority safety officers who spoke of how, as early as September 13, 2001, they had recommended the use of half-face respirators equipped with cartridge filters. He was able to get the safety officers to acknowledge that even those respirators would not protect against organic vapors, such as chlorine and ammonia, or Freon, PCBs, or mercury. And they would not protect against contamination that seeped through the skin from exposure.

Two years into the case, Groner was convinced of the duplicity of the city and government officials as well as their practical, moral, and ethical failures. Yet he knew this did not necessarily prove responsibility for the critical element of causation for the related injuries.

Groner had seen a preliminary report of the toxic elements present in Ground Zero dust.[14] These included asbestos, crystalline silica, dibenzo-p-dioxins (TCDD) and dibenzofurans (TCDF), benzene, lead, mercury, methyl ethyl ketone (2-butanone), polychlorinated biphenyls (PCBs), polynuclear aromatic hydrocarbons (PAHs), and toluene. They had been inhaled by Ground Zero workers or been absorbed through their skin as they worked among the debris, sifting remains either at the Pile or at Fresh Kills. The potential symptoms and illnesses from these compounds ranged from respiratory discomfort to catastrophic lung disease and a host of life-threatening cancers.

WGENB could now show the toxic elements of Ground Zero dust. They could show that among their clients, cancers were being diagnosed several years after exposure that normally appeared only ten to twenty years (or more) later. They had evidence that the lung capacity of some first responders exposed to Ground Zero dust had decreased at a rate ten times greater than normal.

However, the mere fact that a certain population was exhibiting certain illnesses was not conclusive—medically or legally. There were so many other potential contributing factors that could explain the responders' illnesses (genetic, smoking history, prior illnesses, injuries, and other exposures) that establishing a direct connection between Ground Zero exposure and illness that would hold up in a court of law was almost impossible.

Since WGENB's oncologists said that the latency period for developing cancers from Ground Zero exposure was probably around ten years, it was too soon for there to be sufficient cases—or medical and scientific studies—to support the plaintiffs' claims of causation. The facts were running ahead of the science, and the science was just not there yet. There was no understanding, much less proof, as to why some Ground Zero responders fell sick and others did not. Why did some develop certain illnesses and others, different ones? Why were some more sick than others? These were just some of the questions that kept Groner up at night.

Tyrrell was, like his courtroom arguments, practiced and polished. There was something of his military background in the way he presented himself: he dressed conservatively and impeccably, and there was never a hair out of place. His arguments were similarly well-organized and well-researched, and he presented them with great confidence. He was determined to dismiss the case before it even began by arguing that the city and its contractors had been granted immunity.

The New York State Immunity Statute, called the State Defense Emergency Act (SDEA), an archaic statute enacted in the 1950s during the Cold War, allowed for immunity for certain activities for people or entities that were in war-type emergency situations. Napoli, Groner, and their entire legal team were faced with proving the SDEA did not apply to the city, the contractors, and the Ground Zero cleanup. Fighting this would not be easy, all the more so because Tyrrell was one of the smartest and most formidable lawyers they had ever faced.

Denise Rubin, a talented and dedicated Napoli Bern litigator working as part of the WGENB World Trade Center litigation team, was outraged: "[Tyrrell's] position was 'You can't even sue us for this.'" That the court agreed to hear Tyrrell's arguments was one thing— but that doing so halted the litigation and, ultimately, the trial moving ahead was, Rubin felt, a terrible injustice to the Ground Zero responders, whose suffering continued to get worse.

Patton Boggs was a major national firm. They had a deep bench of defense attorneys, and so they produced lengthy court filings and they produced them quickly and often. Nevertheless, Rubin thought WGENB had a better than 50 percent chance of prevailing. It was apparent to her that after the first week to ten days at Ground Zero, the rescue operation was largely over. After that, the city no longer had any basis to consider these injuries as having occurred due to an emergency; for that reason, the city should not be able to claim immunity.

Around Christmas in 2001 Rubin had gone home to Michigan for a few days to see her parents. In the cab from LaGuardia on her return home (she lived at the time about two blocks from Ground Zero), she remarked to the driver, "Oh my God, there must have been a fire out here somewhere. Smell that smoke." He looked at her over his shoulder and replied, "Lady, that's not a fire. That's Ground Zero." Living in Lower Manhattan, Rubin had become so used to smelling the acrid smoke that it took her leaving the city and returning to realize how pervasive it was.

"I get very emotional talking about this," Rubin says now. "Because I spent the next ten years looking at guys in their thirties dragging oxygen tanks behind them. Coming into my office and telling me how they can't work anymore. And they told me about how the chemotherapy made it so they can't feel their fingers anymore. They're lying in bed coughing all night. And they're thinking, 'What's going to happen to my family when I die?'

"I think that all of these guys got a very raw deal from the city. They got a very raw deal from their employers. From their unions to a large degree. They were not getting proper disability. They were not getting good retirement deals. They were having a very hard time convincing anybody that what was making them sick was their exposure to Ground Zero."

PART FOUR

On city, state, and federal levels, there was an ongoing discussion about enacting legislation to aid the plight of Ground Zero responders. Extending the statute of limitations for filing claims would increase the pool of potential claimants. Reopening the VCF or using the FEMA Captive monies to fund a new VCF would resolve the claims speedily. Bringing political pressure to bear on the Captive to disburse its funds could also make a difference in bringing these cases to their ultimate resolution.

From the start, Marc Bern, who had been a steadfast contributor to Democratic candidates in New York, believed politics would play an important role in any resolution of the Ground Zero responder cases. Toward the end of September 2005, he was at a political event where he ran into Senator Clinton and Representative Maloney. They talked briefly about the Ground Zero responders and legislation to monitor their health and treat their illnesses. Bern mentioned that he hoped the victims would be the beneficiaries of the billion-dollar FEMA Captive fund. According to Bern, both Clinton and Maloney looked surprised and told him they had no idea there was a FEMA fund—or that it had been funded to the tune of $1 billion. Both promised to call Bern to get the details.

At first, Gary Acker's doctors didn't know what was ailing him. Then, suddenly, people were talking about "World Trade Center cough," and his doctors decided that Acker, AT&T's emergency specialist who had been almost a month working at Ground Zero, was suffering from that.

His wife, Alison, recalled that, on a July 2002 break from being at Ground Zero, they went up to Lake Placid. It was particularly memorable because, although Gary had never before taken so much as a sick day, after returning from Lake Placid he was sick for most of the next year. He complained about a pain in his side, like there was a fishhook there that he couldn't get out. The pain kept nagging at him. He'd had a kidney stone once, and he thought it might be that again. So that August he went to his GP to find out. Afterward he met Alison at a restaurant.

"I've got good news and bad news," Gary said. The good news was that he did not have a kidney stone. The bad news? He had cancer.

"I'm fine, don't worry, this'll be something we go through," he assured her.

Alison knew this was going to be very challenging. They were young, they had small kids. But Gary was so strong and such a positive person. She knew they would find a way forward.

Some time after that, one of Alison's friends brought her an article in *New York Magazine* about Ground Zero responders becoming ill and a lawsuit being waged on their half. Gary contacted the WGENB law firm, mentioned in the article, and signed on as a client.

After Tyrrell first raised the immunity defense before Judge Hellerstein, Napoli had reached out to the highly respected lawyer Tom Goldstein (who ran the SCOTUS blog, on the U.S. Supreme Court, as well as a clinic at Stanford Law) about helping to prepare the brief. Goldstein had a conflict, so Kevin Russell, who worked with Goldstein and who was very well-versed in appellate work, stepped in. Goldstein and Russell had handled more cases before the U.S. Supreme Court than almost any other law firm. As was increasingly common, a group of attorneys worked simultaneously on the brief, each on his or her own part. "It's a big team effort," Russell said.

Preparations for the brief took months and months of research, an unimaginable amount of discovery documents to review, and the hiring of many experts. They wrote draft after draft before arriving at a final brief worthy of submission. Russell believed, based on the law, they stood a good chance of prevailing before Hellerstein.

Brett Heimov grew up in Avon, Connecticut, just outside Hartford. After graduating from Adelphi University on Long Island as a political science major, he was offered an internship in New York representative Ted Weiss's DC office, where he had worked during college.

The day after Heimov arrived in DC, Weiss died suddenly. Heimov eventually got hired as a staff assistant for Weiss's replacement, Jerrold Nadler. He worked for Representative Nadler for the next twelve years, as his assistant, his staff director, and, for the last five years before 9/11, his chief of staff.

Immediately after 9/11, the New York congressional delegation came together and split up oversight of certain responsibilities, making sure that basic services such as electric, gas, and landline and cell phone service were restored. Nadler, whose district included Ground Zero, made a major effort to reach out to his senior constituents. Some were trapped on high floors of buildings with no electricity; with the elevators not working, they became shut-ins, and Nadler committed to getting them food and medicine to help them survive.

The days following 9/11 were a whirlwind of 24/7 urgency. As Heimov recalls, Nadler was among those asking President Bush for federal aid. "There was not a lot of science behind it," Heimov said. "There was a number floating out there, but nobody knew exactly what to do with it." President Bush and Congress would over time give New York City some $20 billion in aid. The funds were needed not only for the disaster but also to support the businesses in Lower Manhattan. There was a great concern by the federal government, New York State, and the mayor's office that many businesses would flee Lower Manhattan and that the customers of those that remained might not return.

Nadler became a passionate advocate for those working at Ground Zero. When he learned that responders were becoming ill, he pledged to do whatever he could to help them. Several months later, as Congress began to address the bailout package, Nadler's office was immersed in figuring out who was going to get funding. His office made an effort to keep some of the larger Downtown companies functioning by helping them receive the resources they needed. At the same time, Nadler also wanted to help small businesses, such as the corner grocery store that depended on people who worked in the World Trade Center and whose livelihood was basically gone.

Nadler began to regularly receive calls from his constituents complaining about how the air smelled. They complained about coughs, headaches, and, in some cases, rashes. When interviewed for *New York Magazine*, Nadler was quoted as saying, "There may be tens of thousands of people downtown who are slowly being poisoned because their apartments and offices haven't been properly decontaminated, and some percentage will come down with God-knows-what fifteen years from now." When Jennifer Senior of *New York Magazine* asked Nadler if he felt comfortable going to his office on Varick Street in Lower Manhattan, he answered, "Not when I think about it."

Defense attorneys in toxic exposure cases are professional skeptics. Tyrrell and his litigation team did not doubt that many Ground Zero responders had become ill. They didn't question that the workers had been exposed to dust from the site. But they seriously doubted the causation between exposure to the dust and their illnesses—whose severity they also doubted.

Dust was certainly an irritant; the defense attorneys did not disagree with that. Could it cause asthma or lung issues? Possibly. But, as the defense attorneys were quick to point out, the responders were told to wear their masks. The responders might have all sorts of reasons for why they didn't use their masks, but was it the city's fault if they didn't?

The defense attorneys were not without sympathy for the responders who had become ill, but the notion that Ground Zero dust could cause blood or solid tumor cancers was unproven. Even if the population of responders had more cancers than the general population, that didn't prove causation. The defense attorneys were aware that saying so was not a popular view, but it was scientifically correct—and on such facts cases are won.

Still, as time went on and more responders became ill, more and more of them joined the lawsuit against the city and its contractors. In little more than two years, the number of WGENB's Ground Zero clients had expanded from the initial two to several hundred, then to thousands. There were more calls, more injuries—and among those injuries, more cancers—and the number of cases continued to grow.

On April 13, 2006, the *New York Daily News* headline read, "Pols Call for 9/11 Benefits, Full Pensions in Responders' Deaths." There had been a steady litany of calls from (primarily Democratic) politicians, including Jerrold Nadler, Carolyn Maloney, Hillary Rodham Clinton, Senator Chuck Schumer, Attorney General Eliot Spitzer, and Representative Anthony Weiner. However, although there had been bipartisan support from the entire nation to create the original VCF, Republican politicians, particularly those with constituencies far from New York, did not want to write another blank check for New York City. There were wars in Iraq and Afghanistan and other pressing concerns the Republicans preferred to fund.

Maloney had introduced a bill called the "Remember 9/11 Health Act" in 2005 to provide for Ground Zero responders. Unfortunately that bill never made it out of committee, a crushing disappointment to the responders and their supporters. Clinton argued that, at the very least, Congress should authorize funds for medical research and treatment of first responders who worked on the Ground Zero cleanup. She and Schumer had been able to secure Senate funding for the World Trade Center Responder Health Program, a five-year, $1.9 billion treatment program to assess the effects of exposure to Ground Zero dust. Mount Sinai Hospital's treatment program received the greater part of these funds for their five-year study of responders' toxic exposure. That was a small victory, but it would make a great difference to thousands upon thousands of responders and their families.

On the causal link between Ground Zero dust exposure and responders' illnesses, Heimov recalled, "A lot of people said, 'Look, people get sick. You can't prove that it was necessarily connected to that.'" Several dozen cases of sick responders had been profiled in the media, but no one person's case had come to personify the heartbreaking Sisyphean struggle of the injured responders for the public, the press, and politicians to rally around—until the case of James Zadroga.

The *Daily News* pointed out that although Zadroga's death was "directly related" to his work on the Ground Zero cleanup, it was not considered a "line of duty" death. Had he died on 9/11, his family would have been entitled to nineteen years of his full pension; instead, the department awarded his orphaned four-year-old daughter only 75 percent of that amount for the next eight years.

"There is no question that Detective Zadroga died a hero in the line of duty," Senator Schumer told the *News*. "There are others like him who have also been harmed in their heroic effort to save lives after 9/11, and we have to change the pension rules to reflect this sad reality." Clinton called Zadroga's death a reminder of "our continuing obligation to do whatever is necessary to help those who sacrificed their lives and health on Sept. 11, 2001, and in the days and weeks afterward."

Zadroga's death would remain controversial. Kenneth Becker, chief of the World Trade Center unit at the City Law Department, insisted the city did everything it could to protect Ground Zero responders in the aftermath of 9/11—and was looking out for them now: "It should be noted that there is no scientific evidence showing an increase in cancer rates among uniformed services personnel or other persons who worked at the World Trade Center."

The *Daily News* described David Worby as scoffing at Becker's assertion. Worby claimed that Zadroga was not the only death caused by inhaling dust during the cleanup of the World Trade Center site. Even if the city had not recognized their deaths as related to Ground Zero dust, there were laborers, contractors, cops, firefighters, and paramedics who had died from diseases contracted at the site. "The toxins don't discriminate," he said.

The Captive had been in existence for almost two years, and in all that time, those in charge of the fund had not disbursed a penny to the Ground Zero responders. What they had done is pay their staff a salary and paid the legal bills of Warner and Tyrrell and his army of document examiners. In WGENB's view, they were spending the money that had been put aside to resolve claims arising out of 9/11, money that WGENB believed should go to their clients.

Napoli was determined to call bullshit on the Captive. He was deeply offended by the Captive's counsel, Margaret Warner, saying she was working hard to resolve the claims by the Ground Zero responders and that her expenses were mostly related to the litigation.

WGENB's strategy was to put increasing pressure on the Captive from as many sources as possible—the press, politicians, even their clients—ratcheting up the tension to force the city to settle the case and distribute its funds to the plaintiffs. Napoli reached out to Susan Edelman at the *New York Post* with what he knew about the Captive.

In a story published on April 16, 2006, the *Post* reported that the city's $1 billion Captive Insurance Fund was "socked away" while the city denied liability for the ill Ground Zero first responders. A few weeks later Edelman made headlines stating that the Captive had already spent $30 million on overhead, including some $20 million on lawyers' fees. In less than two years, Edelman claimed, Tyrrell had already billed, and the city spent, more money than was necessary or appropriate to defend the city against responders' claims. When Edelman asked those in charge of the Captive for their reaction, they issued this statement:

> The WTC Captive Insurance Co., on behalf of its insureds, is defending significant and complex litigation involving thousands of plaintiffs who have sued the City and many private companies in connection with the heroic and herculean effort to rescue survivors, recover human remains and remove debris on and after 9/11. The court and the lawyers involved are working hard to move this litigation to resolution as quickly as possible. But by its nature, such litigation is inevitably costly and time-consuming. These cases are further complicated by important public policy considerations

and by the dozens of different allegations involving the personal claims of thousands of individuals, potentially against more than 100 defendants. Like those of any other liability insurance company, a significant portion of the WTC Captive Insurance Co.'s expenses relate to litigation.

Edelman's revelations prompted Representative Nadler to write an official request to CEO Christine LaSala of the Captive to provide a briefing on the fund and its expenses. For a sitting congressman to do so was newsworthy in itself, bringing unwanted scrutiny and possible outside oversight to the Captive. Which was the idea.

Dr. David Prezant was firm in his opinion that he had the complete support of the city, the state, and, when necessary, the federal government in detecting and assessing firefighters' 9/11-related illnesses. According to Prezant, both Mayor Rudy Giuliani and Fire Commissioner Thomas Von Essen were supporters of his healthcare initiatives, prior to 9/11 and after 9/11, and had been instrumental in getting the initial FEMA money promised in the first weeks after the attacks. (It was ultimately received in November 2001.) Prezant was the person who coined the term "World Trade Center cough syndrome" in the *New England Journal of Medicine* in September 2002.

Prezant believed that several issues had conspired against a complete protective environment at Ground Zero. First, a rescue effort was going on, staffed by both civilians and uniformed responders. In an emergency situation that involves saving lives, Prezant explained, there's a risk analysis that in an emergency situation favors accepting a slightly greater risk: a firefighter, for example, would accept working in a more risky environment whose safety was more difficult to supervise because of the urgency involved. Second, when you transition to a recovery and cleanup activity, your protective requirements should be much greater because the calculation of risk changes. There is no longer an imperative to rescue, which might overrule the caution of proper and total protection.

To Prezant, what made the situation at the World Trade Center so difficult was that it began as a rescue operation and became a recovery operation. So while the comment by Christine Todd Whitman (among others) that the work environment was safe certainly led to a lot of health issues, Prezant was adamant that that comment was not the only reason the injuries had occurred. Once the responders were working on the cleanup, a greater safety standard should have been upheld. Given that it was not, Prezant was convinced more responders would have more health issues as time went on.

Groner was busy assembling the building blocks of the medical and damages aspect of the case for thousands of clients. Being a trial lawyer meant that you were always learning; it was one of the reasons he most liked being a litigator. A personal injury trial lawyer needs to know as much medicine as his clients' doctors do about their injuries, as much about the science as their scientists, so he can best present his experts, cross-examine the defense's experts, and make their testimony understandable to a jury.

For the World Trade Center litigation, Groner took a lesson in pulmonology from a pulmonologist and read article upon article on asthma, interstitial lung disease, upper-respiratory illnesses, gastro-esophageal reflux disease (GERD), and other conditions WGENB's clients suffered from. Another area of exploration was disability evaluation criteria that dealt with severity levels, and what sort of data was needed to support such determinations.

Demonstrating that Ground Zero dust contained toxic substances and that the responders, whose respiratory protection was inadequate, had inhaled those substances was relatively straightforward.[1] Still, WGENB faced an uphill legal battle. The defense had made the argument that the WTC disaster was an emergency, practically and legally, pursuant to the State Defense Emergency Act. As to the dust itself, it was too soon to know its full health hazards and effects. Moreover, the dust's particulate matter was so small that one could argue that no personal protective equipment, no matter how rigorously its use was enforced, would have worked. Finally, as this was a mass tort—a collection of individual suits rather than a class action—WGENB was required to show the exposure each client had had—which as a practical matter was impossible to assess and impossible to prove.

Proof—proof that inhaling the dust had caused the injuries—was itself a problem. There were cases that had already established what scientific evidence a court would accept as proof. The 1923 *Frye* case created a standard of the "court as gatekeeper" as to what scientific evidence is admissible at trial. However, in 1993, the U.S. Supreme Court in its *Daubert* decision replaced *Frye*'s standards with federal rules that focus on relevance and reliability rather than the opinion of the scientific community. The Supreme Court, however, left it to state courts to decide whether to follow *Frye* or *Daubert* (or a combination of the two). More recently, in 2005, *Parker v. Mobil Oil Corporation*, a New York case, proposed that general acceptance can be proven through legal or scientific writings as well as judicial opinions and adopted criteria for what would be considered scientifically reliable evidence.[2]

These legal standards made proving causation very difficult for Napoli and Groner; they knew it, and the defense knew it. The problem posed by the *Frye* and *Parker* standards was that the medicine was not yet advanced enough and the scientific community was not in sufficient agreement to prove causation. For Napoli and Groner, assembling and submitting the scientific and medical evidence was in great part a strategic bluff. Should they ever arrive at settlement discussions, they wanted to show a credible basis for their clients' pain and suffering.

Given Judge Hellerstein's remarks in his chambers that these victims deserved the FEMA money, Groner hoped that, regardless of their ability to prove causation, Hellerstein would steer the case to a successful conclusion. In this, the press was to play no small role.

PART FIVE

"Something stinks in our city, worse in its way than the toxins that emanated out of Ground Zero," wrote veteran investigative reporter Sidney Zion in the *New York Daily News* on May 18, 2006. "It's the unwillingness by medical and scientific experts to admit that the suffering of firemen, cops and others who heroically cleaned up at Ground Zero can be definitively linked to their time spent at the site after 9/11.... What really is going on, is a fear by the bureaucracy that a decision connecting Ground Zero with health consequences and/or death will result in big time money damages."

On July 23, 2006, the *New York Daily News* launched a series of editorials entitled "9/11: The Forgotten Victims" with the headline "Abandoned Heroes." Over the next five months, led by editorial page editor Arthur Browne, with Beverly Weintraub and Heidi Evans, the *News* hammered away on the treatment of the responders who had become ill as a result of working at Ground Zero. The headlines themselves told a story: after "Abandoned Heroes" came "Death Sentence," "The Making of a Health Disaster," "I Never Complained, nor Sued, nor Will I, but in Case I Die ...," "Save Lives with a $150 Lung Exam," "Please Help Me Go On Living," "Enough Studies: We Need Action," "From New Infamy Must Come Honor." The following year, the *Daily News* would be awarded a Pulitzer Prize for these editorials.

Over a black-and-white aerial photo of the dust cloud over Lower Manhattan, the lead article, "Abandoned Heroes," began, "12,000 brave souls who worked in this toxic cloud after Sept. 11 are sick. For too long, their suffering has been ignored. This must end now." The newspaper called on Mayor Michael Bloomberg to "face [the] WTC health crisis." Having reported on the Captive's spending on defense attorneys and their own salaries, the *News* quoted Worby calling out the city's having spent $20 million "on city lawyers to deny the claims of cops, firefighters and others who were sickened. . . . That money should be used to help these people."

The July 28 story by Corky Siemaszko uncovered that President Bush had signed an executive order on May 6, 2002, which gave EPA Administrator Christine Todd Whitman the power to "bury embarrassing documents by classifying them 'secret.'" This is exactly what the Sierra Club's Suzanne Mattei and others had been claiming for years: that there was a cover-up at Ground Zero and that it reached the highest levels of government. The *News* concluded that at least four of the twelve thousand ill responders had already died. Although by that point WGENB could claim some six thousand clients, it was clear there were still more to come.

The city was put on the defensive, and many Ground Zero responders felt validated by the efforts the *News* was making on their behalf. They had reason to complain: no claims had been paid, and the case was deadlocked, awaiting resolution by Hellerstein of the city's claim of immunity.

Rudy Washington was appointed deputy mayor by Rudy Giuliani in 1996. A graduate of John Jay College of Criminal Justice, Washington had served for the prior two years as commissioner for the Department of Business Services, where he had helped regulate the Fulton Fish Market.

Washington was known as a reserved city official who spoke his mind but shunned the spotlight. In the *New York Times*, Dan Barry said of Washington's behavior on 9/11 and after:

> Many people acted heroically on that awful Tuesday, he among them. After the first tower's collapse enveloped him in a toxic plume, he rushed to City Hall and helped to make some of the critical decisions in those early moments of chaos, when even the whereabouts of Mr. Giuliani was unknown. The quiet deputy mayor spoke several times with Governor Pataki. He telephoned the naval

commander of the Atlantic fleet to check on air cover for the city. He evacuated City Hall and set up shop at One Police Plaza. He quickly mustered heavy equipment and floodlights to expedite the search for bodies and the clearing of debris. He oversaw some of the assistance provided to affected families and businesses. He spent a lot of time at ground zero.

Barry noted that Washington fell sick within weeks of his Ground Zero service and had to be rushed to intensive care due to a bacterial infection that doctors linked to his exposure to the contaminated air at the site. Washington recovered and returned to work, and when Bloomberg became mayor, Washington returned to private life. Over the next few years he became increasingly sick, suffering respiratory and gastrointestinal issues. In December 2004 he filed a claim with the State Workers' Compensation Board for medical expenses and lost earnings. He was denied. It was a year after the deadline for filing for 9/11 injuries. (The rules for municipal employees were different than for police and firefighters.) However, his work-related hospitalization in 2001 should have established his injury within the statutory time.

Washington was forced to file suit, and an administrative hearing had to be held to adjudicate his claim. The judge ruled in his favor.

But the story did not end there. Incredibly, the city appealed that decision. In essence, the city was saying that as tragic as Washington's injury was, it was unrelated to his work at Ground Zero, and even if it was related, he hadn't followed the rules and filed on time. Worse than that, rather than spend money to help a former city official whom many regarded as a hero, the city was going to spare no expense in fighting his claim.

This created concern among the WGENB attorneys. If the city was going to such lengths to fight this one case for simple workers' compensation benefits, how far was it willing to go and how much of the FEMA Captive fund was it willing to spend fighting the Ground Zero responders' claims?

Once again the press relitigated the case in the court of public opinion. The *New York Post* and other newspapers were outraged and called on Mayor Bloomberg to do the right thing. It worked: Barry wrote in the *New York Times*, "When Mr. Washington's claim and the city's idiotic appeal became public last week, Mayor Michael R. Bloomberg asked the city's lawyers to, ahem, revisit the matter. Yesterday, the city's lawyers said that after a review of additional facts, ahem, they planned to drop their appeal."

Although it wasn't their case, WGENB took the result as a victory for their side. They were glad for any good news at that point.

On September 5, 2006, Mount Sinai released "The WTC Disaster and the Health of Workers: 5-Year Assessment." The study, published in *Environmental Health Perspectives*, a journal of the National Institutes of Environmental Health Sciences, was based on medical exams conducted between July 2002 and April 2004 on 9,442 Ground Zero workers, including construction workers, law enforcement officers, firefighters, transit workers, volunteers, and others. The study found that the ailments tended to be worst among those who arrived first at the site, and that high rates of lung "abnormalities" continued years later.

The Mount Sinai study found that almost 70 percent of the 9,442 responders examined had new or worsened respiratory symptoms after the attacks. Among responders who had no health symptoms before the attacks, 61 percent developed respiratory symptoms while working on the toxic Pile; 33 percent of those tested had abnormal lung function tests. Responders had pulmonary abnormalities at a rate double that in the general population. Those abnormalities persisted for months and in some cases years after the exposure.

To Napoli, Bern, Worby, and Groner this was validation of their clients' injuries and claims. For many of the Ground Zero responders who had been treated at Mount Sinai it was confirmation of the positive role the hospital played in their lives.

Some conservative critics disagreed with WGENB's analysis of the report. Michael Fumento of the conservative think tank the Hudson Institute wrote an article asserting that the Mount Sinai study was not dispositive of first responders becoming ill from exposure at Ground Zero. Fumento suggested the responders were suffering instead from stress-induced psychogenic illness and that the liberal scientists at Mount Sinai were espousing the "oddball theory of 'environmental illness.'"[1]

Some scientists and doctors also attacked the studies' methods, data, and conclusions. Anthony DePalma and Serge F. Kovaleski wrote an article in the *New York Times* titled "Accuracy of 9/11 Health Reports Is Questioned." They quoted Dr. Albert Miller, a pulmonologist who had worked at Mount Sinai for three decades, as saying that the hospital's scientists had veered from confirmed objective findings to opinions that advocated the cause of Ground Zero workers. Critical information was difficult to obtain and gathered haphazardly at first, and so the results were criticized as well. Some experts said that of the 69 percent of workers who reported a worsened condition, only 46.5 percent had significant lower respiratory symptoms indicating significant health problems. Dr. Miller called the Mount Sinai report a "public relations extravaganza." DePalma and Kovaleski chided Dr. Robin Herbert for telling the *New England Journal of Medicine* that she was seeing a "third wave" of the disease in the form of cancers. This, the naysayers said, was alarmist.

Of course, many of the defense attorneys were profoundly skeptical of Mount Sinai and its claims. The true motivation, they said, was gaining federal and state grant money. Mount Sinai's Selikoff Center had been floundering before 9/11, they argued, and now, because of the Ground Zero responders, they were flush with funds.

The frequent, sometimes daily barrage of positive and negative information seemingly relevant to the litigation had a profound effect on both the responders and their attorneys, frustrating them and making true progress toward a resolution of the claims appear even more elusive than it already was.

Although Rudy Washington's case was for workers' compensation and not for pain and suffering, such as the Ground Zero responders claimed, it highlighted the fact that many responders had become ill only after the statute of limitations had passed. At the same time, many responders and their advocates were concerned that Washington would remain an exception, someone who received the impossible from the city because Mayor Bloomberg knew who he was, and because Bloomberg yielded in the face of bad press. In response, New York State legislators introduced a law to extend the statute of limitations on filing workers' comp claims. Bloomberg, while still maintaining that New York City had immunity from liability, even from going to trial, did not object to the bill as its passage was spurred because of Washington's illness.

The bill sailed through the New York State legislature and Governor Pataki promptly signed it into law. WGENB hoped the spirit of the bill would quickly make its way into New York courtrooms.

When Candiace Baker was diagnosed with breast cancer, she wasn't feeling sick, and she felt no worse from knowing she had cancer. She treated it as just one more thing she had to deal with. As she was leaving the doctor's office, her best friend called: "Did you hear anything yet?"

When Baker told her that the test was positive and that she had cancer, her friend started to cry hysterically. Baker was the sick one, but it was she who needed to console her friend. "I am fine. I will be fine," Baker told her.

"Did you tell your mother yet?" Baker had not. "But if she's going to react like you did," Baker said, "then I don't think I'm going to tell her."

"You have to!" Baker promised she would.

Baker met her mother, Rosie, for lunch and told her that she had cancer. Her mother broke into tears. "I'm going to be fine" Baker told her. "Are *you* going to be okay?"

As uncomfortable and difficult as those experiences were, they did not compare to having to tell her seventeen-year-old son. "I can say telling my son that I had cancer was probably one of the hardest things I've ever had to do in my life," she recalled at a later date. That was the moment she truly felt the weight she was carrying. She believed she would be fine, but if, for some reason, she was not, she couldn't stand not being there for her son. She didn't know how he'd react. She was afraid. She didn't want to burden him.

But Baker could not put it off. When she told him she had breast cancer, her son, who was six feet tall, hugged his five-foot-one mother, putting his head on hers, and cried. She turned to him and said, "'It's okay, honey, don't worry, I'm still gonna make your car payment.' And you know we both started laughing, and I was like, 'Okay, let's wipe our tears. Enough of this stuff.'"

Judge Hellerstein held two days of arguments on the question of immunity. Kevin Russell handled most of the arguments for WGENB. He had immersed himself in the case, meeting often with Napoli and Groner. Overall, Russell recalled, the feeling was that Hellerstein was favorably disposed toward the victims but seriously concerned about setting any precedent that would hamstring future recovery efforts. "I was particularly hopeful. I was a true believer in our argument that by creating [the Captive] insurance fund, Congress necessarily precluded the defendants from saying that we don't have any liability at all." In other words, it was clear the city would pay claims because the fund for such payment had been created by Congress.

It was not an argument that Hellerstein was inclined to adopt. Instead, his questions indicated that he believed there were too many questions of fact that needed to be decided even to consider immunity.

On September 10, 2006, Katie Couric appeared as a CBS News *60 Minutes* correspondent, reporting on "the dust at Ground Zero." With all the authority that *60 Minutes* brought to any investigation, Couric said that about forty thousand firefighters, police, construction and utility personnel had worked on the Pile. Among those she interviewed was Joe Zadroga, who spoke of how his son, James, became ill after spending weeks working at Ground Zero. "Every morning he would wake up and he said he would be coughing and hacking, and this black stuff would come up out of his lungs. . . . He couldn't figure out what was happening to him." James's cough continued until one morning in 2006, when Joe woke to a strangely quiet house. "I went upstairs, and soon as I opened the door, I saw him on the floor. I didn't even have to go in there. I knew he was gone."

Couric also interviewed Dr. David Prezant, who compared the caustic dust at Ground Zero to drain cleaner. "When you inhale it or swallow it, it's burning your entire nose and airway and stomach."

Christine Todd Whitman was unapologetic when Couric confronted her. "Everything that the scientists were telling us, that the air—ambient air quality in Lower Manhattan, this was not about the Pile, this was about Lower Manhattan—the readings were showing us that there was nothing that gave us any concern about long-term health implications. That was different from on the Pile itself, at Ground Zero. There, we always said consistently, 'You've got to wear protective gear.'" Whitman said she communicated with the city because the city was in charge, enforcing safety. It was their responsibility.

Former mayor Giuliani declined to talk to *60 Minutes* but gave them this statement: "The people who worked at Ground Zero are heroes. The government must do everything it can to make certain that they have the support needed to deal with any problems that may have developed as a result of their valiant service to our country."

The number of ill Ground Zero responders was increasing. And the number of them filing suit against the city was also growing. In the *60 Minutes* segment, David Worby appeared as the representative of eight thousand first responders who blamed their illnesses on the WTC site. Couric asked Worby if the city had told workers to wear respirators and they didn't. He answered, "We had to give them a safe place to work. That was the city and the contractors' responsibility." Worby then went even further, saying, "Let's say that some of my people are personally responsible. They're sick and they were there helping the country as rescue and recovery workers post-9/11. If they're partially responsible, does that mean they shouldn't get medical treatment? Does that mean the government should be in denial about their problems? Of course not."

Worby was making the argument that no matter what defenses the city claimed, at the end of the day, they needed to care for these heroes who put their lives on the line for their city, the nation, and society at large. It was not a legal argument, but a moral one. Then again, by airing a segment on the claims of Ground Zero responders, perhaps *60 Minutes* was implying that this was a case that would be won, if not in the courtroom, then in the court of public opinion.

During the first six months after 9/11 Thomas Ryan, the NYPD officer who was unsuccessful in finding his uncle at the site, was going to at least one memorial service every week. He treated it like a job. But Ryan was unable to talk about 9/11 or what he saw at Ground Zero. For the first five years after the disaster talking about it was just too emotionally difficult. He would just avoid the conversation or walk away.

About six months after Ryan stopped going down to Ground Zero, he developed a persistent hacking cough. Six months after that, he was having asthma attacks so debilitating he felt he was going to collapse. He heard that Mount Sinai was offering a free health clinic for all responders and got permission from the Police Department to go there on police time. It was there that he first learned his lungs were compromised.

Ryan was convinced he became ill as a result of his service at Ground Zero. As he reasoned years later, "It had to be. . . . I was twenty-nine. I'm a nonsmoker, I still am. . . . I never had any problems. I was always healthy. I played sports. If you were to see me now, I'm forty-four, you would probably say, 'That guy's in good shape.' But my lungs are like a coal miner's. They said I have 51 percent or

52 percent capacity. It's just that I have [the respiratory illnesses] COPD [chronic obstructive pulmonary disease], asthma, and RADS [reactive airways dysfunction syndrome]." Ryan continued to work throughout 2006 and 2007 as his illness became progressively worse.

As Candiace Baker would later tell it, the surgeon, still in his scrubs, walked over to her mother, who had been waiting anxiously for seven hours, ever since Baker had been wheeled into surgery, and told her, "Candiace is resting. She should be waking soon." "The surgery went well," he continued. "We got all the cancer."

He paused before adding, "We had to do a double mastectomy, unfortunately. And we had to remove the lymph nodes." He explained that Baker would need to undergo chemotherapy but that she would be able to have reconstructive surgery.

Rosie was in shock. At her daughter's bedside she stood, holding and rubbing her hand.

When Baker came to following surgery, she recalled, "I was in so much pain I couldn't see straight." She grabbed her mother's shirt and screamed, "Do something!" Her mother was screaming too. The nurses gave Baker a shot and she drifted off into unconsciousness.

Baker next woke in the middle of the night: "It was two or three o'clock in the morning, and my youngest sister was sitting by the bed. I remember I woke up and I was looking for my mom and I said . . . I called her by her first name. Her name is Rosie. I call her Rose. I'm like, 'Where's Rose?' . . . My mother would never not be there."

After repeated questioning, her sister explained that their mother was so distressed by Baker's condition that she started having chest pains. "They literally took her to another hospital which specialized in cardiac, and my brother went with her because they thought she had a heart attack when I grabbed her and I was in so much pain."

No one had yet told Baker that the surgeons had needed to remove both her breasts. And they had not told her about the scarring. As she lay in the hospital, there was still no indication that her injuries would be acknowledged or validated by or that her suffering would be compensated by the Police Department, her union, or the victims' lawsuit she had joined.

Litigation in general, and discovery in particular, is often an investigation for truths not offered willingly by the opposing side. Yet lawyers are not trained as historians or as detectives. As a litigator you have to develop those skills: the never-ending search for information, documents, and witnesses balanced by a healthy skepticism toward and distrust of what is presented, all in service of creating a convincing narrative that buttresses your client's cause.

The victims' attorneys dove deeply into the sea of documents provided by the city, its agencies, and contractors and processed through Napoli's formidable infrastructure. What they uncovered were proclamations, orders, correspondence, minutes of meetings, all of which they intended to use to refute Tyrrell's claim of immunity.

If discovery is war via documents, then it was the defense team's strategy to weaponize the withholding or release of sought-after documents. Tyrrell's team at Latham & Watkin would withhold critical documents for as long as possible, bury significant information in a sea of insignificant documents, or swamp the victims' attorneys with more documents than any one legal team could review in a lifetime, much less in the course of a few months or years. These tactics could be very effective, and Tyrrell was a master of them.

Tyrrell's document discovery office gathered, scanned, analyzed, reviewed, and prepared documents for submission to the court or in response to the court's discovery orders. It was a huge engine that produced substantial billings for his law firm. Tyrrell could argue, fairly and with good reason, that this was how major litigation was conducted and that any reasonable litigation defense firm would have had to do the same. Hopkins pointed out that as they were the New Jersey office of Latham & Watkins, their fees were less than what a New York firm would have charged.

Napoli and Bern too were experienced and skilled in mass tort guerrilla combat against major law firms. Using Napoli's infrastructure, they scanned the discovered documents, which over time amounted to millions of pages, into a master database. This allowed them to use optical character recognition technology to search for keywords, such as "Fresh Kills." Similarly, whenever the victims' attorneys prepared a deposition, they would input certain keywords to access all documents that might apply to that witness. This allowed a small firm like the WGENB joint venture to take on a major law firm.

Getting, reviewing, and analyzing the documents Tyrrell and team dumped on WGENB was essential. Just one footnote buried among millions of pages could be the key to defeating Tyrrell's motion to dismiss. Discovery could well prove to be critical to combat his immunity defense of the city. And defeating that motion was critical because at stake was dismissal of the whole case.

Napoli and Groner were all too aware that litigation can also be a war of attrition—no matter the strength of their position, the longer the case went on, the more difficult it was to bear its cost. And the city could choose to keep litigating for many, many more years. Time passing favored the defense—and they were already five years post-9/11 and two to three years into the suit.

Napoli, Groner, and Denise Rubin retained legal scholars and experts to show that after the initial few weeks of the rescue operation, the archaic, 1950s State Defense Emergency Act, which allowed immunity for war-related illnesses within a certain period of time, did not apply to what was essentially a nine-month-long construction cleanup project. They did so not only to rebut Tyrell's continuing claims of immunity that Kevin Russell had presented to Judge Hellerstein, but also to make the case for the city's culpability. WGENB wanted to show that neither the state nor the U.S. government nor any federal agency, such as the EPA or OSHA, or the armed forces had directed the recovery operation—that it was the city's and its contractors' responsibility to protect the Ground Zero responders from toxic exposure, and hence there could be no federal immunity for their actions.

Rubin gathered the sum total of what WGENB uncovered and sub-mitted it to the court in a thirty-nine-page document, "Plaintiff's CMO3 Timeline," which meticulously listed in chronological order the events and specific documents that affirmed the city's control of the cleanup operation, including documents from the Port Author-ity, the New York State Department of Environmental Conservation, and the FDNY, among others, confirming that the city's Department of Design and Construction (DDC) was in control of safety at the site and of transportation of WTC debris.[2]

Among the evidence in Rubin's document was a September 21, 2001, EPA press release stating, "All rescue workers in this restricted access area are being provided with appropriate safety equipment. . . . Available results continue to show that rescue workers at the disaster site are not being exposed to hazardous materials." At the same time, the DDC, in contradiction to the EPA, was recommending, "When working on or around the pile (within 25 feet of the pile), [cleanup workers] should use respiratory protection." The FDNY, for its part, was taking no chances: they too contradicted the EPA's claims of safety. On October 26, 2001, it sent its incident report to all contrac-tors and agencies stating that using a respirator was mandatory for workers above or around the Pile.

Rubin also included ample evidence that the city's contractors were aware of the toxicity of Ground Zero dust. Between September 13 and 22, 2001, OSHA took air samples to test for toxins and found asbestos that exceeded OSHA's limits as well as elevated dioxin and PAH levels.[3] Compliance and enforcement of safety procedures were also major problems. There was a constant stream of reports that non-construction persons were not wearing the proper exposure protection. Numerous documents demonstrated that DDC and the individual contractors were responsible for moving debris and for maintaining proper health and safety standards—and that workers were not wearing their respirators, that respirator use among workers was declining, and that little was done to ensure better compliance.[4]

1. Firefighters work amid clouds of smoke at Ground Zero on October 11, 2001, one month after the terrorist attacks on the World Trade Center. AP Images.

2. (*top*) Workers wearing respirators sift through debris as it passes by on a conveyor belt at the Fresh Kills Landfill, looking for human remains and personal items from the World Trade Center attacks. AP Images.

3. (*bottom*) James Nolan, a construction worker and Ground Zero responder, on March 12, 2010, in New York. AP Images.

4. Governor George Pataki (*left*), Mayor Rudy Giuliani, and Senator Hillary Rodham Clinton tour Ground Zero on September 12, 2001. AP Images.

5. Detective Candiace Baker. Courtesy of Candiace Baker.

9. Marc Bern addresses the press on the steps of the federal courthouse, following a hearing with Judge Hellerstein to discuss the settlement agreement, March 12, 2010. Christine LaSala, president and CEO of Captive Insurance Company, stands behind him. Credit: Lucas Jackson/ Reuters Pictures.

10. The Hon. Alvin K. Hellerstein. Credit: Marilynn K. Yee/*New York Times*/Redux.

11. Bill Groner, from a 2010 feature in the *New York Times*. Credit: Fred R. Conrad/*New York Times*/Redux.

12. *From left*: Lead defense counsel James Tyrrell; former Victims Compensation Fund special master Kenneth Feinberg; plaintiffs' attorney Bill Groner (*partially hidden*); Captive Insurance Company outside counsel Margaret Warner (*partially hidden*); Captive Insurance Company president and CEO Christine LaSala; and New York City corporation counsel Michael Cardozo gather to announce settlement of the Ground Zero responders' World Trade Center litigation. Credit: John Marshall Mantel/ *New York Times*/Redux.

13. Candiace Baker in 2018. Courtesy of Candiace Baker.

Finally, WGENB discovered that on April 10, 2002, at a meeting of government and insurance agencies (DDC, New York Department of Health, OSHA, Port Authority of New York and New Jersey, the FDNY, who were co-incident commanders of the site, and Liberty Mutual) they agreed on transferring control of the Ground Zero site back to the Port Authority—meaning that the city had control until then. This was confirmed by documents showing that on May 10, 2002, the Port Authority regained control and responsibility for the site, as further confirmed in a July 8 letter from DDC to the Port Authority.

The memos, with their alphabet soup of agency initials, were mind-numbing, technical, and, often, boring. But what they had to say—that the city was in charge of the Ground Zero cleanup and that officials knew the air was not safe and that proper safety procedures were not being followed—that was damning.

Since his cancer diagnosis, Gary Acker, the AT&T disaster communications team leader, had taken to stopping by the Worby Groner office before each doctor's visit. He would ask Gina about her day and about the cases, and if Paul was in the office they would chat. It was a ritual Acker felt brought him good luck.

Which it did—until it didn't. By the time Acker was diagnosed with multiple myeloma, a plasma cell cancer, in August 2005, it was already in advanced stages and had spread to his bones. For the next month he underwent chemotherapy every day. He tried to remain positive, upbeat, strong. He remained loyal to his employer, about whom he would never say a bad word. He talked about wanting to take another hunting trip with his sons. He held hands with Alison as they took this journey together.

Following chemo, Acker needed to undergo a stem cell transplant, which, in itself, is a risky procedure. The body becomes very vulnerable to infection, and sometimes the patient's system just gives out and closes down. Even if patients survive the procedure they are kept in intensive care for around a week, during which time things can be touch-and-go. Acker underwent the procedure, but it took its toll. "I have no energy. My energy level is down," he said, "but I am alive."

"I know why I got sick," he said. "We had no masks, no respirators. The company and the city provided nothing." Still, he said, "No matter what the outcome, I would do it again in a heartbeat."

Acker represented the innate nobility and selflessness of so many of the Ground Zero responders. What they were enduring was not fair or just. WGENB had to find a way to drive the litigation to a resolution that benefited people like Gary Acker.

In October 2006, while WGENB was immersed in populating their database and tending to the overwhelming amount of paperwork caused by what was now approaching ten thousand plaintiffs, they experienced a sudden jolt of excitement when Judge Hellerstein's chambers alerted them that he was ready to issue his opinion on Tyrrell's defense argument that the city and its contractors had immunity from Ground Zero responder claims.

The defense had argued that they were entitled to government contractor immunity, by which companies that are contracted to do government work enjoy the same immunity as the federal government. Judge Hellerstein, however, found that the City of New York was sufficiently in control of the Ground Zero site that it was not doing the bidding of federal agencies. As Mayor Giuliani and his successor, Mayor Bloomberg, were the prime movers in the recovery, the city was not a federal actor, nor was the city entitled to the immunity granted by the federal Stafford Act.

Regarding the city's claim that it also had state immunity under the SDEA, Hellerstein ruled that there were many factual issues to address regarding whether defendants had state immunity, and they were better addressed at trial and for a jury to decide. Accordingly, he concluded that the first responders' cases could proceed.

Hellerstein also felt compelled to point out that although it was not usual practice for the government to create a fund to compensate plaintiffs in a litigation, "here, the City was given one billion dollars to assure against liability, loss or expense."

"What, one may ask," Hellerstein wrote in his decision, "was the City, and Congress, contemplating if not the kinds of suits as those over which I preside?"

After John Feal's epiphany at McDonald's, he decided, "I'm going to up my game. I'm not going to feel sorry for myself. I'm going to decide to fight back because obviously the way I'm fighting now is not doing me much good."

Around this same time, Feal's mother (with whom he was very close) was diagnosed with cancer. He was struck by how she never complained, and he decided to adopt the same attitude: less talk, more action. He began to help other responders who were fighting for their benefits, telling them, "This is what I did, that's what I did, and you should do this, you should do that." When they followed his advice, they found it helped them.

Feal believed that no one—no construction worker, police officer, firefighter, emergency medical technician—should have to go through that process alone. And no hero should have to hear "no" as many times as they did. He decided to start a foundation, which eventually became the FealGood Foundation. The original concept of the foundation was "to be a Band Aid," to help responders put food on their table or pay their utility bills or give them gas cards or get them to chemotherapy, to help stand proud again and be recognized for their heroism. With the FealGood Foundation, Feal had found his purpose.

Napoli and Groner thought the time was ripe to approach the defense about settling the case, not only because of Judge Hellerstein's comments but also because Tyrrell had refused to talk settlement until the immunity defense was resolved. Not settling would mean years more of discovery, more expenses, and more risk in appearing before a jury. It made much more sense to use the $1 billion FEMA fund to pay valid claims now.

At least that was how Napoli and Groner saw it. However, much to their surprise, Tyrrell filed an appeal to Judge Hellerstein's decision and refused to talk settlement. The defense team were confident that they were right on the law and that the Second Circuit Court of Appeals would agree with them. And if they had to argue their case all the way to the U.S. Supreme Court, they were prepared to do so.

This was a huge punch to the gut. Groner couldn't believe that Tyrrell would take this position, much less that the Captive and the city would support it. In essence they were saying, "We will go to any length to dismiss these cases." The city was in effect saying, "We prefer to pay our lawyers their exorbitant fees rather than give a dime to Ground Zero responders who acted selflessly for the city and who are now suffering and may well get much sicker." Both positions were offensive, and both benefited Tyrrell, who was earning a direct percentage of the billings on this case.

Brian Shoot, a partner with Sullivan Papain Block McGrath & Cannavo, was widely regarded as one of the top appellate attorneys in New York State. Shoot was incensed as well and wrote to his colleagues defending Ground Zero responders:

> This has gone into the realm of the surreal now. Please correct me if I've missed anything here: The corporate contractors, all of whom were handsomely paid, and some of whom might be likened to war profiteers, should be commended for their "noble and swift action" and "swift and heroic" action in "speedily and decisively tak[ing] action to save lives and restore society . . ." (Brief. p. 26). However, the men and women who were actually sustaining permanent injuries that would in some cases result in their deaths, wearing masks which the "noble" defendants had KNOWINGLY misrepresented to be safe, should AGAIN be treated as fodder and made to wait upon each new defense scheme to avoid any and all responsibility or accountability for their actions. Is that about right?

It was a scathing indictment of the defense.

Napoli and Groner were in agreement: this was war. They needed to attack on several fronts in order to pressure the city and the Captive and force their hand to settlement. WGENB planned to fight Tyrrell in the courts with new lawsuits against the Captive, at the political level with federal and state administrative inquiries and investigations, and in the press.

WGENB had top appellate lawyer Kevin Russell preparing to argue before the Second Circuit Court of Appeals on the issue of immunity—and to the U.S. Supreme Court, if necessary. At the same time, Bern and WGENB's political consultants renewed their conversations with Representative Nadler, to investigate the Captive and question their expenses. Nadler called upon the inspector general of the Department of Homeland Security to open an investigation into why the Captive had not disbursed any funds to victims and whether it was misusing government funds by spending so much on the legal defense and its managers' own salaries and expenses.

Through their political connections, WGENB also worked on getting the New York State insurance commissioner to investigate why the Captive was not settling cases or making disbursements. Under New York State insurance law, insurance carriers have various requirements regarding setting up reserves for claims and resolving claims. On July 17, 2007, Napoli launched an aggressive play against the Captive, having three Ground Zero responder victims sue the Captive directly. A St. Vincent's Hospital health care worker assigned to the World Trade Center (then suffering from cancer as well as lung and gastrointestinal diseases) and two NYPD detectives (one with severe lung disease, the other with leukemia) filed suit against the Captive Insurance Company, claiming it had misused its funding by spending it on legal and administrative fees rather than on injured workers, and that it had concealed its misuse of public funds. "Despite the payment of tens of millions of dollars for claim defense and administration, not one penny has been spent to compensate workers injured by exposure to toxic substances during their heroic work at Ground Zero."

Marc Bern was quoted in the magazine *Business Insurance* saying the suit needed to be filed "because the captive insurance company has been acting recklessly and failing to do what was intended of them with the billion plus dollars that was given to them by Congress." WGENB had filed suit not only against the Captive but also against the Captive's board of directors, including its president, Christine LaSala, and Mayor Bloomberg. Bern explained that his firm was asking that the Captive's board be replaced and that control of the Captive be taken away from the city.

WGENB was more than willing to make the press an ally and use them as part of their strategy of attacking the Captive on as many fronts as possible. It was a momentary marriage of convenience, of course; at such time as it suited them, the press could turn against WGENB. However, Napoli was eager to reach out to journalists, including Susan Edelman at the *New York Post*.

Soon after Napoli filed suit, the *Post* carried the following headline: "WTC INSURE WA\$TE." Wrote Edelman, "The WTC insurance fund has spent close to $74 million on overhead and legal bills so far—but paid just $45,000 to one worker who fell off a ladder." Edelman made public LaSala's salary of $350,000 as well as $20,000 in health benefits. She also cited records showing that the Captive had paid out $45.7 million thus far to law firms defending the city and its contractors.

Edelman reiterated WGENB's contention that the Captive was falsely interpreting its stated purpose to "protect" the city by spending its funds to defend claims against the city, rather than for the benefit of those Ground Zero responders who became injured as a result of inhaling dust at the World Trade Center site and the Fresh Kills Landfill. The suit argued that the Captive was created specifically for the benefit of the workers exposed to toxic dust from Ground Zero, citing a May 2002 request from the city to Congress saying that "toxic chemicals emanating from the WTC debris site" made insurance "absolutely vital to protect the city and its contractors," which was the purpose of the $1 billion FEMA funds Congress awarded the city. Edelman also mentioned a 2003 press release issued by Governor

Pataki and Mayor Giuliani that specified that the Captive was created "for the city to expedite the payment of claims." To Edelman, that meant paying the claims of Ground Zero responders. Napoli was using the press to rattle the Captive's cage.

Many Ground Zero responders were less concerned about their asthma and more concerned about developing cancer in the future; many were most concerned with how to support their families should they become too ill to do so. At the same time, the Captive wanted some protection against future claims. If WGENB could find a way to allay the responders' fears about their future and also find a way to reduce how much the Captive needed to keep in reserve to protect against future claims, that would go a long way to removing the stumbling blocks to a settlement.

Napoli and Groner discussed a couple of novel ideas. One was to approach insurance companies about developing a first-ever cancer payment policy, whereby, in return for a premium paid now, the responders were protected should they receive a cancer diagnosis within the next ten or twenty years. Another idea was to create a separate second policy to cover all future claims from existing clients and from those not yet in the suit. To that end, perhaps $100 million could purchase $500 million or $1 billion of indemnity. Doing so would also decrease the Captive's concerns regarding future liabilities.

New York State's Insurance Commission would need to approve the Met Life policy, which was not going to be easy to sell. Napoli and Groner approached a number of insurance companies, but none was interested in writing a policy protecting against future claims. Met Life, however, was willing to explore the idea of a cancer payment policy.

Baker was sent back to work after having her bilateral mastectomy. She was then going through chemo. One of her bosses saw her at work and asked, "What are you doing here?"

"They told me to come to work," she replied.

"You need to go home," her boss declared. "You're like a liability here. If something happens to you, how can we even explain it? Why are you even here? I don't know why they sent you back here."

Her experience before the NYPD medical board was even worse. One of the doctors must have been in his late eighties, Baker guessed. His hands were trembling while trying to take her pulse and listen to her chest with his stethoscope. He then asked her to open her robe and he examined her surgical scars. "Detective Baker," he said, "I see you have cardiac issues and orthopedic issues and cancer issues. What else is wrong with you?" She found that terribly condescending and disrespectful, the whole experience awful and inhumane.

When President George W. Bush announced his proposed budget for 2006, buried among its provisions was a cost savings measure by which the U.S. government was going to reclaim $125 million in workers' compensation funds earmarked for Ground Zero responders to pay for medical expenses and lost earnings, which had been made available to New York State in the wake of 9/11. The Bush administration's position was that they were just reclaiming funds that had not been used because the state's needs "were not as large as initially feared."

The Ground Zero responders and New York's political leaders were incensed. A bipartisan group of twenty-three members of the New York congressional delegation, including Senators Clinton and Schumer, as well as Mayor Bloomberg and Governor Pataki, all voiced their objection. That $125 million was meant for processing claims for "the thousands of 9/11 responders who still need our help," as Representatives Nadler and Maloney put it. According to Pataki, those funds were to be made available "until expended."

"With thousands of 9/11 responders still injured, it's wrong to pull back promised federal aid that could be used for their medical treatment and other needs," said Maloney. "I cannot accept the idea that these funds are not needed when so many of the 9/11 responders who have contacted me say their biggest frustration has been with their workers' compensation claims. We need to use these funds to assist those that were injured as a result of the terrorist attacks."

Maloney and Clinton reached out to injured responders, among them John Feal, to help rally public support for the funds and to lobby Congress not to defund them. They introduced the Walsh Amendment, attached to Katrina emergency funding, which also would prevent the cancellation of Ground Zero funds. As was captured in the first episode of *Sierra Club Chronicles*, entitled "9/11 Forgotten Heroes" (available on YouTube),[5] Feal drove a van filled with fellow Ground Zero responders to Washington to speak to the senators and representatives. In the video, Feal appears in a sleeveless T-shirt, his biceps heavily tattooed, roaming the hallways of the Congressional Office Building, climbing the stairs, riding the escalators, and following the underground passages to buttonhole every representative he could, shaking their hand and introducing himself: "How are you? John Feal, injured 9/11 worker—looking for your support for the Walsh Amendment, to keep the money in New York."

The Walsh Amendment failed to pass. However, Feal and his fellow FealGood Foundation responders continued to lobby the press and Congress to keep the funding.

Finally, in late October 2005, Senators Clinton and Schumer were able to attach an amendment to the Labor–Health and Human Services Appropriations bill that restored the $125 million to New York City. Maloney and Representative Maurice Hinchey offered their own matching House amendment, and after a short conference negotiation, the final bill was adopted. It was one small victory for the Ground Zero responders at a time when there had not been many.

By the end of 2005 Judge Hellerstein had become frustrated by how little progress had been made in the litigation. He had tried to get the plaintiffs to submit detailed and accurate information about their injuries, but he believed he had received incomplete and inexact filings.

The WGENB lawyers were doing the best they could. Their explanations for the deficiencies in their filings were various. For one, the data for the clients' injuries became outdated almost as soon as they were submitted because the plaintiffs were constantly going to doctors; some conditions would get better, though more often they got worse; and new conditions were diagnosed. Further, from a purely practical and administrative perspective, managing and accurately reporting the million-plus data fields pertaining to an ever-increasing number of clients was inevitably going to yield some errors and inaccuracies.

Hellerstein, a former major Manhattan law firm litigator, wanted Napoli's work to be as polished as Tyrrell's. That was the standard for litigants in his court. Tyrrell knew this and, in Groner's opinion, made it a point to highlight any WGENB error to throw a negative light on the clients and their injuries. But Napoli was a street fighter, straight out of Queens, and he had neither Patton Boggs's resources nor the Captive's checkbook. WGENB's resources were focused on battling Tyrrell and winning the cases, not on ensuring every "i" was dotted and "t" was crossed in their filings. He was well aware that those court filings wouldn't make a difference in any final settlement. When the case settled, then WGENB would ensure that all the medical records and filings regarding precise injuries were error-free.

Be that as it may, Judge Hellerstein felt that at a minimum he needed to know how many qualified plaintiffs there were in the suit and how many had serious injuries. As each side in the litigation had completely different notions of which plaintiffs had serious injuries (or injuries at all) and in what numbers, this was difficult to assess. Each side was immersed in the sea of documents produced in discovery. To Hellerstein the case was as good as deadlocked. However, he was determined to use his judicial power to move the parties to a resolution.

Hellerstein was a great admirer of Judge Jack Weinstein, who had pioneered the use of "special masters" in complex litigations. Special masters are court-appointed officials (most often lawyers, legal experts, law school professors, retired judges) who are delegated to ensure compliance with judicial orders, assess evidence, and act as a liaison between the judges and the parties in a case, depending upon the judge's needs and desires and the specific aspects of the case. Rule 53 of the Federal Rules of Civil Procedure allows a federal court to appoint a master to report to the court. Accordingly, on October 17, 2006, Hellerstein announced that he intended to appoint a special master to help organize the case and aid in creating a transparent, verifiable system that compiled the number of plaintiffs and categorized the severity of their injuries.

In the fall of 2006 Aaron Twerski was dean of Hofstra Law School. When Hellerstein asked him to act as special master in a big case, he decided that he wasn't going to do it by himself. He suggested bringing on James Henderson, a professor at Cornell Law School, a leading expert in the fields of product liability and tort litigation, with whom he had worked for some twenty-five years.[6]

Twerski, the son of a rabbi and a descendant of several Hasidic dynasties, had graduated with a degree in philosophy as well as a degree in Talmudic law. He had been a trial attorney with the Justice Department's Civil Rights Division before teaching at Harvard, the University of Michigan, Boston University, and Cornell Law School.

Twerski and Henderson made for an interesting pair. One was tall and Nordic in appearance; the other short with a long white beard. One of the attorneys would later describe them as the "Mutt and Jeff" of personal injury law.

Napoli told the court that the plaintiffs' attorneys supported the installation of special masters but argued that it would be preferable if the masters were chosen by agreement between the parties rather than imposed by the court. He was less polite in an email to Groner: "Having read some of Henderson and Twerski's writings, if these guys are chosen the case is over. They are bad, bad, bad. I spoke with people who know them as well. They are defense minded, anti-consumer, pro-business, and anti-plaintiff lawyers."

WGENB filed their objection to Hellerstein appointing the special masters. And although Groner agreed with Napoli's concerns, he was more ambivalent. He was well aware of Henderson's pro-defense leanings and agreed that having defense-minded special masters could be very harmful; however, he knew Henderson personally and thought highly of him. Prior to his tenure at Cornell Law School, Henderson had taught at Boston University Law School, where he was Groner's torts professor, and Groner had worked as Henderson's research assistant the summer after his second year. If they were to have a special master, he preferred that it was someone he knew.

Despite their objection, on December 12, 2006, Hellerstein announced the appointment of Twerski and Henderson as special masters for the case. For Groner, that Hellerstein had gone ahead regardless of their objection demonstrated, if it wasn't already clear, that the judge was going to impose his will on this case.

In appointing the special masters, Hellerstein encouraged both sides to carve a settlement. He urged Tyrrell and the Captive, despite their legal stance to the contrary, to use the $1 billion fund for the benefit of the victims—rather than "as their personal piggy bank."

When Napoli argued that the victims' claims were greater than $1 billion, Hellerstein chastised him as well. In one notable exchange in court, Hellerstein told Napoli, "Forget about the law. Forget about analyses. Ask yourself the most basic practical question that you have to ask as a plaintiff's lawyer: What can I do for the people who have entrusted their most precious asset to me as a lawyer? How can I bring a return so they can enjoy it and their children can enjoy it in their remaining lives?"

The judge was unusually blunt in criticizing both sides for pursuing what he believed was their own interest, for maximum advantage and maximum potential gain. This was Hellerstein at his most cynical, but both sides understood that he was goading them toward a settlement.

Cynthia Mahoney was born in Aiken, South Carolina. She was trained as an EMT and became an Episcopal nun and chaplain. She had been assigned to a convent in Lower Manhattan just a few weeks before the events of September 11, 2001.

On September 11, Sister Cindy, as she was known to all, rushed to the site to help. For the next five months she volunteered her services: she worked with the fatality team of the city's Medical Examiner Office during and in the aftermath of the disaster; she blessed human remains as they were extricated from the rubble at Ground Zero; she offered prayers and comfort to the workers there, as well as to relatives of the dead when they came to the site. The *New York Post* called her the "Angel of Ground Zero."

Sister Cindy was an example of the self-sacrifice and integrity of those who volunteered at Ground Zero, and who, as a consequence, paid with their health. Over the next few years, she suffered from chronic obstructive lung disease, asthma, and other respiratory and gastrointestinal diseases. She called upon David Worby in August 2006 to become her guardian and ensure that when she died her body would be autopsied in hopes of helping other ill Ground Zero responders and that the results would be used in the lawsuit. She became so sick and destitute that she returned to South Carolina to be cared for by relatives.

Cynthia Mahoney died on November 1, 2006. Worby, per Mahoney's request, made sure an autopsy was performed by a pathologist in South Carolina, and the findings were reviewed by Dr. Michael Baden, who had been the New York State medical examiner. Though the autopsy was inconclusive, both doctors believed there was no plausible explanation for Sister Cindy's symptoms other than exposure to Ground Zero toxins. This information was duly noted in her medical file, and despite her passing, her estate continued in its suit against the city and its contractors.

Senator Clinton told the Associated Press, "The death of Sister Mahoney is yet another tragic reminder that Sept. 11 continues to take lives."

Worby, who prided himself on his lawyering and his reputation in the legal community and among judges, was concerned that Hellerstein's admonishing of WGENB did not bode well for their lawsuit. Worby was also concerned that Hellerstein's criticisms would create a perception with clients that they were not being properly represented—eroding trust between attorney and client.

But Napoli was dismissive of Worby's concerns. He knew something that Worby didn't: he was having lunch with Tyrrell to propose the start of settlement negotiations. Following the lunch, Napoli sent a December 22, 2006, email to Tyrrell, which began, "Thank you again for lunch. As we discussed, I indicated I would take the first crack at a preliminary structure for a global resolution. Attached please find plaintiffs' proposal. Please review this proposal. While a lot of work remains to be done, I believe it can be accomplished in short order. I think this proposal takes us a long way to actually resolving the litigation. Merry Christmas! Happy New Year!!" Napoli titled his document "Proposed Structure for Global Resolution of Ground Zero Respiratory Claims."

Napoli divided the resolution process into five distinct phases. First, they would determine how much money was available for settlement (not only from the Captive but also from private insurance companies, the Port Authority of New York and New Jersey, corporate defendants, and possibly the purchase of additional coverage, as well as potential further monies from Congress). He opened the door for mediation to accomplish this, perhaps by Twerski and Henderson. Next, they would create an injury matrix using standard American Medical Association guidelines for respiratory and GERD injuries, and determine the numbers of injured, the type of injuries (i.e., respiratory-asthma, GERD, cancer, etc.), and the criteria for determining the severity of the injury.

Napoli suggested they also determine the potential liability of other possible defendants (such as the Port Authority) in order to maximize the funds available for settlement. Finally, after determining how to distribute funds to present claimants, the claimants would provide full releases, all done upon the court's approval. To ensure that all claims were legitimate, Napoli suggested they be overseen by a review board and/or allocation neutral (an independent party who reviews distributions and adjudicates contested claims).

As for future claimants—those responders who were presently without injuries or whose injuries were mild but who, in time, might develop more serious illnesses (which may or may not be related to their work at the WTC—Napoli proposed using some of the settlement funds to purchase insurance policies. Any remaining funds could be invested at a conservative 5 percent interest rate for use in the future. "For example, applying a 5% interest rate to $100,000,000 for 15 years would yield $207,890,000; for 20 years the yield [would be] $265,330,000."

The proposal was bold, impressive, and ambitious. Napoli predicted that there would be more than forty thousand claimants, the number of Ground Zero responders that Mount Sinai had estimated.[7]

The settlement scheme, like the lawsuit itself, did not cover all possible injuries that resulted from Ground Zero service. Many responders were traumatized by their service and suffered PTSD and other psychological ailments, including anxiety, depression, and rage. It affected their professional and personal lives. However, those ailments were not dust-related, and the case focused specifically on illnesses caused by the toxic air.

Still, Napoli had offered a framework for settlement. He was pleased with himself and had every reason to celebrate New Year's with good cheer, hoping that the case would soon be over.

PROGRESS

PART SIX

At the start of 2007, Napoli and Groner believed a settlement was possible. (Trial lawyers are eternal optimists.) Despite the fact that the immunity appeal was still pending and the Captive's managers had shown no inclination to disburse funds, they were convinced Napoli had opened the door with Tyrrell.

Judge Hellerstein, for his part, was eager for the special masters Twerski and Henderson to end what the judge perceived as a stalemate between the parties by tackling those issues that bedeviled him: determining how many valid claims existed and what percentage of those injuries were severe. In a case that had already gone on for several years, the special masters felt they could play a pivotal role in moving the litigation forward. They prepared a questionnaire they hoped would bring the parties one step closer to trial or create a basis for settlement.

What Hellerstein, Napoli, Groner, and the special masters did not know was that Tyrrell had other plans. He entered a motion to halt any discovery or any work by the special masters until the immunity question was resolved—meaning after all appeals were exhausted. His argument was that if the appeals court found the city and its contractors immune from suit, then there would be no trial and hence no need for discovery or for the special masters.

It was a very smart strategic move. On the one hand, it appeared as though he was acting in the best interests of his clients by trying to end the case. However, what Tyrrell was creating was delay, and as the case dragged on that meant maximum billable hours for him and his team, while the Captive's funds sat unused, accruing interest, and the plaintiffs' attorneys, who were not being paid, became increasingly financially stretched.

Tyrrell had filed an appeal on the issue of immunity with the Second Circuit Court of Appeals, just one step below the U.S. Supreme Court. Usually you need to wait until the end of a case to appeal. However, there is an exception for an immediate appeal where you are not arguing the merits of the case but rather a threshold issue, in this case the immunity defense.

Tyrrell applied to Hellerstein to allow him to immediately go to the appellate court. Hellerstein rejected his motion. Tyrrell also asked the district court to stay the proceedings before Hellerstein (in essence, to halt the legal proceedings); they too refused. Tyrrell then used a procedural move and, despite not having permission from Hellerstein, went directly to the Second Circuit and submitted a motion compelling Hellerstein to stay the Ground Zero responders' litigation pending Tyrrell's appeal. Judge Peter W. Hall, who was on the motions panel of the appellate court, granted the stay.

Russell then filed a motion to dismiss the appeal, and, at the same time, WGENB started the arduous and months-long process of briefing the underlying merits of the appeal. Both of those issues ended up going to the three-judge Second Circuit appellate panel assigned to the case. In light of the appeals court's stay of the case, Hellerstein issued his own stay of discovery and a stay of all work by the special masters until the immunity argument was resolved.

Tyrrell had managed to stop the case dead in its tracks while the city was going to the appeals court to try to overturn Hellerstein's rejection of his motion and asking the court to dismiss the responders' lawsuits. This was a devastating turn of events for the victims and their attorneys, whose costs were mounting. WGENB estimated that they had already invested some $20 million in costs.

For Patton Boggs, it was a tactical win as Tyrrell's dedicated discovery center in New York continued to examine and digest documents.

To spearhead WGENB's attack on the political front, Bern traveled to Washington DC and engaged Mark Childress, a lawyer, lobbyist, and former adviser to Senator Ted Kennedy and Senate Majority Leader Tom Daschle. Childress would later serve as President Barack Obama's deputy chief of staff. *BuzzFeed* would characterize him as "the most powerful man in the White House you've never heard of."

Bern had also enlisted Brett Heimov, former chief of staff to Representative Nadler, who had gone into private practice as a political consultant. Heimov informed Bern that Representatives Nadler and Maloney, along with Senator Clinton, continued to discuss possible legislative hearings and initiatives to address the plight of the Ground Zero responders. However, they were meeting resistance from Republican legislators. Bern asked Heimov to come up with strategies to compel the Captive managers to disburse their funds, as well as legislation to benefit the responders.

On the municipal front, Mayor Bloomberg publicly argued that Congress should be the ones compensating Ground Zero responders. As concerned the Captive, the city's position remained that such monies were meant for the defense of the city and not for the benefit of the responders. As mayor and chief financial executive for New York, Bloomberg was impelled to protect the city from financial liability. No one knew how many individuals would have ascertainable injuries from inhaling Ground Zero dust, and to what extent and at what cost the city would be held responsible—and what other liabilities might still be on the horizon. However, this very understandable obligation to protect the city financially stood at odds with Bloomberg's other responsibility: to take care of the responders, many of whom were city employees and citizens of New York who were injured serving the city. It outraged Groner that the city did not direct the Captive to pay out its $1 billion in funds to the responders, who were the constituency he would have to call upon and need to rely on should there be ever be another 9/11-type emergency.

If they were ever to arrive at a settlement, the plaintiffs' attorneys needed mastery of their clients' individual health conditions. Years earlier, doing so for thousands of clients would have been an almost unmanageable task, requiring legions of attorneys, paralegals, and legal assistants. Now, however, firms with mass tort experience, such as Napoli Bern, used computer-driven data to handle complex litigation; it was still a time-intensive process, but in the law, as in much of contemporary society, the tech-savvy had an edge.

Nurses were hired to review every page of every medical record in WGENB's complex database: dates of doctor's visits, symptoms, tests done, test results, diagnoses, medications. This was made all the more complex by the hundreds of different diagnoses that the different doctors used to describe the multitude of injuries they were seeing. Many of the responders' injuries were getting progressively worse, and each new diagnosis and doctor visit needed to be recorded and evaluated.

Barbara Krohmer, a licensed nurse, was overseeing the day-to-day operations of the Medical Database collection, input, analysis, and assessment and worked directly with Groner and Napoli over the years. She was an extraordinary talent, dealing not just with the data and records of thousands of clients but with staff, nurse consultants who did the data input, outside medical consultants, and thousands of clients whose medical issues or questions couldn't be handled by other WGENB staff. At different times during the litigation, there were more than a dozen nurses working around the clock. It was as if a medical office was embedded in the law firm.

Tyrrell, DiMuro, and the defense team questioned various conditions the Ground Zero responders complained of suffering, including the harmful effects of having World Trade Center cough. "It's just a cough," DiMuro said, more than once. "It goes away." Despite the victims' hacking, persistent coughs and the black sludge they coughed up, DiMuro remained skeptical. Moreover, he had doubts about anyone who developed the cough *after* they finished working on the cleanup. "Months after? Not medically possible," he insisted.

Although the toxic nature of Ground Zero dust and debris may have been challenged by New York City and its defense attorneys, the medical establishment was becoming more and more convinced. In a 2006 article in the *American Journal of Respiratory and Critical Care Medicine* several investigators reported that pulmonary function in the year after the disaster showed a reduction in lung function about twelve times as severe as that predicted for a single year of aging. Medical monitoring for up to twelve months after the Towers' collapse showed persistent respiratory abnormalities.

On May 31, 2007, the *New England Journal of Medicine* published "The Legacy of World Trade Center Dust" by Jonathan M. Samet, MD, Alison S. Geyh, PhD, of Johns Hopkins University, and Mark J. Utell, MD, from the University of Rochester. Given the prestige of the *NEJM*, this article had a great impact on the medical community.

The authors noted that "World Trade Center cough," which had been recognized as early as 2002, had developed in some firefighters who experienced substantial and probably permanent loss of lung function. Ground Zero dust had been sufficiently analyzed, they asserted, that its content was not likely to change. The respiratory illnesses detected in the responders were consistent with "airway injury resulting from inhaled particles and gases."

After many years of listening to the defense declare that there was no medical or scientific basis to believe that working on the cleanup of Ground Zero was the cause of their clients' illnesses, these articles gave the attorneys at WGENB much needed hope that scientific evidence might yet validate their claims.

For James Zadroga, Sister Cindy Mahoney, and other responders who had died, it was their survivors, the press, and outside medical examiners and experts who, in addition to WGENB, insisted that their deaths were related to their work at Ground Zero. The City of New York had never confirmed the link—until May 2007, when the city medical examiner for the first time officially linked a death to Ground Zero dust exposure.

Felicia Dunn-Jones, a forty-two-year-old civil rights attorney who'd been caught in the dust cloud, died five months after 9/11.

Dr. Charles S. Hirsch, New York City's chief medical examiner, was certain "beyond a reasonable doubt" that the exposure to Ground Zero dust had contributed to her death, which he ruled a homicide.

This was a huge admission by New York City that Ground Zero dust could kill. For the attorneys at WGENB it meant that the estates of those who lost loved ones after being exposed to Ground Zero dust had a greater chance of proving causation and getting not only validation but compensation and closure. For the victims who were still alive, however, it confirmed their fears that their illnesses could worsen and might even prove fatal.

Also in May 2007, Mayor Bloomberg called on Congress to reopen the VCF, over which he had no control, for the benefit of Ground Zero responders. He even suggested he would transfer the Captive's $1 billion, over which he did have control, to the VCF. Bloomberg still wanted the city absolved but, for the first time, acknowledged that the FEMA funds should be used to benefit the injured responders.

However, even if Congress did reopen the VCF fund, it had no power to stop the litigation. Removing the FEMA funds would end the insurance protection granted to contractors and expose them and their insurance carriers to greater liability. And it could take years before the city settled any litigation. The only real effect of Bloomberg's well-intentioned announcement was to add more uncertainty among the responders about the litigation.

Oral arguments before the Second Circuit Court of Appeals on the issue of immunity had been set for October 1, 2007. Despite having won this argument in the lower court before Judge Hellerstein, the WGENB attorneys had been working on the appeal since 2006. Napoli, Groner, and Rubin were optimistic but also anxious: they knew no win was guaranteed. Kevin Russell had been reviewing his arguments with the WGENB attorneys and was ready. Brian Shoot, a partner at Sullivan Papain who represented hundreds of firefighters, had submitted a separate brief for which he consulted closely with Napoli, Groner, Rubin, and Russell.

Given that the stakes were so high—thousands and thousands of Ground Zero responder cases were on the line—WGENB made a concerted effort and were able to submit several amicus briefs (supporting legal briefs) from relevant police and firefighter unions and other associations of workers at Ground Zero. It was important to show the court the widespread support for the plaintiffs in the appeal.

For the defense, Tyrrell and Hopkins were convinced they would prevail at the Second Circuit, that the law was on their side. At the same time, the defense needed to continue to prepare for eventual trial should their appeal not succeed.

In August 2007 there was a surprise development: Napoli received a call from Tyrrell, who had rebuffed all Napoli's prior overtures. Tyrrell told him that he and Margaret Warner were prepared to start confidential settlement discussions on behalf of the Captive and the defendants.

Finally! It was the call the plaintiffs' attorneys had been waiting for. The timing made sense: it was smart to start settlement discussions when both parties were unsure of the future and were vulnerable—it made both sides more reasonable.

Shortly after Tyrrell's call (and most likely not coincidentally) the *New York Post*, Fox News, and other press outlets that, until then, had been so pro–plaintiffs' attorneys that Groner referred to them as their co-counsel, began a stream of attacks on WGENB, accusing them of seeking to enrich themselves at the victims' expense and saying they would soon collect some $400 million in lawyers' fees.[1] Groner, who had long feared the press would turn on them, suspected Tyrrell as the source.

The $400 million figure sparked outrage from the public and dissension among WGENB's clients. It didn't matter that the facts were wrong. (The WGENB attorneys would earn nothing if they lost the case, and if they won, they would get a percentage of what the responders received, which, after expenses, was certain to be much less than $400 million). The victims were in ill health, and some were getting worse. They could no longer do the jobs they loved. They were angry that after all this time and the suffering of both them and their families, they had received nothing. Confronting all these unpleasant truths drove a wedge between some clients and their attorneys, causing them to question their faith in WGENB.

On October 1, 2007, an unusually mild morning in New York City, the attorneys entered the federal courthouse in Lower Manhattan to make their arguments before the Second Circuit Court of Appeals. The three-judge panel consisted of Richard Wesley, Jon Newman, and Sonia Sotomayor (prior to being elevated to the U.S. Supreme Court).

The issues before the court were twofold: Was this an issue that the appeals court should hear (did it have the jurisdiction to hear this case)? And if they did have the authority to hear this case, were the city and its contractors protected by immunity from being sued for the respiratory injuries suffered by the Ground Zero responders?

Everything was riding on this court appearance, and a tremendous amount of work on both sides had gone in to being prepared for this day. The court was filled with attorneys from both sides, each scrutinizing every look on each judge's face and on the faces of opposing counsel to gauge the temperature in the room.

Tyrrell had arrived like the general of an army (which in some ways he was). Everything about his bearing and dress said "Solid." As the appellant in the case, he was slated to speak first, but before he had even had time to introduce himself to the court, Judge Sotomayor launched in with "You've got three principles at play here, all of which suggest we don't have jurisdiction. You have the Supreme Court telling us immunity should be rarely granted. You've got the state saying it favors suit rather than nonsuit, and you have language that is, at best, ambiguous. How do we have jurisdiction?"

As Groner would say at a later date, "It was a 'Holy Shit!' moment." Clearly, Sotomayor understood the issues in the cases deeply and was wasting no time in hammering Tyrrell. When he tried to regain his footing, she held fast, saying that the real question was whether or not this court should be reviewing this matter. Judge Wesley then took up the cudgel, also knocking back each of Tyrrell's attempts to argue a basis for immunity. The judges were insistent that Tyrrell address the threshold issues first—which threatened to knock him out before he even got to his best arguments for immunity.

There were several memorable exchanges. Judge Sotomayor took Tyrrell's position to outrageous contentions, asking if a guard at the WTC shot everyone who came within ten feet of Ground Zero, would he then have immunity for his actions. Tyrrell answered that intentional acts would have immunity. Sotomayor was aghast: "You truly are arguing that the New York State legislature intended the City and its contractors to have immunity [for] anything you want to do so long as you think it's going to help the activity . . . whether that understanding is reasonable or not?"

At one point Tyrrell said, "I'm confused, your honor." And Sotomayor responded, "You're confused because you're not explaining—you're not following the law."

It did not get much better for Tyrrell from there. Judge Wesley challenged him on what the law actually said, and, disputing Tyrrell's recollection, added, "I'd be willing to bet good money [that I'm right]."

Finally, Tyrrell asked, "Shall I get back to my argument?" To which Sotomayor responded, "I think you should defer to your colleague."

The true knockout punch came when Judge Newman said that he could not understand why the Captive had not distributed its FEMA funds to the victims. "Clients are ill and dying, it just cries out . . . with a billion dollars sitting there available but not yet distribute[ed]—for all sides to do what was done in so many other situations . . . [to] set up a claims distribution mechanism, instead of all the discovery motions. Hire Kenneth Feinberg . . . the way he distributed the Victims' Fund."[2]

Here was the Second Circuit, just one step below the Supreme Court, who, rather than merely interpreting the law before them, was complaining about why the responders weren't being compensated for their injuries.

Hopkins thought, "What the hell does that have to do with anything? We're here arguing about this law." As he saw it, this was the perfect opportunity to uphold and enforce a law that was already on the books. But the court was looking for a way around the law. Hopkins was surprised because the Second Circuit was quite renowned as a preeminent federal appellate court, and he had expected a much clearer analysis of the law.

It was now Russell's turn to speak for WGENB on behalf of the Ground Zero responders. Russell felt they had a strong argument that these claims fell outside the scope of the Stafford Act and the New York State Defense Emergency Act and that, consequently, there could be no federal or state immunity for the city and contractors. At the same time, he recognized that a year earlier Judge Hellerstein, who seemed very sympathetic to the victims, had indicated he was also very concerned about not issuing a ruling that would set a precedent for future disasters. If ever there was another emergency, no one wanted any hesitation on the part of any city to direct all personnel at its disposal to the rescue, recovery, and cleanup operations. The judges on the Second Circuit were likely to have the same concern.

WGENB's strategy was to come up with plain language and technical arguments that would make the Second Circuit comfortable that ruling in their favor would not hinder saving lives in the next terrorist attack. WGENB argued that within days of 9/11, the city and its contractors had decided that safety protocols were needed and were put in place, but they were not followed. The court, in WGENB's opinion, could rule that the city had not followed the rules they themselves had set; the court would not have to say anything about future incidents.

Seeing the judges take on Tyrrell so strongly encouraged Russell. Given that they had tackled Tyrrell on the issue of jurisdiction, he thought he would start talking about the merits of their arguments against immunity. But Judge Wesley cut him off, saying, "I thought you were going to talk about [the] jurisdictional [issues]." This was a strong indication that the Second Circuit would decide the appeal on the lack of jurisdiction without having to address the specific immunity issues.

Still, Judge Newman was interested in the practical aspects of the case and, like Judge Wesley, was engaged with the question of why the parties had not yet arrived at a settlement. As Newman noted, it was "a rare case where they have a billion dollars of federal money on the table."

Although it was expected that the Second Circuit would take several months to issue their written opinion, just four days later the court lifted their stay, allowing the tort cases to proceed under Judge Hellerstein.

This did not mean that WGENB had won their case. The Second Circuit still needed to issue their ruling on the jurisdictional question and possibly on immunity as well. However, in lifting the stay, the judges were saying that they recognized that delaying the cases was harmful. They would now take their time to issue their written decision on all the issues.

A November 25, 2007, article in the *New York Post* by Edelman was headlined "9/11 Suits in Legal Limbo." The article detailed how WGENB had submitted a request to Hellerstein to proceed immediately with the trials of three of the sickest Ground Zero responders. Time was running out for these three heroes, who were, Napoli told Edelman, on death's door suffering from lung disease. It was Litigation 101 to get cases to trial if you wanted to get the defense to offer settlement money—and this was yet another way to jump-start the case again.

As the *Post* reported, Hellerstein held a meeting in chambers to hear details of the two NYPD officers and a Ground Zero morgue volunteer whose cases Napoli hoped to argue right away. But while expressing sympathy for the responders, Hellerstein denied WGENB's request for immediate trials for the three. Instead he approved the hiring of a technology consultant to help the special masters set up their own plaintiff database. To the victims' attorneys it was an unnecessary, inefficient, and costly undertaking that was duplicative of their own efforts. But to Judge Hellerstein and Special Masters Twerski and Henderson, it was the only way to build an objective database.

This was a case where what appeared in the newspaper on any given day might seem to impact the course of the litigation.

On December 14, 2006, Ken Feinberg published a *New York Times* op-ed calling for "a fair deal for 9/11's injured." As the VCF administrator who had awarded over $7 billion to the families of those murdered on 9/11, Feinberg was very aware of the Ground Zero responders' litigation. He held a unique position as an impartial observer who had also had personal experience awarding compensation for 9/11 victims and their families in ways that most everyone had found just. As an admirer and protégé of Judge Jack Weinstein, he also had the respect of Judge Hellerstein. So for Feinberg to voice his opinion on the editorial page of the *New York Times* was significant.

In his op-ed, Feinberg argued that the principles used to make awards with the VCF should be used as a blueprint to resolve the current World Trade Center litigation and to quickly get money into the hands of recovery workers and others. "More than $1 billion in public funds is currently available for distribution as part of the initial federal appropriation earmarked for New York City's 9/11 recovery. If you add financial contributions from those contractors and others involved in the litigation, and supplement that with funds from various city charities, a total of at least $1.5 billion is available to settle the pending lawsuits—more than sufficient to pay all eligible claims, as well as lawyers' fees and costs."

As with the 9/11 VCF, Feinberg said, the neediest victims—those without a financial safety net—should be the priority. He concluded, "Just as the 9/11 fund should be viewed as a unique public policy response to an unprecedented national calamity, so, too, would this settlement be considered a one-time solution to all remaining physical injury claims occurring at the World Trade Center."

Following Feinberg's op-ed, Carl Campanile, a reporter for the *New York Post*, wrote, "The Mayor's Office is giving 'thoughtful consideration' to a plan to compensate thousands of sick World Trade Center rescue workers who can prove they fell ill after laboring at Ground Zero—potentially settling a nasty negligence suit they have filed against the city." Napoli was quoted as saying Feinberg's proposal could be a breakthrough to end the case: "We endorse the concept of distributing money to our hero rescue workers for their injuries—in line with what happened with the Victim Compensation Fund. We endorse the concept of developing a plan for restitution without further litigation."

And still no progress was made.

WGENB continued to wage war on all possible fronts. On the political front, Mark Childress and Brett Heimov' s lobbying efforts were yielding results. In what was seen as a major development, on December 4, 2007, the inspector general for the Department of Homeland Security announced it was launching an investigation into the Captive and why it had not disbursed any of its $1 billion but was instead spending its funds on fighting claims from Ground Zero responders. The inquiry was launched upon a request from Representative Nadler.

Christine LaSala, president of the Captive, was already a figure of some controversy in the press. On January 23, 2007, on *Fox 5 News*, the local Fox affiliate news program, consumer reporter Arnold Diaz, as part of his *Shame on You* series, confronted LaSala on the sidewalk in New York, asking her, "When are you going to start paying any money to the sick and injured World Trade Center recovery workers?"

"You know there's active litigation going on," was LaSala's response. To which Diaz replied with righteous indignation, "But you were given a billion dollars, [and] you haven't paid out one penny in two and half years." LaSala just repeated, "No comment, no comment," as she tried to walk away.

Diaz pointed out that LaSala earned $350,000 a year, and Representative Maloney wondered what it was LaSala was doing beyond collecting her salary. Diaz also pointed out that the Captive had already spent $100 million of its funds on defense attorneys, as well as for extravagant expenses, such as $1,250 for a single dinner and $342 for a night at the Waldorf Astoria.

On January 8, 2008, LaSala announced that she was stepping down from the Captive as of July 1. She was a very qualified insurance executive who had taken on a difficult job, one that didn't earn her a lot of friends. Groner found her to be very smart, candid, and honest in their dealings. She had all the hallmarks of a good negotiating partner. However, if she was the roadblock to a settlement (and Groner did not know if she was), then she should be replaced.

Nadler and Maloney released statements after LaSala's announcement. Nadler said, "Anyone who is proud of the fact that the Fund has more money now [i.e., because that money was invested and earned interest] than when it first started fundamentally misunderstands its purpose. The funds were provided to help workers who continue to suffer because of their exposure at Ground Zero, without bankrupting the City and contractors. While Ms. LaSala protected the City and contractors, she clearly failed to help the workers. I strongly encourage the Captive Board to select a new president that will fulfill the Fund's original intent and mandate."

"Sick 9/11 workers have filed thousands of claims against the Captive over the last three years," Maloney stated, "and I'm sure that many—if not most—of these claims are valid. If the Captive is going to continue its blanket refusal of these claims, it'd be cheaper for them just to buy a rubber stamp than replace Ms. LaSala. . . . The millions Ms. LaSala spent on overhead during her tenure could have done a world of good for suffering 9/11 heroes."

Former mayor Giuliani would receive a similar reaction when in February 2007 he announced his plan to run for president, standing in front of his new headquarters near Ground Zero. Laying responsibility for the Ground Zero responders' illnesses and deaths at Giuliani's feet, Edelman reported in the *New York Post*, "At least 204 Ground Zero rescue and recovery workers have died since 9/11—succumbing to a range of cancers." The *New York Times* would charge that Giuliani's legacy was clouded because he "ran a slipshod, haphazard, uncoordinated, unfocused response to environmental concerns."

On March 26, 2008, at 9:48 a.m., Napoli received an email from the clerk's office of the Second Circuit Court of Appeals. The court had rejected the defense's claim that the appeals court should decide their claims of immunity for the city and its contractors and ruled that the case should proceed before Judge Hellerstein.

Obviously Tyrrell and Hopkins were disappointed, but they were now eager to press the litigation forward. If they could not win peremptorily on the law, they were confident they would do so on the medical and scientific evidence DiMuro had gathered.

Upon hearing the decision, Michael Cardozo, the city's corporation counsel, said, "We are disappointed with the court's decision. However, we are confident that as the facts unfold in the District Court, the city and contractors will be found to be immune from lawsuits over our response to the terrorist attack."

"What this means is that victory is going to take longer to achieve, and we're going to have to get into the underlying facts of the case," said Scot C. Gleason, senior counsel in the city's Law Department.

Groner couldn't get over this statement. "Victory" as the city's counsel meant it would result in denying their clients, ten thousand sick and dying rescue workers, a single penny of the billion dollars Congress had set aside for them. It was shocking and shameful.

Representative Nadler had pushed for a congressional hearing to investigate the status of compensation for 9/11 illnesses. It was now more than six years since 9/11 and the end of the cleanup at Ground Zero, and Nadler wanted to put the responders front and center again in the nation's consciousness.

On April 1, 2008, Chairman John Conyers Jr. (D-MI), opened the hearings: "While [Mayor Bloomberg] has worked hard to fix this mess left by his predecessors, [the city has] taken an adversarial stance against the victims of this environmental tragedy."

Several Ground Zero responders attended the hearing. Among them, Mike Valentin, a tough undercover detective, who read aloud his statement, was particularly affecting. Valentin was a burly bull of a man with blond hair, cropped short and brushed back, and a blond goatee setting off his ruddy complexion. But his forceful exterior belied his scarred insides.

Valentin explained that, born in the Bronx, he was second-generation NYPD and had been working undercover for the Manhattan South Vice Unit. On the morning of September 11 he was wakened by his wife, who told him that a plane had hit the World Trade Center. After watching the second Tower fall on TV, Valentin rushed to join other colleagues, with whom he drove to the 7th Precinct, located in Manhattan's Lower East Side, all of them desperate to get to Ground Zero.

> When we arrived at the 7th Precinct, a young woman was walking past the Precinct, covered with what looked like powdered cement. Her face was covered with powder except for circles around her eyes—but you could see the look of horror in her face.
>
> Later that afternoon when 7 World Trade Center collapsed, I was standing only a block away. The scene was surreal—I remember feeling like I was watching a disaster movie. Quite simply, I could not believe what I was seeing with my own eyes. But if that scene was surreal, it did not begin to let me know what waited for me in the days and weeks to come. During the next few months, working in and around the World Trade Center site, I saw things that were unimaginable—the sights, sounds and smells of those months were burned into my memory for the rest of my life. Looking back now, my memory of 9/11 seems like one long nightmarish blur from beginning to end.

While working at Ground Zero he began to suffer chronic problems: "I coughed so hard that I actually developed back spasms." Although in October or November 2001, he had a chest x-ray that determined his lungs were clear, over the next few years he suffered from lung and sinus infections, burning inside his ears, and night sweats and would undergo four surgeries to examine or remove tumors, as well as his gallbladder.

Valentin testified that he was also diagnosed with GERD, esophagitis, sinusitis, thickening of the pleural lining of his lungs (which is indicative of asbestos exposure), pleurisy (a very painful inflammation of the lining of the lungs), severe ankle swelling, and severe throat pain twenty-four hours a day from the excessive stomach acid production. His illnesses had financial consequences as well. "Because I am unable to work, I had to sell my house in 2005 and today, my wife and our children and I live with my parents. . . . As a result of my illnesses, I am more than $160,000 in debt. I worry about my children's future, and whether I will be around to see them grow up."

Valentin cited Officer James Zadroga as "a hero who died of 9/11 illnesses with his baby daughter by his side—only to have Mayor Bloomberg sully his memory with public statements implying that Zadroga had caused his own death by abusing his pain medications—pain medications that were kept under lock and key by his father to prevent even an accidental overdose."

These men and many more died because they put their City and their duty ahead of their own safety. They died waiting for their government to do the right thing and provide for their health care and for the support of their families.

Even now, many police officers are being denied the three-quarter salary line-of-duty pensions they should have received, and instead are only given ordinary disability. Even to get that much, we have to face a maze of bureaucracy that is frustrating, demoralizing and needless.

In 2003, you and your colleagues allocated a billion dollars through FEMA to provide the City of New York and its debris removal contractors with coverage for claims arising from debris removal performed after [the] collapse of World Trade Center buildings on September 11, 2001. . . . Today, we know that the Captive . . . is a national disgrace. . . . I can't believe that my Congress would have set aside a billion dollars to have that money go to pay insurance executives and law firms hundreds of millions of dollars to fight the very heroes that money should have been helping for these last five years.

Valentin called on Congress to retake control of the Captive's fund and direct its use for the benefit of the Ground Zero responders, concluding, "We are only asking that our city and our country help us now in our own hour of need."

Valentin had held the room rapt. There was little that could be said after he spoke. If ever a case was made for the Ground Zero responders, that was it. And yet, still nothing happened.

One of the behind-the-scenes heroes of WGENB's battle on behalf of the Ground Zero responders was Larry Casey, the joint venture's chief information technology expert. Casey was an outstanding talent who had created a series of databases and computer programs specific to Ground Zero. Having him at the helm was critical for WGENB to do their work. Casey was supported in this essential and crucial work by Chris Farrish and Fred Kaiser. All three labored around the clock creating reports, doing database compilations and computations, and working on WGENB technology. Together they constituted one of WGENB's greatest resources.

The following email from Casey, dated April 27, 2008, gives some indication of the progress being made: "Good News! In an effort to increase the overall performance of the database I have been reviewing all views, tables, stored procedures and functions that reference client exposure. I found that the 'caps' were slowing down the system because 2 important fields that we use in applying the 'caps' were not indexed. . . . As a result, a calculation that previously took over 14 minutes now takes 6 seconds! . . . And can be run at any time, day or night."

This was a huge improvement. Reports that analyzed millions of data fields were critical for WGENB to understand, qualify, and quantify the tens of thousands of illnesses their clients had. Reports were being run 24/7. Reducing the run time for just one of those reports to six seconds would allow more reports to be generated and more information to be understood and would allow the lawyers to better represent the responders. Over the next several years, they would run thousands of analyses and construct many hundreds of compensation models using the data.

Casey had created a list of injuries for what were now WGENB's 10,205 clients who had a total of 36,843 medical conditions. At the same time, Groner finally found a respiratory illness severity scoring system that could factor in the enormous complexities in the case. It was all starting to come together.

Computer reports aside, it was incredible to think that in six years, Napoli, Bern, Groner, Worby, and all the attorneys in the WGENB joint venture, who had started with a handful of cases, now had more than ten thousand. What had been a snowball was now an avalanche.

Judge Hellerstein's core discovery order compelled each side to identify and submit the names of victims' medical providers, exchange medical data, and identify medical criteria. However, following a May 29, 2008, conference before the judge, it was evident that the two sides remained far apart about the most basic facts in the case.

The defense continued to refuse to accept that most of the plaintiffs were actually ill or that their illnesses were caused by working on the Ground Zero cleanup. The city contended that only 30 percent of the claimants had any possibly related illnesses, and none of these were severe. This gap between the two about how many were seriously ill was a major factor keeping the parties from making progress in court or having meaningful settlement discussions.

So WGENB continued to make their case in other venues. On July 2 the *New York Post* published Edelman's story "9/11 Illnesses 'Get Worse'": "Of 10,000 Ground Zero workers suing the city, medical records show 67 percent suffer respiratory ailments and 45 percent have a gastrointestinal disease, their lawyers claim."

The attorneys at WGENB spent a great deal of time developing compensation models to present to the Captive as part of a settlement negotiation. This was certainly among the most complex mass tort in U.S. history, and convincing the Captive to settle the case for what WGENB thought a reasonable amount was no easy task.

In broad strokes, they hoped to arrive at a lump sum, an amount large enough to provide all their clients with a reasonable payment for their pain and suffering. WGENB was considering two approaches to negotiate what that lump sum should be. The "top-down approach" was to prove to the Captive that the injuries were worth cumulatively more than the Captive's billion dollars, so the Captive would agree to offer the full billion less an agreed-upon reserve for future claims. The "bottom-up approach" required making determinations on individual case settlement values and extrapolating that based on each individuals' injuries.

Napoli and Groner believed that to get Margaret Warner, the Captive's attorney, to agree to a top-down approach using the FEMA funds, they needed to establish two matters. The first was to convince her that the Ground Zero responders' claims were worth far more than $1 billion, so capping the settlement using the available Captive funds was a sound financial bargain. Second, Napoli and Groner needed to know the minimum amount the Warner desired to keep in reserve against future claims.

Groner had already been working on developing a point system and injury matrix to use for distributing a lump-sum award, which required injuries to be objectively verifiable and defendable. This was difficult and highly complex work. He needed to establish a set of master rules that could be applied to ten thousand individuals who were exposed to Ground Zero dust in different circumstances. How to compare and score the injuries of someone who had five days of exposure in September right after 9/11, compared to someone who got sick the following May? Someone working at the World Trade Center site itself, compared to the Fresh Kills Landfill? This was a litigation, not a victim compensation fund, so these injuries needed to be weighed in light of how a jury would view the chances of proving causation in each case.

Too many rules would be unwieldy; too few would run the risk of being inaccurate. Groner saw his job as making sure that his clients got recovery awards that were closely aligned with their specific circumstances. A system that created false positives, by which a person was awarded points that overstated his or her actual injury, was as bad as a false negative, a system that understated injuries. To refine this system, Groner was regularly having Casey run the database against new rules. He would see what one individual would get under the new rule and decide whether that best reflected the client's medical injuries.

Myriad factors would impact calculations, such as the location where clients worked, the days they worked, as well as preexisting conditions and whether the person was a smoker (and how long and how much), among many other factors. What was their doctor's diagnosis, what medications were they taking, and what treatments had they had (including surgery)? Was their condition expected to get better or worse? The goal was to have enough rules and factors to yield a fair result. Groner worked at this matrix for several years.

The managers of the Captive finally agreed to hold a meeting so that Napoli and Groner could make a presentation on three of their most serious cases (the three cases Napoli had wanted Hellerstein to take up first). Napoli hoped these cases would demonstrate why his settlement demands were realistic.

"I ask you to listen closely to them and their stories," he said. Each was compelling, very human and relatable. "Listen to them breathe, listen to who they are. Because these are the cases that are going to drive this litigation." The message was not subtle: Juries will do whatever they can for these heroes, and if they find for these three, they can find in similar large dollar amounts for thousands of first responders.

Napoli seemed to be making the bottom-up argument—that trials for a few would set the precedent for the others to earn the same or more. But what he was really doing was making the top-down argument, of which step 1 was demonstrating that the Ground Zero responders' injuries would easily top $1 billion.

Napoli and Groner had learned that the defense was basing their estimate for their comprehensive settlement on a sample of cases, so they did the same, calculating that their sample was representative of WGENB's ten thousand cases within a margin of error of 5 percent. Groner rose to present a statistical sample of five hundred cases, their illnesses, their medications, the trends of their illnesses. He was not arguing the merits of valuing individual cases; instead he was demonstrating how extrapolating the value of sample cases indicated potential liability in excess of $1 billion.

"In short," Groner said, "we have performed the most far-reaching and advanced analysis thus far of the Ground Zero injury severities." Both Napoli's and Groner's approaches, different though they were, yielded liability valuation in excess of $1 billion, a vastly larger number than the Captive or the defense favored.

What they were asking for, Napoli said, was to get as great value as they could from the Captive: first, by having the Captive declare how much of the $1 billion FEMA fund was available to be disbursed to their clients (or how much was to be kept in reserve); second, by enlisting the Captive's help in trying to get more funds from some of the underlying insurers, such as Liberty Marine, and other potential contributors, such as the Port Authority.

Warner remained resistant and expressed several concerns: she was worried that new legislation being proposed in New York and Washington DC might have provisions allowing the Ground Zero responders in the case to opt out of any settlement and sue the Captive directly. Further, if not all plaintiffs opted in to a settlement, the Captive would need to keep greater funds in reserve. Finally, she was concerned that in the end, Hellerstein might not approve any settlement they made. Clearly settlement was still far away from possibility, beached for now on a distant shore.

PART SEVEN

Andrew Carboy had a nickname for Tyrrell. He called him "King James" because "it was hard to make a deal with the King."[1]

Over time, both Groner and Napoli found it easier to have candid conversations with DiMuro rather than Tyrrell. DiMuro was willing to talk about how he saw the cases, what defenses he believed would carry weight, what he thought the defense would never agree to, and where they might find common ground.

DiMuro was up-front that his point of view was that of a seasoned defense attorney who brought a cold-eyed and doubt-filled view to most plaintiffs and their claims. He weighed all claims against whether they could have been caused by other factors, what could and could not be medically proven, and what could or could never be proven in a court of law. DiMuro, it was fair to say, believed in only what he couldn't dismiss, and he felt he could dismiss a lot of the plaintiffs' claims. For instance, when provided with what WGENB believed were some of their best cases—of responders suffering from respiratory diseases—he easily dismissed many of them as having already been longtime smokers. He believed that WGENB's clients, no matter how sick, would have a hard time proving their illnesses were legally attributable to Ground Zero exposure.

When Groner put forward new medical studies confirming that the responders' respiratory illnesses and the lung scarring were due to the caustic nature of the dust and the presence in the dust of silica, glass, and other irritants, DiMuro dismissed these as well, as another instance of treatment centers giving biased info to justify their diagnoses and get more funding.

DiMuro had definite notions as to what Ground Zero responder illnesses the Captive would or would not compensate. There was no medical evidence or scientific studies of people who developed cancer in less than four years after exposure. Anyone who had developed cancer that fast, he argued, did not do so as a result of Ground Zero. He would have excluded emphysema too unless there was no prior smoking. He did not believe there should be any compensation for conditions that were precancerous, were preexisting or were now aggravated. Many responders complained of multiple dust exposure injuries, some primary and some secondary injuries. DiMuro wanted to allow only secondary injuries that were moderate or severe, and to remove all orthopedic injuries, psychiatric injuries, and cardiac injuries, which he viewed as being unrelated to dust exposure.

Groner went back and forth with DiMuro for more than a year. DiMuro would goad him, asserting that in his estimation only 10 percent of their cases were serious injuries. Groner's response? Even if DiMuro's absurd assessment was correct, 10 percent of ten thousand cases is one thousand cases. And an award of $1 million for each would yield $1 billion. Those nine thousand other cases were therefore certainly going to bring the total value of their cases to more than $1 billion.

But DiMuro had decades of experience in toxic exposure injuries, and it was his job to limit his clients' damages and disbelieve plaintiffs' counsel. Groner didn't remotely agree with DiMuro's assessment of responder illnesses. He wasn't even sure if DiMuro believed it himself. But it gave him a good indication of what WGENB was up against.

In the years since the terrorist attacks, the weeks leading up to September 11 each year had become the occasion for Ground Zero–related press releases, press conferences, and news stories in all forms of media. It was also the time of year filled with promises from politicians that the time had come (finally!) to take care of the Ground Zero responders.

In the lead-up to the seventh anniversary, in 2008, CNN ran a story by Andrea Kane, "9/11 Survivors Troubled by Asthma, PTSD," which detailed the ongoing health issues of responders whose condition had become worse over time. A similar theme coursed through Brandon Keim's story on *Wired*, "9/11 Health Problems Could Worsen," for which he interviewed Mount Sinai's Dr. Philip Landrigan, who described the dust cloud at the WTC site:

About two-thirds of the mass consisted of pulverized cement. It was extremely caustic, with a pH between 10 and 11. The effect on a person's sinuses, bronchi and trachea would be like inhaling powdered Drano. The pH of Drano is around 10 or 11—the only difference is that this was a dry powder. The particles adhered to the lining of airways, creating searing and burning.

We think that accounts for the fact that a substantial fraction of people who inhaled it now have restrictive lung disease. Their lungs have scarred, diminishing total lung volume: studies from the fire department indicate that firefighters caught in the cloud lost very significant amounts of lung volume, equivalent to what a normal person would lose in 11 years of normal life.

Those folks lost in one day what normally takes 11 years. In addition to the cement, there was pulverized glass: the outer skin of the buildings was glass that shattered and turned into microscopic spicules and shards. That compounded the damage caused by the cement. Those were the two materials that accounted for most of the respiratory problems we see to date.

Dr. Benjamin Luft, head of the Long Island World Trade Center Medical Monitoring and Treatment Program, weighed in as well: "It is extraordinary that approximately 30 percent of the responders still suffer with very significant problems seven years later. And now, we must be vigilant in detecting the long-term [effects] of the toxic exposure and monitor our patients for the development of cancers and autoimmune disease."

Dr. Luft had himself gone to Ground Zero several days after the attacks. "I witnessed the smoldering destruction and the all-pervasive dust," he would later recall, "inhaled the caustic odor that permeated the air, and was humbled by the extraordinary response. As a trained clinician and scientist, I observed a situation containing all the ingredients needed for the development of significant mental and physical disease as well as social disruption to those who responded."[2]

As the child of Holocaust survivors, Luft knew the importance of recording testimony. As a physician and a medical researcher, he was impelled to heal and care for the sick as well as to gather the data to document, track, and treat them. In what befell the Ground Zero responders, he had found a mission.

Luft's voluntary clinic for responders to address their mental and health needs led to his establishing a seminar course for medical students, 9/11: The Anatomy of a Health Care Disaster. As part of the course two responders were interviewed about their experiences. Their testimonies and their impact on those who heard them were so profound that, according to Luft, it led to his establishing an oral history project for responders that in time led to a book, a documentary, and an oral history archive that was donated to the Library of Congress, where it can be visited and accessed today.

In order to increase pressure on the managers of the Captive to disburse its funds, WGENB worked to initiate a two-pronged investigative attack at the state and federal levels. Napoli drafted a letter to Eric Dinallo, the New York State insurance superintendent, asking him to investigate and intervene in or assume control of the Captive, if necessary, so as to fulfill its mandate by disbursing its funds to the Ground Zero responders.

On the federal level, WGENB had been waiting for the report of the Office of Inspector General (OIG) of Homeland Security for some six months. The OIG's mission includes promoting effectiveness, efficiency, and economy as well as detecting fraud, abuse, and mismanagement in their programs. Finally, in June 2008, the OIG released "A Review of the World Trade Center Captive Insurance Company," a forty-nine-page report. It noted that of the approximately ten thousand claims, only six suits for broken bones were settled for some $320,000, yet the Captive had thus far spent $103 million on legal fees.

The OIG made several recommendations for the Captive to improve its financial reporting process. Yet, to the disappointment of WGENB and the Ground Zero responders, the OIG did nothing to force the Captive to use its funds to start settling responders' claims.

Napoli remained undeterred. In order to sow discord among the defense, WGENB exacerbated the long-standing friction between the city and its more than 150 contractor defendants. Right after 9/11, the city had lobbied Congress to cap the city's liability exposure at $350 million. However, the city had not secured the same exposure cap for the contractors. Susan Edelman aired their dirty laundry in the *New York Post* in an April 13, 2008, article, "$$ War with 9/11 Contractors," which began, "The city and its contractors have become embroiled in an explosive rift over who's responsible to pay 9/11 workers sickened during the World Center cleanup. Splitting with Mayor Bloomberg for the first time, the contractors were now contending that the city has no financial cap on [the contractors'] liability for claims from the cleanup. The contractors have filed bombshell court papers saying they could be left holding the bag for potentially enormous costs if the burden of compensating sick 9/11 responders shifts to them."

Not all the press about the Ground Zero responders was favorable. An article by Jennifer Kahn in the *New Yorker* magazine's September 15, 2008, issue, "A Cloud of Smoke: The Complicated Death of a 9/11 Hero," revisited the story of James Zadroga. In the grand tradition of upending accepted fact and goring sacred cows, Kahn cast doubt on whether Zadroga's death was in fact attributable to inhaling Ground Zero dust. Much as the city's medical examiner did, she found damning that Zadroga may have been a drug abuser and left the impression that his death was drug-related, that his respiratory ailments were more consistent with inhaled drug abuse. Much was made of the fact that the contaminants found in Zadroga's lungs had passed from the blood stream rather than lodged in the lung tissue, implying that this was more likely the result of intravenous drug use than from breathing toxins.

It had been said that Zadroga's wife's unexplained death was the result of a heart ailment or possibly a brain tumor. However, the *New Yorker* article reported that it was, in fact, due to drug abuse as well. The picture was not a pretty one and left the impression that Zadroga was not the hero the press had made him out to be. At the very least, it demonstrated the great difficulty in attributing medical causation resulting in death to Ground Zero dust inhalation—something many doctors and other health officials were wary to admit.

Many of the victims and their supporters were shocked by what they saw as an attack on the deceased. What was the point of sullying Zadroga's name? Gina Barrese expressed the feeling many had: "They say he was a drug addict. So what? Maybe that was because of 9/11. It doesn't mean that Ground Zero didn't make him sick."

Napoli was a person of great charisma when he wanted to be. He was also Machiavellian, often in strategic ways that worked to his and his clients' benefit. He bullied, blustered, overwhelmed, and exhausted his opponents on his way to victory. That was his style, and it had worked well for him. As one of his associates said, tellingly, "Paul has a talent for pissing people off. But you can't argue with his results."

When he was getting nowhere with Tyrrell, Napoli turned to DiMuro. When he was getting nowhere with either, he turned to the Captive and its outside attorney, Margaret "Peg" Warner. Napoli's relationship with Warner was complicated. To her detractors, she could appear haughty and, at times, seem to act as though Napoli, his legal practice, even his way of practicing law, was beneath her. She played her cards close to the vest and acted as if all the cards were in her hands. Accordingly Napoli alternated between bringing on the charm and showing her what a street fighter he was.

Napoli regularly scrutinized the minutes of the Captive's board meetings, which he had fought to get copies of. (As a public entity, their records were supposed to be made public.) In the August board meeting, by way of explaining why they wanted to keep their funds in reserve rather than disbursing them, one board member explained that the defendants were against settling. That was news to Napoli. Useful news. News that reporters such as Edelman at the *New York Post* would be interested in. The *Post* ran yet another article emphasizing that the Captive was using the funds to enrich the defense attorneys rather than paying heroes' claims or settling the cases.

Napoli sent Warner an email asking if she was ignoring him. Warner responded, "Paul, I am not ignoring you, but perhaps I should. . . . I hear that you have Sue Edelman on the trail again. Surely, Bill [Groner] and you know that a reversion to tactics . . . will close minds and doors. And fast. . . . I will try to call you at some point in the afternoon."

Napoli was outraged by Warner's contention that his behavior would "close minds and doors." He blasted back, "You yourself said that litigation is in full force. You cannot have it both ways. Settlement talks do not occur without talking and having meetings. If the Captive truly wants to advance talks, then they certainly have not shown it, and the parties on our side believe the Captive's talk is simply hollow 'rhetoric.'"

It was on! Warner then sent Napoli a blistering letter which said in part:

You have brought thousands of cases by individuals who allege no present injury. This is a disservice to those of your clients who truly may be injured and who can prove those injuries are the result of their heroic work at Ground Zero. It also wastes the limited taxpayer money appropriated to ensure that all of the WTC Captive's insureds do not face financial exposure arising out of their own heroic efforts. . . . Although you complain that the costs of defending these numerous cases is eroding the resources available for settlement, litigation tactics you continuously chose to deploy have increased significantly those costs. You have failed to respond meaningfully to Judge Hellerstein's core discovery, including by withholding or not producing pre-9/11 and other medical records necessary to evaluate crucial issues such as the severity and alternative causes of many plaintiffs' alleged injuries.

Napoli answered, "The response was nothing short of sophomoric. My clients' injuries are clear, there are plaintiffs *dying* every day from these injuries."

As Warner and Napoli continued back and forth, Edelman's headline in the *New York Post* on November 30, 2008, as if on cue, blared, "Stox-Socked Fund Pays Lawyers, Stiffs Heroes": "The insurance fund created to cover claims by Ground Zero workers is losing millions of dollars on the stock market while spending mounting sums on lawyers and overhead, raising fears that little will be left for sick and dying 9/11 responders. . . . The fund lost more than $7 million alone in the three months ending Sept. 30, records show." Napoli was quoted as saying, "It's a travesty that the lawyers and administrators given the task of distributing these funds have reaped all the money to compensate themselves."

Warner was incensed. She emailed Groner, "I will not countenance schoolyard tactics. If David [Worby] and you were serious about settling these cases, you would bring Paul in line."

When Warner canceled their next meeting, Napoli cajoled her in an email: "If we stopped talking every time a news article was written we would never talk." He then turned the charm offensive back on, and soon enough he and Warner were telling the court that the various letters they had sent complaining about each other were only temporary disputes.

As Napoli and Warner battled it out in emails, Groner and DiMuro continued to dance around what would yield a settlement that Napoli, Tyrrell, Warner, and Hellerstein would all accept.

DiMuro was a daunting adversary. With decades of product liability and toxic exposure defense experience and years of studying WGENB's cases and clients' medical records, he knew more than Tyrrell or anyone else on the defense about damages, Ground Zero dust causation, the real potential value of WGENB's cases, as well as the potential exposure to the city and its 150 contractors. As DiMuro was in charge of the medical and scientific experts, he mirrored Groner's expertise on the responders' cases and injuries. The two could go back and forth over scientific minutiae like teens on rival high school debate teams.

DiMuro liked that Groner was something of a wiseass. One day in court, Groner had told him, "You know, if you lost twenty pounds, you'd be good looking." DiMuro laughed—but he also started going to the gym. The friendship between adversaries grew from there.

Groner suggested DiMuro have dinner with him and Napoli. They ended up at a steakhouse in Midtown and talked about their lives, personal and professional. They opened up to each other and said things they promised not to repeat. Finally, Groner asked, "How do you put up with Tyrrell?" DiMuro admitted his frustration and his personal disaffection for Tyrrell, his tactics, and his personal ulterior motives. DiMuro estimated that he had already billed some $200 million for his firm and had personally raked in almost $14 million. "It's Tyrrell's philosophy to be billing as long as he can, up to and past the settlement."

Groner saw his opening: "If you were in charge, don't you think you and I could settle this with the Captive?" DiMuro supposed they could.

Groner kept pushing: "Out of the billion in funds that you have, how much would you ultimately pay to settle?"

"I don't know," DiMuro replied. "I don't think the city will ever go above $600 million." For Groner, this was a key moment. DiMuro had shown that he was his own man and that they could communicate honestly with each other. "Oh my God," Groner thought, "we do have a chance of settling this case."

As special masters, Aaron Twerski and James Henderson were determined to get a more detailed picture of the plaintiffs. There were long negotiations among the parties regarding discovery questions. When the special masters' first set of questions did not yield enough information, they sent a greatly expanded set. At one time, Twerski said, there were about twelve hundred questions. These were then winnowed down to three hundred, which was also deemed too many. Eventually they would bargain the total down to thirty-five questions.

According to Twerski, the most important thing that happened was that the masters got a chance to look at all of the injuries. They determined that most were respiratory, for which the American Thoracic Association had established standards for severity. So they were able to rank them as well as factor in preexisting conditions and contributing factors, such as if the plaintiff was a smoker. "When we got the medical conditions right, we got the severity chart right. That was key."

Once Twerski and Henderson had a sense that the majority of the ten thousand plaintiffs did not have severe conditions, they became convinced a settlement was possible. According to Twerski, at the beginning the plaintiffs' attorneys said $1 billion was not enough. However, once Twerski and Henderson deduced that the majority of injuries were not the most severe, they deduced that the Captive's $1 billion would suffice to cover all the plaintiff settlements. Twerski and Henderson's figures and observations, based on their own database, gave Hellerstein increased confidence of reaching a settlement.

The Captive had organized a meeting with WGENB and Sullivan Papain to discuss settlement. Groner had reason to be optimistic that his conversations with DiMuro meant that a settlement was possible. Yet as the Captive and the defense made clear, the parties were still extremely far apart. So much so that Groner wondered why they had even called a meeting. The defense's position didn't leave room for a middle ground.

Groner left that session thinking there was no reason to come back, until DiMuro walked up to him and whispered in his ear, "We had another $50 million to offer today but chose not to for strategic reasons."

Groner was stunned. He asked DiMuro why he would ever share this confidential information. Doing so could put his job—if not his career—at risk. DiMuro answered that his duty of loyalty was not to

Tyrrell, who he was convinced did not want to settle, but to his clients, the defendants. By sharing confidential information, he hoped to keep Groner coming back to the negotiation table and settle the case. After this, Groner started affectionately calling DiMuro "Deep Throat."

DiMuro recalled, "We fought like cats and dogs every day [during the negotiations]. I didn't like Paul being so flippant and arrogant. But that was Paul. Bill was more of a fighter, but in the beginning, Bill would make comments that would drive me insane because I thought they were completely wrong." For example, Groner told DiMuro that many of his clients had "rhinosinusitis that was extreme," and he'd have medical reports to back it up. But DiMuro didn't consider extreme rhinosinusitis a valid condition. "I had the best ENT guys in the city, and they had never heard of it." Rhinosinusitis, yes—that DiMuro saw as a not significant condition. But an extreme form? DiMuro didn't buy it.

Then Groner and DiMuro discovered that they both had gone to Boston University School of Law. "That was an ice breaker," DiMuro recalled. "When you're with people a long time, you start talking about their wives and their kids and it becomes a more friendly relationship. And then it became a more respectable, professional relationship, because we could then both have our points of view and not yell at each other." Groner was passionate in his beliefs, DiMuro in his. But DiMuro came to respect that Groner knew the medical aspects of the case. Napoli, DiMuro said, "was more the hammer for the negotiation."

Often DiMuro and Groner did not agree. For example, Groner had discovered that many of his clients who had significant respiratory problems nonetheless had normal chest x-rays and normal pulmonary function test results; proving these clients had respiratory disease in light of having normal test results was a big problem. But Groner learned that within the pulmonary system there are small airways called bronchioles, and if those become inflamed and narrowed they could cause serious breathing conditions that would nonetheless not show up on pulmonary function tests. Yet DiMuro was adamant that if it did not show up on the pulmonary test, it didn't matter if some-one had shortness of breath or difficulty breathing; it meant he or she did not have an injury.

As DiMuro discovered, "You could reason with Bill." They could disagree and still remain courteous. And they grew to trust each other: "If I told Bill something, it was the truth. If Bill told something to me, it was the truth." That trust became necessary in establishing a back channel during the negotiations. That way, when there was an impasse, DiMuro could go to the Captive board and say, "Look, I've had a discussion with Bill. I believe him. I think that's where they are, and I think I can work this portion out." Bottom line: "[We] knew we were going to get to the number and that we [could] get there in an amicable way."

Judge Hellerstein had tasked the special masters with developing a plaintiff database of medical injuries and severity requiring hundreds of thousands of data entries, which was informed by frequent con-versations with the attorneys at WGENB and Patton Boggs. WGENB was playing along with the special masters in countless meetings to create a mountain of information that, in Groner's estimation, would never make a difference. They were doing so just to appease the judge.

Along with building their own databases of plaintiffs and injuries, Napoli and Groner were having secret negotiations with the defense, informed by their even more secret conversations with DiMuro.

On a brass-tacks level, DiMuro and Groner and their respective teams worked at defining categories of injuries, differentiating injury severities (such as different levels of asthma severity), and discussing adjustments for factors such as age, length of time exposed, preexist-ing illnesses, and multiple injuries. DiMuro wanted offsets for smok-ing, alcoholism, diabetes, and hypertension. He was friendly but tough.

As conflict escalated between Napoli and Warner, DiMuro reached out to Groner via email, drenched in friendly sarcasm: "Seems like everyone is getting along. The good cop, bad cop thing really seems to be working. It seems that I will have to intervene and save the day." Groner understood that it was up to him and DiMuro to pull each side back from the brink.

Groner shared with DiMuro that they were working on a plan to insure the victims with a cancer disability policy covering them going forward, should they develop cancer in the future. DiMuro let Groner know that of the various blood cancers, the defense would, in his opinion, reasonably agree to cover only a few, such as acute myeloid leukemia, chronic lymphocytic leukemia, Hodgkin's and non-Hodgkin's lymphoma, leukemia, lymphoma, and myeloma. Groner thought the defense's agreement to pay for *any* cancers was a concession, and all the more so given that WGENB's own oncologists could not yet prove they were related to Ground Zero dust and debris, and Dr. Howard from NIOSH had said such proof was still "beyond science."

DiMuro said the Captive was not inclined to cover (nonblood) solid tumor cancers, as they are most often not respiration-related and medical causation would be impossible to prove. On the other hand, nasopharyngeal, esophageal, and liver cancers, all of which he was unconvinced were related to Ground Zero exposure, were nonetheless, in his opinion, Groner's strongest solid tumor cancer causation cases. That DiMuro was sharing this information increased the feeling that they were working together toward a solution to these and hundreds of other issues rather than in opposition to one another.

Judge Hellerstein knew as well as anyone the old adage "If you want to arrive at a settlement, set a trial date." Once the immunity challenges were behind them, he renewed his efforts to have trials commence.

WGENB was also eager for Hellerstein to set a first case for trial. Napoli and Groner had already spent almost a year having conversations with the Captive managers and the defense, trying to arrive at a number from which to craft a settlement. They had made the case to the Captive managers that if they tried the first case and WGENB won a million dollars, the Captive was in trouble. And if they lost, WGENB had over nine thousand other cases with which to set a level for payouts.

At the same time, if they did win a million for their first case, some or many of their other clients would expect receiving the same or more. And it was clear that the court system could never handle ten thousand separate trials.

On February 19, 2009, Hellerstein issued his "opinion discussing methodology for discovery and trial of sample cases," a fifty-five-page order (fifteen pages of decision with forty pages of exhibits), which read like a draft law school article on his personal case management methodology. He discussed the history of the case, how he'd handled it thus far, and his plan to bring the cases to resolution. Having decided to treat the World Trade Center litigation not as a class action meant that each case was separate. However, as it would be impossible to try more than ten thousand cases, Hellerstein announced they would begin with twelve. He hoped that those cases would establish certain outcomes that could be extrapolated or used as the basis for a comprehensive global settlement.

Accordingly Hellerstein announced that trials would begin on May 16, 2010, almost nine years after 9/11 and seven years after Worby and Groner had filed their first case. The most severe cases would be tried and resolved first. At Hellerstein's direction, the special masters had selected 225 of the most severe cases; of that group, they would choose six—two selected by the defendants, two by WGENB and the plaintiffs' attorneys, and two by the judge himself. Those six cases would then proceed forward with full discovery, including perhaps dozens of depositions per case, document and medical record exchanges between the plaintiffs and defense attorneys, and physical examinations by defense doctors.

Hellerstein noted that although Congress had given the city $1 billion to cover cleanup claims, $191 million has already been eaten up by the Captive in overhead and legal costs and another $14 million has been lost in recent bond investments. Hellerstein chastised the Captive and the defense attorneys, pointing out that given what they were billing, delays only benefited their earnings.

Napoli and Groner were well aware that the court had not yet allowed discovery beyond what was necessary for the challenge to the claim of immunity. They would have an immense amount of work to do, both in the short term and most likely over the next several years if Hellerstein kept to his schedule. And even if Hellerstein was able to meet his ambitious schedule, the number of cases they would try would be negligible compared to the thousands of plaintiffs. One way or another they would have to find a better way to resolve the great majority of cases.

At the same time, Hellerstein's plan would create more work for Tyrrell with his document discovery center, where he had already processed millions and millions of documents and deposed many plaintiffs.

Some at WGENB were concerned that in announcing his roadmap to holding trials, Hellerstein was signaling that he was against settling. Moving ahead to trials, in their opinion, favored the defendants, who were more prepared and had greater resources. There was skepticism that DiMuro could ever help broker a settlement and that perhaps his "candor" had been a defense ploy. Groner disagreed, arguing that by forcing some trials, Hellerstein was just laying the groundwork for a potential future settlement—one that he believed DiMuro would be instrumental in helping them achieve.

Following Hellerstein's order, the first six cases were chosen. However, on March 3, 2009, one of the outside attorneys representing a non-city defendant emailed, "According to Tyrrell, for what it is worth, the insurance carriers do not want to settle now or soon but want to drag this case out for as long as possible because of the economic crisis." There was no way to know if the email was just bluster, but it made sense. After the 2008 economic collapse, including the failure of several insurance companies, those raking in large fees wanted to keep doing so, and those insurance companies still in business wanted to delay all potential payouts.

Meanwhile, Christine LaSala had decided not to leave her position as president of the Captive after all. Her salary, however, having been much impugned in the press, was "voluntarily" reduced from $350,000 to $234,500. This was good news, as LaSala was a smart, hard-working insurance executive who would push for settling the cases for the benefit of the city and its contactors.

At the end of April 2009, Napoli and Groner met again with the Captive managers. This time it was Warner's turn to present. Groner was guardedly hopeful that this meeting would yield the break they were waiting for, the opening that would allow them to negotiate in good faith to some disbursement for the afflicted Ground Zero responders.

Warner was a serious corporate litigation attorney. Her presentation was deliberate and contained no frills. After all the promises and important advances, Napoli found her offer completely underwhelming. It represented very little acknowledgment of WGENB's prior presentations and hewed to the defense's positions, offering up just a fraction of the funds the Captive had at their disposal. After the meeting, Napoli sent Warner an email: "In all frankness, Peg, the offer was meaningless." He pointed out that it was only marginally higher than the previous year's offer.

Napoli was irate and decided to dig in. If they wanted a fight, he was going to bring it. WGENB's position had always been that if they were to go to trial, it would take only five hundred cases being paid out at $2 million each to eat up the entire $1 billion Captive fund. Napoli emailed, "The offer conveyed was insincere and seems purposefully intended to discourage further negotiations—all of which begs the question of why you even wasted our time."

Napoli threw new energy into trial preparation. Conversations between him and Warner continued to fly back and forth by email. At the same time, Napoli, Groner, and DiMuro continued their back-channel discussions.

Patton Boggs had complained to the court about WGENB's alleged failures to comply with discovery orders, and WGENB had complained about Patton Boggs, which now delivered to WGENB a giant mound of documents, including a hard drive with 350 GB of documents and some 3 million hardcopy pages. A favored tactic of well-staffed law firms with deep pockets, it's called a data dump and is intended to cause distress and distraction to your adversary. They were betting or hoping that WGENB could neither spare the manpower nor spend the money on processing all this information.

In July, however, things started to break for WGENB. On July 28 Hellerstein held a hearing to announce that there would be no delays for the trials he had scheduled to start the following May. He was particularly tough on the defense and the Captive.

Tyrrell had been making motion after motion and argument after argument to try to have the court dismiss various groups of cases, but Hellerstein generally wasn't having it. At one point he told Tyrrell, "I'm not sure I'm bound by either side's briefs. . . . In many senses what happened at the World Trade Center was unique. I feel hesitant and awkward in trying to apply a statute that would potentially cut off a substantial number of people's recoveries. . . . I think we are all gripped by the immensity of the issues and the practical consequences it has on tens of thousands of lives." Tyrrell's many defenses, even when not successful, demonstrated the entrenched nature of the case. It did not look like resolution was going to come easy, or soon.

And then there was the jalapeño margarita breakthrough (or "halopenia," as it was called in an email at the time).

Napoli had continued to engage with Warner throughout the summer, convinced that cases like these settle "with love, not war." Groner considered Warner an excellent corporate attorney but was annoyed at what he perceived as her immovable default position of "You guys have to bring your number down." He also felt she played her cards too close to the vest and simply didn't demonstrate the flexibility that negotiations require. Or perhaps she was playing "cold" to get WGENB to lower their demand numbers. Whatever the reason, Groner felt he and Warner didn't have an open dialogue about a potential resolution and wanted to break that log jam.

Thus he and Napoli made a plan to invite Warner out for drinks after the Hellerstein conference to see if they could make any personal headway. Hellerstein had just battered the Captive in the hearing, and it showed on Warner's face. She looked like she needed a drink. She'd brought along the Captive general counsel David Biester, whom she had jokingly referred to as "her bodyguard."

What Napoli and Groner had worked out in advance was counterintuitive: rather than giving Warner an ultimatum, "a last chance opportunity to tell us how much of the $1 billion they needed to keep in reserve or we come for that and more," the plan was to avoid talking business. Just when Warner expected them to press their advantage, they wouldn't. Let her relax and drop her guard. They would take off their lawyer hats, get silly, and then leverage whatever information was retrieved over the next several weeks and months.

As soon as Warner sat down, she said that she was not sure about their next meeting, scheduled for late August. It was futile, she said, unless Napoli and Groner came down from their number. At this point the parties were hundreds of millions of dollars apart. Groner, on cue, said, "Peg, let's not talk business. Let's just enjoy a drink, and talk about family." And that's what they did for the next hour. They all talked about their kids, their families, their lives. There was plenty of laughter; Biester's wife was nine months pregnant with their first child, and they teased him about how his life was about to change forever.

Warner ordered a jalapeño margarita. "We did anything but talk about the case," Groner recalled. The only exception was when they talked about Hellerstein and how the defense got their heads handed to them in the court conference earlier that day. Groner suggested that Hellerstein would never dismiss the case. The one time Warner reiterated, "You guys have to come down in your numbers," Groner, in an attempt to keep it light, said, "Yeah yeah. We come down, you come up, up and down, na, na nah nah na." And they all laughed and didn't speak of it again.

Although the mood was light and casual and they maintained a certain silliness, they were all aware that the substance behind their conversation was anything but casual. The lawyers on both sides had spent years in litigation warfare, regularly deploying take-no-prisoner tactics. The short time spent drinking together created a personal connection that Groner believed advanced the cause of settlement.

Several days later, at 9:00 a.m. on Friday, July 31, Warner sent an email to Napoli saying that she needed to speak to him and Groner; it was important. And when Warner said something was important, that meant it was urgent.

In the phone call to Warner, Napoli and Groner learned that she was peeved because she had heard that they had been talking to allocation neutrals (expert consultants who would come in to validate agreed-upon awards and hear the appeals of any clients who disagreed) and telling them the case was going to settle soon. She was angry because the negotiations with WGENB were confidential, and any breach threatened settlement.

Groner explained that he had approached an expert who could assist the parties to someday help administer a settlement. Warner then launched again into "You have to come down with your numbers." Napoli and Groner kept their response light. And then Warner said, "You know there is a magic number that we will never go past."

This was a major admission. Napoli and Groner had been trying for several years to get the Captive board to share how much money they wanted to keep in reserve so they could arrive at a global top-down number to resolve the litigation.

Trying to keep the mood casual, Napoli mentioned the jalapeño margarita, and then asked, "How much is it that you won't go over?" Warner answered that she would tell them the number at some point, but it certainly wasn't in the ballpark of what they were asking. Groner's best guess, informed by his conversations with DiMuro, was that Warner wanted to keep at least a third of the funds in reserve.

Knowing that and being able to use that figure as the basis of their ongoing negotiation was a breakthrough.

Napoli didn't respond but ended the call very politely. And after he hung up, he and Groner mused about how their love fest with Warner and the jalapeño margaritas were paying off.

Negotiating is a dance, one that includes no small amount of theater. You do your best to have your opponent be the first to name a number, and then, upon hearing it, you show surprise, disgust, or warm acceptance, depending upon your strategy and how close the number is to where you want to go. In similar fashion, you never want to tell the other side what your bottom line is because doing so takes away the negotiation play.

With regard to Warner's admission about having a magic number, there was no way for Napoli and Groner to know if she let that accidentally slip or told them on purpose. That was what made negotiating challenging (and somewhat exciting). One never knows, but for Groner, Warner had suddenly catapulted the negotiation into a higher gear.

What Groner said to Warner about Hellerstein's never dismissing the case seemed to stir her to action. She emailed Napoli, "We agree that it is high time for both sides to engage in a candid back and forth process. . . . The WTC Captive has invested an extraordinary amount of thought, effort, and money preparing for our discussions. This meeting is crucial—it may well be the last chance to see if we can bridge our valuation chasm before the demands of all-out discovery and trial preparation crush the process. I reiterate that we need to see substantial movement from you as a sign that you are serious about arriving at an attainable resolution. We are on at 9:30 on August 25 at McDermott's offices in New York."

Groner, feeling their moment was at hand, suggested he would try a new approach for the August 25 meeting. "I am going to stop negotiating and lay my cards on the table," he wrote in one email. He told Napoli of his confidence at arriving at a deal with the Captive: "I am in the zone and I want to play this out—I can totally pull this off—tell me if you like it." Groner then laid out a twenty-point settlement plan. His "declining reserve" proposal was to have the Captive pay the full $1 billion less an agreed-upon reserve for future claims for a certain number of years. Each year, based upon the number of new claims, the Captive would release more of the reserve to the responders, and do so until all of it was paid.

But at the August 25 meeting, despite all of Groner's preparations and plans, Warner was not interested in a declining reserve or any twenty-point plan. Instead she made her own presentation, upping her offer significantly but still substantially less than what Napoli and Groner hoped to arrive at. They decided to let her offer dangle while they continued to pursue other avenues to bring pressure on her and the Captive.

Groner's phone was ringing. It was DiMuro. "It passed unanimously," he said.

"What passed?" Groner asked.

"Oh, come off it. You know full well what I'm talking about. This has you written all over it."

"I really have no idea what you are talking about."

That was how Groner learned that legislation informally called "Jimmy Nolan's Law" was introduced in New York to extend the deadline allowing Ground Zero workers to file claims for their injuries.

Once Groner had a chance to look at the bill, he deemed it "a potential grand slam." Napoli heard that the announcement of the bill so concerned the Captive that they held emergency talks (which explained the call from DiMuro).

The funny thing was that Worby had to remind Groner that the bill was actually Groner's idea. Several years earlier, New York State assemblyman Nick Spano was in a tough reelection race; he was about to lose to Andrea Stewart-Cousins. Spano had reached out to Worby asking what law he might introduce that would help the police, firefighters, and other Ground Zero responders in his district. Worby in turn went to Groner, who made several suggestions, such as declaring that the New York State Immunity Act did not apply to the responders or that certain injuries were recognized as being related to Ground Zero dust or a law that would extend the deadline for Ground Zero workers to file a claim. It was this third suggestion that had become Jimmy Nolan's Law. Groner had completely forgotten about it.

When Groner told this to Napoli, Napoli was convinced that Groner had come to him and that it had been Napoli's idea. Groner agreed it was possible. There was no ego issue between Napoli and Groner; they were in this together as a team with one common goal: to win the case for the responders.

Jimmy Nolan was a carpenter who lived in Yonkers. He was working on construction at New York University in Greenwich Village when he heard about the attacks on the World Trade Center. Nolan rushed to Ground Zero and spent three weeks working, even sleeping, there. When he became ill several years later, the time to file a claim had passed. Jimmy Nolan's Law was meant to extend the time for 9/11 workers such as Nolan to file their claims. It unanimously passed the New York State House on June 22, 2009, unanimously passed the New York State Senate on July 16, and was sent to Governor David Paterson for signature on September 4. Paterson then had ten working days to act on the law.

Passage was not a sure thing. Mayor Bloomberg opposed the law, worried that it would increase the city's liability, and thus weaken the city's finances, and there was a possibility Paterson would not go against the mayor. Accordingly, WGENB was mobilizing support to get the bill signed. They hired Spano, who had lost his election, and Gene DeSantis as lobbyists. Bern enlisted a politically savvy public relations firm to strategize about whether Paterson would sign the bill into law. He learned that the key person to lobby was Paterson's chief of staff, Larry Schwartz.

Groner and Bern were marshalling all forces; strategy meetings were held; all support letters they received were forwarded to Larry Schwartz. Spano let Groner know that Bloomberg was "going hard" against the bill and had weighed in personally with the governor, so

Groner wrote Paterson, saying, "We urge you to sign Jimmy Nolan's Law into law. The brave men and women who are its beneficiaries deserve nothing less."

Keith Silverstein, an attorney who had excellent relationships with many labor unions and who had referred many clients to WGENB over the years, made a last-minute appeal to his various constituencies to voice their support of the bill, writing, "Mayor Bloomberg is vehemently opposed to this bill, [and] he and his staff are demanding that the Governor not sign it." Silverstein called on the unions to have their members call Schwartz to voice their support. Numerous unions complied and sent letters urging the governor to sign the bill into law.

Bern found a message on his voice mail: "Hi! This is David Paterson. Can you please give me a call?" The governor did not give a reason for wanting to talk.

Bern was surprised. Was Paterson calling him about Jimmy Nolan's Law? Bern asked around, and the best possible explanation was that Bern had been identified as a large donor to former governor Mario Cuomo. Paterson was doing his own fundraising, and the call appeared to have been made from Paterson's election headquarters.

The timing, however, was suspect. To make this call for a donation during the ten days he had to sign the bill would be not only inappropriate but unethical and possibly illegal. When Paterson's chief of staff, Larry Schwartz, was asked about this, Paterson at first denied having made the call.

However, WGENB's phone system was such that Paterson's voice mail was easily transferred into a digital format and forwarded to Schwartz, to expose the truth. On September 16, Bern met with the governor at 3:00. Paterson explained that he wanted to talk about the bill, which he was inclined to sign. However, Paterson said, he was also meeting with representatives from New York City, at 5:00, and they would try to argue against his signing. Paterson promised, "If they come up with anything, I will call you," adding, "If I don't, I will sign it at 7:00 p.m." That was the extent of their conversation. Bern waited by his phone.

That night at 7:00 Paterson signed into law Chapter 440 of the laws of 2009, Jimmy Nolan's Law. He expressly credited Bern's efforts when signing the bill.

As a result of Jimmy Nolan's Law, thousands of existing claims against the city were refiled and strengthened, and many responders who hadn't yet filed claims were able to do so.[3] Groner hoped this would push the Captive one step further toward a resolution. It would not return Jimmy Nolan to health, but it was an acknowledgment that for his service he was owed better from the city.

PART EIGHT

In early December 2009, the Captive settled its multiyear dispute with Lloyds of London, one of the insurers of the WTC. Because these monies would be added to the Captive's funds—and, in principle, meant that the Captive now had more money from which to forge a comprehensive settlement—Napoli wanted to be party to the settlement and get access to the complete details. Warner refused. Napoli, undeterred as usual, protested to Hellerstein in a letter to the court, after which Warner agreed to allow Napoli to see the signed settlement but not to disseminate it.

Groner, seeing an opportunity to move the negotiations along, told Napoli he was prepared to play bad cop and contact Warner directly with his own negotiation strategies. Napoli held Groner in check, for the time being, as he continued to alternately cajole and hector Warner.

There was still a large gap in settlement numbers between the parties. WGENB wanted the Captive to pay out most of their funds to the responders, and Warner wanted to keep a large portion in reserve. She was distressed that Napoli and Groner were asking for more than she said she would ever consider.

DiMuro, who was in secret contact with Groner and Napoli, told them that he was pursuing a separate channel with the Captive, waiting for the right opportunity to talk to LaSala, the Captive's president. He was more receptive to WGENB's number but was not sure the Captive board was. Groner promised to update DiMuro as each offer progressed.

Napoli thought the time had come to close the negotiations.

The Ground Zero responders' mass tort lawsuit proceeded on two different tracks. On one, after more than a year and a half of secret negotiations between the Captive and WGENB, they were making some progress. The Captive managers suggested they simplify the process of categorizing the injuries and their severity: divide the injuries into just four levels of severity and have different payment amounts for each tier. There was an elegance to that simplification of injury categories that Groner liked.

On the other track, Hellerstein, unaware of what the lawyers were doing, was pushing ahead in his own manner. He issued his roadmap for the case in early December 2009, calling upon the attorneys to break the victims down into five groups (based on the severity of their injuries), and then provide the court with the first group, all of whom needed to have thirty-five agreed-upon data-entry points complete. From that group the special masters would have ten days to identify two hundred severe cases, twenty-five cases selected randomly, and four hundred additional cases selected randomly. Five days later each side would have to identify two cases from each group for discovery and trial. In forty days' time, they would populate the first twenty-five cases—the "A" cases—and then the special masters would select two other cases to go to trial. A week later they would repeat the process with "A2" cases, and then again with "A3." If all went according to Hellerstein's plan, the data entry and information for the list of cases would be complete by January 1, 2011.

Many involved in the confidential negotiations continued to feel that the court's database was an enormous waste of time, money, and effort, which they needed to give obeisance to in order to appease Hellerstein, while they were secretly closing in on a settlement.

WGENB and the Captive were distrustful of Hellerstein, concerned that he would get involved in the nonlegal details of injuries and compensation in ways that were more appropriately left to the parties to negotiate. The fear among the attorneys was that, because this material was 9/11-related, Hellerstein was going to demand to be involved.

Christine LaSala wanted the case settled, and to that end she sometimes cut off litigation avenues that Hopkins and DiMuro might have pursued. At the same time, she didn't want to be paying for any cases that the defense felt were not legitimate. DiMuro and his medical team felt that there were cases with minimal injuries that were not significant, and at first LaSala was not inclined to pay any of those claims. However, she came to realize they would have to pay some minimal amount because, as DiMuro saw it, Napoli and Groner were not going to go to a client and say "You're not getting anything." In DiMuro's pragmatic view, any settlement would mandate an opt-in threshold that would require a high percentage of the claimants to sign off on the settlement. No one was going to alienate a claimant, as too many rejections would imperil the entire settlement.

According to DiMuro, LaSala's issue was that she had a mandate to protect the contractors. Once Napoli and Groner's demand came under $1 billion, she still needed to reserve money for future claims. But once LaSala believed that was possible, the case was going to settle. Settling sooner made sense to LaSala because Tyrrell's legal fees were too high. It was costing her more for Tyrrell per month than many of the survivors would receive in a settlement.

Although LaSala never let on to the victims' lawyers, she was insistent about settling to the defense attorneys. DiMuro recalled, "She yelled at me one day. She said, 'This case is going to settle. So you're either on the train or off the train.'" DiMuro had told her, "I'm on the train. I get it."

Napoli now turned his full attention (and sometimes fury) to trial preparation, with a 24/7 urgency. He was a harsh taskmaster. To give some indication of the intensity of trial preparation, here are the assignments given out by Napoli at a trial prep meeting held Monday night, December 14, 2009:

Chris LoPalo was put in charge of proof charts, assigning attorneys to the more than 150 defendants, as well as getting transcripts from Carboy's office. Tate was tasked with gathering keyword searches; Justin needed to circulate his memos on defendants; Barbara was in charge of trial memos; Patricia was the keeper of all trial spreadsheets. Bing needed to amend trial complaints to add the city and Port Authority; LoPalo would also circulate certain relevant transcripts;

Tate and Paul would tackle certain experts; while Bern would prepare others; Barbara would deal with the oncologist; Denise would deal with *Parker v. Exxon Mobil* (the new standard for introducing scientific experts); Neil Theis would prepare for the pathologist; Bern would call experts Carl Thurnea and Stackpole; they would speak to Kennent, a disability expert; LoPalo would handle Joe Cipolla Kamela, Neiderman, and Groth; Bern would deal with Stahl. And so it went.

Tension and tempers ran high. There was a lot to do, and during times of stress Napoli's default setting was to push staff to their limits; managerial pleasantries gave way to blunt, terse, demanding, even belittling comments—as if doing so was the best way to get a superior result. By midmonth Groner reported to a colleague that he was "hardly talking to Paul."

Napoli didn't care about what didn't matter to him. He could be flippant, sarcastic, and dismissive, badgering colleagues and adversaries alike. To arrive at a result he was happy with, he could spend a great deal of energy being unsatisfied, criticizing, complaining, being pessimistic sometimes to the point of paranoia—because the adversaries were often truly coming after him. What he said one day was not necessarily what he would say the next day. Yet he could then charm his way into everyone's good graces.

Groner, by contrast, was more even-keeled and consistent. Methodical, logical, and up for war-gaming every possibility, he was always responsive and looking to engage—it was part of the reason he developed friendships with opposing counsels such as DiMuro.

Over the years of nonstop partnership and near constant interaction, Groner and Napoli got along extremely well. Yet given the intense pressures that abounded, it was inevitable that Groner would at times get singed by Napoli's flame throwing.

Further, Groner was frustrated on several counts. After almost seven years at a 24/7 pace they had felt close to settlement on several occasions. However, they remained far enough apart from the defense that they now had to prepare for trial. This meant greater exhaustion to follow. Each trial would cost a huge amount of money and bring unknown results at a time when the WGENB joint venture's money was stretched. All this could bring anyone to the end of their rope.

Groner was burned out; he needed a few days off, a vacation. But he could not walk away. He believed strongly this was more than a billion-dollar case, and settling for less was going to shortchange their clients. On the other hand, there were stark realities: thousands of responders wanted compensation now, and closure, and to end the nightmare the litigation had become. Success at trial was not guaranteed, and there was simply no way for the court system to try so many cases. WGENB had incurred tens of millions of dollars in overhead and expenses at high interest rates, causing financial burdens, while the defense had ample funds to litigate for many more years. A reasonable offer had to be considered and presented to the clients.

On December 23, DiMuro sent warm regards and wished Napoli Merry Christmas. Groner also spoke with DiMuro, who reported that there was no new movement on numbers or on values for certain conditions, and no unanimity among Patton Boggs attorneys as to either.

DiMuro had reviewed sixteen trial cases thus far and estimated that at least four were worth more than a million dollars, while four others were absolute winners at trial for the defense. DiMuro said the Captive board did not believe Napoli and Groner's initial trial cases were particularly strong. They had looked at a bunch of trial cases and weren't convinced causation could be proven on any of them. He believed that if the Captive board looked at Napoli and Groner's true severe disability cases (not just the randomly chosen ones), they would find those more convincing, but, DiMuro added, "they aren't doing that."

Over the many years of litigation, Andrew Carboy's most astonishing moment came in 2009, during the deposition of Tennyson Hedley, the head of FDNY OSHA. (The Fire Department had their own internal Occupational Safety and Health Administration.) Hedley revealed that they had fewer than seven hundred respirators for ten thousand members on the morning of 9/11.

"It took six years to get to the point where I got that testimony," Carboy said. "Under the federal law, the FDNY was mandated to have a respiratory protection plan. This guy didn't even know it existed. He didn't even know where to find it."

To Carboy, this was an outrage. From day one, the FDNY had known that they were not providing sufficient protection. This was information that Patton Boggs and Tyrrell should have revealed from the start, in the earliest discovery. However, as Carboy related, Tyrrell and Patton Boggs took the position that as the FDNY's protection was formulated before 9/11, the defense was under no obligation to share any of this information. In other words, they knew about it, and they withheld it.

Patton Boggs had given the plaintiffs' attorneys some 22 million documents that totaled approximately 80 million pages as part of their attempt at invoking immunity. Yet all those documents were dated after 9/11. Carboy's point was that it didn't matter what post-9/11 documents the defense shared if a plan had been in place before the attacks: "You had a plan in place before there was terrorism, and you didn't follow the plan." That was something that should have been disclosed from the beginning of the litigation.

Beyond that, Carboy argued, although the collapse of the Twin Towers was an extraordinary, unimaginable event, building collapses were not a new phenomenon. They happened frequently in New York City (albeit on a much smaller scale). Carboy argued that FDNY protocol in the case of a building collapse is that you have to wear your mask. The FDNY knew this, but they didn't have a sufficient number of masks.

According to Carboy, Tyrrell's response was, "Well, we didn't give you this information [that the FDNY both required masking and yet didn't have enough masks] because it didn't happen after 9/11." The duplicity, from the FDNY and from Tyrrell, was staggering.

Carboy had one more takeaway from this experience: the firefighters must have known they didn't have adequate protection. Still, they rushed in; they saw horrors never imagined; death was all around them, and they continued to do whatever they could for others, for their city, and for their country. "They did it compulsively. It's a duty. It's a calling, and that's why they went back day after day, even when it converted to a recovery."

Napoli and Groner could respect the work of Tyrrell, Hopkins, and DiMuro—even when they violently disagreed with them—because they all believed that the American legal system demanded the strongest possible advocates. The adversary process that is the cornerstone of the system demands that each side muster the best evidence they can and the best arguments they can make (regardless of their personal opinion of the case or their client) and do their best to challenge the other. Although the standards of proof and the evidentiary rules may differ between a civil trial and a criminal trial, in the end a judge and/or jury decide what is more reasonable to be true based on what was presented in court. And, as has been remarked upon many times, although it is not a perfect system, no one has found a consistently better one to adjudicate guilt or innocence or find fault under the law.

Personal injury attorneys often see themselves as David fighting Goliath. At the same time, the attorneys defending those clients being sued see themselves as champions of hard truths and defenders against false claims. It was this same adversarial system that allowed for Groner and Napoli to advocate in support of the injuries and illnesses afflicting the responders having been caused by exposure to Ground Zero dust—even when medical science did not fully support their contention. And it allowed for DiMuro to doubt and challenge those very contentions.

In representing the city and its contractors, it was DiMuro's job to find fault with the plaintiffs' medical evidence. And he was very good at his job. He continued to be skeptical of medical and scientific studies that sought to prove causation between exposure to Ground Zero dust and the illnesses responders were experiencing. "You have to look at who's authoring the reports, and you have to look at the information that it's based upon. And then, finally, you have to look at the conclusions that are reached based upon that information."

DiMuro's mantra in doubting the researchers and research programs was simple: "Follow the money." For example, he recalled deposing Paul Lioy, who'd been hired by the city to test the dust. He asked why, if he found no asbestos danger, and many years had gone by since 9/11, he was still studying asbestos. According to DiMuro, the answer was because that is how you get more grant money.

DiMuro did not believe the studies were conclusive: "What I generally say to folks is, Read the study and look for certain words in the study. When you see the word 'suggest,' it's suggested. It doesn't mean anything. It means 'maybe, maybe not.' Which is not right. If you see 'possible,' those are all buzz words that allow additional research."

Mount Sinai Hospital, DiMuro believed, was also chasing the money. He claimed that their Selikoff Center was losing money prior to 9/11 and that following 9/11 it became a profit center. As he was quick to point out, no one goes to the Mount Sinai or Stony Brook program without believing they are suffering from symptoms caused by Ground Zero exposure. And in no case do the doctors say, "'You must have had that before.' Or 'It must have been caused by something else.'" He pointed to the fact that there are no cases of Ground Zero responders going to either of the programs who were found to have no illnesses as a result. "To have no cases where that is found is statistically impossible." Therefore, DiMuro reasoned, you can't really trust the programs' conclusions.

DiMuro did not believe the doctors involved were bad people, or that the responders did not have the illnesses they had. He just believed that the presumption of illnesses had tainted every element of the illnesses, from symptoms, to diagnoses, to what the medical centers treated and what the press reported. Regardless of what the plaintiffs, the public, or press believed, DiMuro needed only to assert that science had not proved causation from Ground Zero dust.

"I believe that some of the guys who had been there early on, and developed symptoms early on, have a higher rate of respiratory ailments. . . . I'm not going to debate that one, because that follows typical medicine. . . . [However,] when I hear that World Trade Center dust was special or you hear David Worby talking about the effect being 'synergistic,' [that is just wrong]."

DiMuro had hired a chemicals exposure expert, an army colonel and asked him about the chemicals present at Ground Zero, their dispersal and the dangers they posed. DiMuro's expert told him that with chemicals, "you need pressure, you need time, you need it to be in a medium that's going to stay around. Just because you have molecules that come together, it's not like pouring cream into coffee."

When the chemical expert examined what was found at Ground Zero, he concluded, "Basically, you don't have enough benzene. And it would take a year for the benzene, it would have to be under pressure, heated to a certain amount to form this molecule. Then you'd have to be exposed to it for a while." He asked, "Did you have people passing out?" Groner and Napoli had no one who claimed they passed out from chemical exposure. DiMuro concluded, "There was no evidence of a synergistic relationship between the chemicals present—just Worby saying so."

"I don't believe the cancers," DiMuro continued. "I've worked on cancer cases for thirty years. There are certain carcinogens, but just because you get a whiff of them doesn't mean it causes cancer. One of my experts said toxic benzene exposure was possible 'if they waded around in it or breathed it for a couple of years.' Bill would say the fires burned for three weeks or that inhaling that smoke was cancer causing. Our guys were saying, 'Unless somebody stuck their head in the plume, yeah, maybe.' But none of the guys ever said they put their head over a plume."

That was how DiMuro saw it. Not only was he entitled to that opinion, but as defense counsel, he was tasked with arguing for it as vigorously as possible. The American legal system depended on it. Two different sets of beliefs, opinions, and arguments battling it out, with a judge and jury delivering the closest approximation of truth that in any given case can be proved or arrived at. Or not.

Candiace Baker found it hard to express how much her sickness changed her life. She knew only that it affected her deeply.

In discussing her breast cancer, she explained, "Between the surgeries and the scars, your self-esteem is different, you don't feel as attractive, you question your femininity." And there were other ways that Baker felt her illness set her apart: "I remember going to one of my doctor's appointments, and the doctor said to me how many children did I have? I said I have one biologically, and I have two that were foster kids that I was going to adopt. And the doctor said, 'That's good because you wouldn't want to get pregnant during this.' And I'm like, God. And then being told, 'Oh well you'll never have children again.' Those decisions were things that were taken from me without choice. Those are things that I had no control over.

"Being sick you realize that, at least in my case, you lose control over a lot of different things. Growing up, if there was a test, I studied, I got 100. If it was a course, I studied my butt off, I got an A. There was no manual for this cancer. There was no manual for the respiratory illnesses, and there was no manual for the gastro illnesses. And, as you're going through chemotherapy that makes you sick as a dog, you no longer recognize yourself in the mirror. You're going through things that there was no manual for. There is no instruction. There is no guide. There's no one to take you by the hand and say 'Oh, here, this is what it's gonna be like when your toenails fall off in the shower.' No, there was nobody there for all of that."

On December 30, 2009, Margaret Warner reached out to Napoli, telling him, as she had several times before, "January 7 is an important meeting." He took this opportunity to come down hard on her, emailing, "It is time to agree on the money. You need to put up more now. I told you where we are. Put it up so we can wrap this up already." He closed with "Happy New Year to you and your family."

Warner reiterated, "January 7 is an important meeting," which seemed to set Napoli off. He replied, "I have heard 'important meeting' before (a few times). You need to agree to our money demand,

and the rest will fall easily into place. Please stop delaying and put up the money. Happy New Year!"

Once WGENB brought their number under $1 billion, DiMuro knew the case was going to settle. He recalled an associate's predicting settlement early on in the case. The associate had spent the day fighting Napoli during witness depositions. Napoli was resisting having his client give any answers on medical questions. When the opposing attorneys said they would file a motion with Hellerstein to force him to comply, Napoli's response was "Do whatever you want. I really don't care."

Napoli's style of litigating, DiMuro said, could be distilled as "Never comply with anything, until somebody makes you do something." This made sense in New York courts, where it was hard to get sanctioned or for a judge to actually compel an attorney to act. DiMuro surmised that there was no way to have a personal relationship with ten thousand clients. That many clients was all about having leverage. He took all these signs as evidence that Napoli was never going to trial—he was gaming for settlement.

And, in truth, DiMuro agreed that the case would settle. The elephant in the room was the Captive's billion-dollar fund. No one was going to return the money if it wasn't used. As long as none of the clients had to go into their own pocket to settle, no client was really in a position to complain about a settlement. And that, DiMuro believed, was the bottom line.

Tyrrell was not leading the secret negotiations between the Captive and the victims' attorneys. DiMuro believed that LaSala and Warner had decided that "if Jim was part of the settlement negotiations, all he would do is throw monkey wrenches into it." Tyrrell's priority was sustaining his team at Patton Boggs, who had dozens and dozens of lawyers working on different aspects of the Ground Zero litigation.

According to DiMuro, "Jim's motto is 'Every battle should be won on the last day with the last bullet from the last gun.'" Meaning, you billed to the hilt, and then you settled the case.

As a corporate mass tort or class action defense attorney, Tyrrell rarely took his cases to trial. He would win by having the case dismissed because of the statute of limitations, a jurisdictional or procedural question, or by settling for a minimal amount after having driven the plaintiffs into the ground with years upon years of expenses. His clients liked his results, and his law firms liked them as well.

One of the largest defense expenses was for document review. DiMuro described Tyrrell's document review enterprise as like "a hamster on a wheel." DiMuro thought it a waste, and all the more so because he thought WGENB was never going to look at all those documents. If, for some reason, either side actually needed a document, they were going to ask the city for it. You didn't need an office in New York going over millions and millions of documents. But to DiMuro it was a way to justify the increased billings—and for Tyrrell to profit from it personally.

At a certain point, once LaSala had decided the case should and could settle, DiMuro recalled, she also decided she didn't want Tyrrell at the settlement meetings, concerned he would report back to the contractors and say things that were going to derail the settlement—because doing so was in Tyrrell's best financial interest. For settlement leadership, LaSala turned instead to DiMuro.

DiMuro responded, "You're the client. You want to settle this thing, my job is to help you get there."

So, after that, at every settlement meeting, DiMuro sat with LaSala, Warner, and their associates on one side, Napoli and Groner on the other with Carboy and Papain.

As DiMuro recalled, "Tyrrell was not permitted to come to those meetings. In fact, he was livid and he said, 'Well, you don't know what you're doing.' I said, 'Jim, LaSala's settling the case. She doesn't want you there because she understands you're making personally $14 million a year. You have a strong motivation for the case to go on forever. I don't.'"

According to DiMuro, LaSala also had strong arguments with Warner about arriving at a settlement. Warner refused to allow the Captive to be taken advantage of by Napoli and Groner, and she was very reluctant to go as high as they wanted. At one point, DiMuro and Warner told LaSala that Napoli and Groner's demand was simply too high. As DiMuro recalled, LaSala told him, "Your boss is burning through money." It made more sense to LaSala to pay more than others thought wise rather than spend more months paying the exorbitant Patton Boggs fees. As far as settlement was concerned, DiMuro remarked, "the train had left the station."

In the first days of January 2010, WGENB and the Captive were still far apart on the global number, but the attorneys on each side had been working through the other complex issues so that if they reached agreement on the amount, the rest could fall into place. On a daily basis this meant that the summary of the settlement deal points, or the "term sheet," as it was called, was being continually revised, commented upon, negotiated and renegotiated, and there were constant adjustments, adjustment factors, and medical criteria changes.

Traditionally the responsibility of a plaintiff's personal injury lawyer with a single client is to get as great an award as possible, and the defense tries to pay as little as possible. It's not about what is fair but rather what each side will agree upon. In a mass tort situation, when you have a lump sum settlement, you need to decide, aside from the global amount, how to distribute those monies as fairly as possible among the clients.

How much each Ground Zero responder received was the product of a negotiated set of formulas and metrics and adjustment factors between the victims' counsel and the Captive. As a starting point, those people with the greatest injuries should receive more than those with lesser injuries. Determining how much more was more complicated. Doing so required looking at intra-injury severity differentials, meaning if someone had asthma, they would look at the four different levels of asthma and compare the pain and suffering the person had at each level. The parties also looked at inter-injury severities, meaning they would compare the points awarded for, say, asthma level 2 and GERD level 2, which would again depend on the typical amount of pain and suffering the person experienced.

WGENB came up with enough factors that differentiated people, but not so many that it would make the administration of awarding points impossible. For example, for asthma they looked at the severity level of pulmonary function tests and medications taken, while for COPD they would look at either pulmonary function tests or carbon monoxide diffusion capacity tests or cardiopulmonary stress tests. For interstitial lung disease, they looked at pulmonary function tests, but for sarcoidosis only they looked at CAT scans. Points were then adjusted upward or downward for smoking history, preexisting disease, age, dates of exposure, duration of exposure, and other factors.

Since Groner saw his job as making the system as perfect as it could be in terms of relative fairness between clients, he and the entire WGENB medical-legal team continued to test to make sure there were no false negatives. For example, someone with interstitial lung disease might be a false negative because the condition required a test of total lung capacity (TLC), but not all pulmonary function tests gave a TLC score, and thus some clients with significant pulmonary disease did not have the tests to support the severity.

At the same time, Groner's conversations with Met Life for a cancer disability policy, which had been ongoing since 2008, were also nearing what he believed would be a successful conclusion. Met Life, proud of having been a New York City institution for over one hundred years, was very interested in doing something for the Ground Zero responders and agreed to develop with WGENB a first-ever cancer disability policy. The plan was to create a policy for any responder who settled his or her case and later developed cancer to receive a $100,000 lump sum payment. This would, if all went well, give some financial assistance, albeit modest, to the many responders who were cancer-free but greatly concerned about the future.

At the January 7 meeting there was some readjustment of the injury tiers and awards. Groner was optimistic, feeling that although they remained far apart on so many levels, including a final number, the final details, getting Judge Hellerstein's approval, and getting almost all of their clients to opt in to the agreement, much was coming together. They were entering the home stretch.

The Captive's attorneys were resisting weighting some surgeries above others given the problems with causation. (How do you deal with lung transplant patients who were smokers?) The compromise suggested was to create a category of "additive payments," or additional payments, to individuals based on circumstance, to be negotiated and capped at a certain number of points. They were making progress.

At his first court conference of 2010, in January, Judge Hellerstein wasted no time in asking Napoli and Tyrrell to acknowledge that settlement negotiations were proceeding and that there was a draft settlement agreement. Neither the judge nor the special masters had been consulted to craft the settlement, so Hellerstein was now asking for details. Napoli demurred, saying they had signed a confidentiality agreement.

Hellerstein, who always pushed for transparency, then asked to hold an off-the-record session in his chambers to garner the particulars of a potential settlement. This was perhaps only the second time in all the years of this litigation that Hellerstein had done so. (The first was when they discussed the immunity plan.) Off-the-record in-office sessions Hellerstein reserved only for the most critical issues, which concerned explaining or hearing about the trial's progress or direction rather than attending to legal motions, orders, or in-court matters.

As they moved into February, the settlement negotiations continued, herky-jerky, seeming to make progress but still failing to close the gaps between the parties that would amount to a global resolution.

In parallel with the conversations, trial preparation for the forthcoming May trials continued. The defense took the deposition of Dr. Spiros Demetris, who had treated an NYPD officer who was among those chosen for the first set of trials. The detective had worked for less than a week at Ground Zero before he developed a severe hacking cough and COPD, which causes a permanent and progressive thickening of the airways that results in severe breathing problems. Before Ground Zero, COPD was traditionally a smoker's disease. Demetris's testimony was a good reminder to the victims' attorneys of why they had been waging this fight for so many years. He told the attorney, "I've been doing this for twenty-five years and I can't recall another time a thirty-two-year-old came in with COPD."

When the defense attorney tried to impugn Dr. Demetris by implying he was a paid expert, he shot back, "I'm not here today because I'm being paid. I felt very strongly about what was going on with him, and to me it was very mind boggling that [the union doctors denied the patient's disability]. All they have to do is meet him. . . . I don't know who reviewed the case for them, but if they examined him, how could they come to a different conclusion?"

In some ways, this back and forth was the crux of the case: a very serious injury to someone in the prime of life; an illness that is usually associated with smoking and that has never before been known to be caused by dust inhalation; and a doctor who is saying it was clearly caused by the dust.

Demetris spoke of the dangers from all the particulate matter in the air at Ground Zero: "It's like working at a demolition project, only at an atomic bomb scale."

On February 5, 2010, the *New York Times* broke a story they titled, "As Trial Date Nears, Efforts to Settle 9/11 Responders' Lawsuits Yield a Draft Plan." The attorneys at WGENB were caught off-guard. They were operating under a strict confidentiality agreement and had maintained secrecy for almost two years. They had no idea who leaked the story.

Attorneys on both sides refused to comment, but Judge Hellerstein told the *Times*, "The parties have been working very hard. . . . There have been intensive discussions going on looking to settlements of individual cases and globally of all cases."

Mayor Bloomberg's spokesperson, Jason Post, said that the mayor did not want the Ground Zero responders going into court to prove the city responsible for their illnesses because, according to the mayor, the city wasn't responsible. Instead the mayor was in favor of lobbying Congress to pass a bill offering federal relief to people harmed by working at the site. "We would rather stand with the responders before Congress than fight them in the Courts," Post told the *Times*.

This was disingenuous. Mayor Bloomberg was saying that he preferred the city avoid admitting any liability and that if he could blame Washington, he would do so willingly. As mayor of New York, Bloomberg was doing his job to protect the city financially from lawsuits, but there were ways for him to do his job that would have benefited the responders sooner, and without imperiling a settlement.

In a *New York Law Journal* article that appeared that same day, Judge Hellerstein admitted that he did not know how much money was being discussed for the settlement. But he warned, "I should also tell you that because of the extraordinary public interest in this case and because of the limited nature of the funds that are available for settlement, there will undoubtedly be fairness proceedings that will be part of the settlement."

On February 7 the *New York Post* revealed that the managers of the Captive had already spent "$275 million between 2004 and Dec. 31, 2009 on defense lawyers and administrative costs"—fighting against the responders rather than using the funds to aid them. The *Post* did not look upon the victims' attorneys as much better. Under the headline "9/11 Billable Billions," the newspaper claimed that the victims' attorneys in the case "could bag up to half the Billions available" and that as a result "workers are livid." The *New York Daily News* reported an unsubstantiated claim that the plaintiffs' attorneys would be collecting as much as $400 million. Both stories were premature and based on faulty presumptions.

The media's focus on fees had the effect of stoking ill feeling among WGENB's clients. A single article like the *Post*'s, before the attorneys could even present the complete settlement to their clients, was going to make its acceptance that much more difficult. The false information on fees could stir up resentment and cause any settlement to fail at finding widespread consensus, putting the parties back into never-ending litigation.

Gary Acker was never a spender. The money he made went to his boys, to their college, to the house—never to himself. However, one day, when Acker was still in remission, he was staring at a Corvette. He had loved Corvettes his whole life. Alison, who couldn't imagine what he had gone through and survived, told him, "You know what, I don't care. We don't even have the house anymore. If you want that car, honey, you get that damn car."

Acker got the Corvette. He loved having that car—behind the wheel, he felt like himself; he was no longer a cancer patient; he was free; he could go wherever he wanted. A few weeks later he got Alison a Corvette too, the same as his. There was nothing he enjoyed that he didn't want her to enjoy as well. That was just the sort of person he was.

At the start of February 2010, the Associated Press seemed to be devoting great energy to holding to account the Ground Zero responders suing the city. The AP reported that a New Jersey cop claimed to be Downtown while duty logs showed him working in his home precinct, and that another cop had asserted he was too sick to work before he claimed to be on the Pile. WGENB was steadfast that these were just outliers—their cases had been vetted, and among more than ten thousand victims, no more than a handful were mistakenly accepted.

The *Daily News* cited the cases of one NYPD and several FDNY officers whose data wrongly showed that they had cancer. The *News* noted that Hellerstein had faulted WGENB for failing to deliver accurate case histories to the defendants. The report concluded, "It's time to get real, Your Honor," calling on the judge to verify the claims.

This did not look good for WGENB. The media was taking isolated and uncorroborated information and making it seem pervasive, putting WGENB clients in a bad light. Napoli emailed Groner, "These reporters are assholes." DiMuro chimed in: "More good press; my only question is how Worby gets the lead and not the guy who is actually doing the work—Groner."

The next day Groner reached out to find a PR person who would take charge of rebutting false claims and making sure that their story got out there. He was referred to Ellen Davis, a graduate of Boston University School of Communications and then Georgetown Law, who worked for ABC News in the White House and for political consultants. Bern, who was handling public relations, agreed to hire her.

On the NBC radio network, Napoli and Groner conceded that given their thousands of clients, some mistakes had crept in, but they assured everyone they had been working to correct those few cases that were the exceptions, not the rule.

WGENB strongly suspected that all this negative disinformation was leaked by Tyrrell. This was part of the psychological warfare common in litigation—you wound your opponent where you can, when you can. However, in this case, as they were closing in on arriving at settlement, the timing seemed wrong. Could Tyrrell be trying to blow up the settlement in order to further drag out the litigation? Was he hoping to make his own legal fees seem less outrageous? It was hard to say. Many at WGENB and elsewhere felt that he stood to profit most from a settlement falling apart.

Groner reached out to Warner to rein in Tyrrell, saying in an email, "This type of press is very damaging to our joint interests; the AP is apparently on a crusade or tirade and I am not sure how much this is fueled or encouraged by Jim T but to the extent it is, please shut this down immediately. We should chat sooner rather than later about whether there should be any corrective action by us jointly to correct the record and I would appreciate your thoughts on this; we have come way too far for this type of mis-information to be disseminated." Warner said she would tackle the problem on her end.

However, the week of February 8, 2010, found Groner increasingly frustrated with Warner. He felt she was playing some game regarding the funds at her disposal—funds that no company or individual had personally paid for—while he and Napoli were negotiating on behalf of responders who were sick and not getting better. There were moments when Groner wanted to call off the negotiations, but Napoli persevered when Groner faltered, and vice versa.

By the start of the next week, Warner was finding Groner a more reasonable negotiating partner. He had worked out with Napoli and Papain where they stood in terms of a final global settlement number. By February 15, they were close.

On the morning of February 16, Groner was out of the office, dressed in a T-shirt, and unshaven, holding his smartphone to his ear as he listened to Warner. The difference between the parties had narrowed considerably. Yet the gap that separated them was significant. The Captive was always going to keep some funds in reserve and pay out the rest. The question remained how much of each. Groner was looking for the maximum, and Warner, who was still looking to keep funds in reserve for future claims, was holding to the lower end of the range.

However, that morning on the phone, they were able to finalize a clever solution that spoke to both their concerns by using a sliding scale of payouts. They crafted a settlement amount that started at $575 million (the city, its contractors, and the Captive could then say they settled for less than $600 million) and, depending on the number of claimants who opted in to the settlement and the number of new claims filed in the following five years, could rise to $657 million (as high as Warner would go and significantly higher than she had ever offered).

"Let's button this up," Groner said. Warner suggested they have a conference call the next day with Napoli, Papain, Tyrrell, and LaSala to confirm their agreement. Groner assented. Then the call was over.

In the privacy of his home office, Groner raised his arms to signal he'd made it across the finish line.

But he was more relieved to have arrived at an agreement than he was satisfied by the negotiation. He felt strongly that the Ground Zero responders, based upon their serious, progressive, and persistent injuries and disabilities, were entitled to much, much more. However, at this point, he accepted that this was the best result he could get. It was a settlement award that WGENB and Sullivan Papain were ready to recommend to their clients, and the responders deserved to have closure on their claims. Still, many details remained to be worked out.

On February 20 Warner sent over a detailed term sheet, to which Napoli, ever the fighter on every detail, commented to Groner, "This sucks." The Captive's continued insistence on reducing the amounts of awards for various tiers Napoli called "bullshit." The devil was in the details, and Napoli and Groner both brought a hawk-like attention to making sure their clients were not ill-served by the particulars of the settlement. The ensuing battle was over hundreds of details. For example, the Captive's attorneys continued to reject payments for conditions they deemed not verifiable, such as solid tumor cancers (which were difficult to prove as having been derived from toxin exposure). The debates were granular: determining which of the dozens of disease names in dispute could be grouped as the same (COPD and small airway disease, for example); what diagnostic criteria (as opposed to severity criteria) were required to be considered for compensation; what qualifications were needed for the severity criteria in the forty-plus severity categories. Each of these contained myriad subissues that were argued over and over again.

The negotiations over the details felt never-ending. There were times when Joe Hopkins's instinct would have been to just say no and walk away. However, the client—in this case, the Captive and LaSala—would send them back to work. It was clear to Hopkins that the Captive was going to arrive at a settlement.

Nick Papain was a highly respected member of the personal injury bar and a past president of the New York State Trial Lawyers Association. Sullivan Papain represented the firefighters union, and Papain and Carboy represented some five hundred firefighters who were part of the Ground Zero litigation. Their participation and agreement were necessary to any settlement and resolution of the case. Papain was a zealous advocate for his clients, and that sometimes brought him into conflict with Napoli, whose focus was on WGENB's clients.

By February 20 all parties were deep into the negotiations on the final details. Groner was essentially negotiating the medical issues, and Napoli the scores and scores of nonmedical issues. At 12:30 p.m. Groner emailed Worby, "All hands on deck to get signed deal which should be any minute." At 5:18 p.m. Groner was still optimistic: "10-hour marathon and still going on term sheet but really getting there." The next day he remained positive, declaring, "We are really close."

Later that same day Groner was decidedly less sanguine, admitting that they were not even close. WGENB and Sullivan Papain, despite being aligned during the many years of litigation, now diverged with respect to certain issues. Sullivan Papain represented solely firefighters, while WGENB represented many different groups of responders. Any issues that could take money away from the firefighters became a major source of contention. At one point Napoli and Papain were fighting over certain injuries and values ascribed to those conditions that the firefighters suffered from. Tensions were high and things were said out of the heat of the moment. Groner emailed Worby, "This will take hours as Paul and Papain are at war. In front of all, Paul tells Nick: 'You have no idea what the fuck you are talking about.'" Papain, also a fighter to the end, responded in kind.

Groner commented, "Really ugly and a bit of fun but I am exhausted." At 8:09 p.m. he wrote, "Leaving Grand Central now after long day. Very very close to deal. Thursday morning conference call for a few hours should wrap it." "Should" carried little weight. The negotiations continued on for long days and nights.

During the last days of February 2010, there was concern on all sides about leaks to the press and the damage half-information and misinformation had caused, and that it could wreck the final settlement process. Each side was going to have to present the settlement to their clients, and that was best done in a calm and reasoned atmosphere in which a sensible cost-benefit analysis made the case for acceptance.

Marc Bern, together with Ellen Davis and Lanny Davis (no relation), an attorney and political and public relations consultant,[1] drafted a proposed "stand-by statement" to stave off reporters: "The attorneys continue to work together to resolve this very complicated and difficult litigation in a manner that will be fair to all parties involved. There is no resolution at this point, so any story would be based on speculation."

Over at the Captive, David Biester, concerned about the press, sent a March 6 email with the heading "Silence is golden." The pursuit of a settlement at the same time as Hellerstein continued to push both sides toward trial made for potential breaches of confidence. As Biester pointed out, "We have a report that plaintiffs' counsel at a deposition right now is asking public questions to Patton Boggs about how close we are to settling etc. We have all worked very hard together to keep this under control. It would be most unfortunate for the lid to blow now."

The next day, March 7, 2010, Warner brought her own pressure to bear on the proceedings, writing Napoli and Groner, "As I discussed with Paul about an hour ago, time is fleeting on the Term Sheet. You received at 1:05 this afternoon our final Term Sheet and nearly all Exhibits. The remaining Exhibits will be sent as soon as possible. We need your agreement on these no later than Monday." She added, "We are working on immovable, urgent deadlines occasioned by the meeting with the judge on Thursday. In order to be authorized to sign the Term Sheet, we must have an agreed, final document on Monday."

Groner emailed Worby on March 8, "Been working straight for the last 72 hours. They gave us 'final' term sheet on Saturday. Still have 5–10 issues, 3–5 of which are very important, and they won't budge. On a negotiation call now. It's very ugly. I hate these people."

He relayed to Napoli his most recent exchange with Warner over his list of issues. Warner said she was not going to negotiate over them, then asked Groner, "So, do we have a deal?" To which Groner replied, "No."

Warner could not tell if Groner was merely posturing. She then asked whether, if there was no deal, they should cancel their next meeting. Groner held firm and replied that as things stood, it didn't seem like any further meeting would be necessary. The implication was clear: the deal was in trouble, and he could live with that.

However, before the moment was lost, Groner added that *he* still wanted to negotiate the remaining issues. So, as he saw it, if Warner maintained that the issues were nonnegotiable, then they had nothing more to discuss, but if she was willing to negotiate, then they could work to resolve the issues and make a deal. It was up to her. It was a gambit on Groner's part to see if Warner would indeed compromise further.

A few hours later the Captive did make some concessions on some of the side issues relating to peripheral cases. After another conference call with Warner, Groner emailed Napoli, "They blinked."

March 9 began early for Groner. At 3:58 a.m. he emailed Napoli, "You up?" At 4:10 he sent another email: "I say we wait to see if they move on the issues related to responders who worked at the piers and on the barges." An hour later, getting more revved up by the minute, he sent Napoli a detailed email outlining several options Napoli should propose to Warner to resolve outstanding issues concerning limiting barge and pier workers' liability, how to rate asthma in the settlement, and ways Ken Feinberg might mediate, arbitrate, or decide some of the outstanding issues between them.

At 5:38 a.m. Groner emailed Worby, "We should wrap this up today."

Two hours later, Groner emailed Napoli again, this time with the full draft of an email he wanted to send Warner to resolve their outstanding issue with regard to an extra cash contribution to the monies available to the victims.

An hour later Napoli was asking Groner if he'd heard anything back.

At 12:41 p.m. Ryan Smethurst sent the final proposal from the Captive on surgeries.

Groner emailed Napoli, "This is going pretty darn well."

Napoli responded, "Boy am I smart."

To which Groner replied, "Smart in agreeing with my recommendation."

At 10:42 p.m., Groner emailed, "We are Done."

At 3:38 the following morning, DiMuro emailed Groner, "Just heard [about the settlement]: Who caved?"

Napoli, however, was not done, emailing Groner, "The time line is off. It will take 5 years to get [the settlement claims processed and paid]. We need to revisit the time line." Under the terms of the settlement they were negotiating, WGENB and Sullivan Papain would have ninety days to get 95 percent of their clients to sign off and opt in to the settlement. Otherwise no deal.

At 4:20 a.m. Groner emailed Warner that in the event Hellerstein did anything other than approve their settlement, they should extend the time required for claimants to opt in and sign the documents that released the city and its contractors from liability for the Ground Zero responders' injuries.

At 5:33 a.m. Warner emailed Napoli and Groner that she would call around 10:00 a.m. "Attending to some last minute 'constituency issues'" (meaning some of the 150 clients she represented).

At 7:07 a.m. Napoli emailed, "We need to prepare a statement to our clients when they call us about the settlement. We need to tell them a copy is available on our website and we will be working to put together their claim forms, to submit to them for approval."

The rest of the day passed with documents emailed back and forth and emails commenting on emails, plans being readied in case there was a settlement and in case there was not, all amid phone call after phone call.

At 8:26 p.m. Warner wrote, "On behalf of everyone, thank you for your hard, careful and persistent work in getting this Term Sheet into final, signature-ready form. We appreciate your efforts."

At 10:20 p.m. a final term sheet was emailed to the parties on all sides.

Warner than sent Napoli and Groner an email about press strategy:

We understand, agree and have taken measures. Assuming Monday proceeds appropriately, we want Nick (Papain) and you to meet Tuesday afternoon with [their adviser] Lanny Davis. (The meeting should begin at 2:00.) The purpose of the meeting will be to lay out our thoughts and plan, for you to provide input and for us all to agree on a consistent, coordinated "roll out."

Please be aware that for many, important reasons through Monday, only McDermott and Chris (LaSala) and Dave (Biester) will possess knowledge about what transpired in yesterday's negotiations. It is imperative that none of your offices assume otherwise in their respective interactions relating to the litigation. I cannot stress enough the sensitivity and importance of this embargo from the WTC Captive's perspective. If you have any concerns or questions, please call me at my office.

It fell to Ryan S. Smethurst, Warner's co-head of McDermott Will & Emery's insurance litigation team, to supervise and do a great deal of the detail work in reaching a settlement agreement on behalf of the Captive.

Arriving at a settlement both sides would sign was not without its last-minute glitches.

At 2:29 a.m. on March 11 Warner sent the following email once more to all: "On behalf of everyone, thank you for your hard, careful and persistent work in getting this Term Sheet into final, signature-ready form. We appreciate your efforts."

Despite Warner's declaration, at 4:05 a.m. Napoli found some errors in the documents that he felt were critical to address before any signing could take place.

At 5:25 a.m. Ryan replied to Napoli, "I have tried to call you twice. Please call on my cell. . . . We have a proposal as to how to address all but one of the issues you raised this morning."

Shortly after 6:00 a.m. Ryan emailed all, "Paul and I have resolved all of his issues this morning on the basis I discussed earlier with Peg. Please call Paul or me if you have questions, but this is done."

The attorneys gathered on the morning of March 11, 2010, at the offices of McDermott Will & Emery at 340 Madison Avenue, not far from Grand Central Station. Warner had booked a large conference room. Around a long table were set out around a dozen copies of the settlement agreement. Among those present were the six signatories to the agreement: Warner (as counsel to the Captive), Tyrrell (as counsel to the insureds), and Napoli, Groner, Papain, and Carboy (all as plaintiffs' liaison counsel). LaSala and Biester were also present.

At 8:29 a.m. Groner emailed that the deal signing had been held up "because they [were] locating special pens." Which may seem silly but, as far as the attorneys were concerned, when you have a signing of documents memorializing such a momentous accomplishment, those little keepsakes are meaningful.

That morning Bern had Ellen Davis prepare a press release that said in part, "This case is one of the largest mass tort litigations in the country. It also is unique, given the complex legal, factual, medical, scientific and public policy issues presented in the wake of the 9/11 terrorist attack on our country."

With the pens located and handed out, each of the attorneys took their turn going around the conference table and signing each copy of the agreement. At 12:20 p.m., after the signing was complete, Groner sent the following email: "Now all done. Still confidential."

The attorneys gathered at one side of the conference room to take a group photo to memorialize the moment. In the photo, LaSala is holding a copy of the signed agreement and has a big smile on her face. Tyrrell, Napoli, and Groner are smiling too.

However, this settlement would not be effective until it was presented to the claimants and 95 percent had agreed to it. And before it could be presented, as far as Judge Hellerstein was concerned, no settlement was official until they presented it to him and he approved it.

Still, the next morning they would wake to this lead article in the *New York Times*:

Ground Zero Workers Reach Deal over Claims
by Mireya Navarro

A settlement of up to $657.5 million has been reached in the cases of thousands of rescue and cleanup workers who sued the city over damage to their health, according to city officials.[2]

FAIRNESS

PART NINE

On Thursday evening, March 11, 2010, the media revealed that a settlement had been reached in the case officially known as *In Re: World Trade Center Disaster Site Litigation*. Press accounts reported that plaintiffs in the suit would receive between $575 million and $657.5 million from the Captive, depending on how many adopted the settlement. There was the possibility of tens of millions more in settlement funds, from other ancillary lawsuits that WGENB were in the process of settling (with the Port Authority, the barge operator, and the construction companies in charge of doing the work at the Fresh Kills Landfill). The Captive would keep more than $250 million in reserve for future claims.

The draft settlement agreement was almost a hundred pages long, with page upon page of negotiated compromises, definitions, terms, and adjustments, followed by even more exhibits explaining the matrix of injuries and the severity index. Nonetheless it was far from a done deal; there were still some serious benchmarks to reach. The settlement required a 95 percent opt-in, which meant that if only 9,499 victims signed on for the settlement, it would not take effect. It was going to be challenging to get 9,500 to agree to anything, much less a very complex settlement agreement in just three months' time.

There was another issue: how to estimate what the settlement meant financially to each victim. Their awards would be based on how many points their verified medical condition and injuries scored (overseen by an allocation neutral), and what each of those points was worth was a function of the total number of points awarded to plaintiffs—neither of which was yet known. The plaintiffs were going to have to agree to the settlement based on an estimate of what they would receive, which could vary greatly;

some clients would receive just a few thousand and others more than a million dollars. Not surprisingly, many of the victims who'd been suffering for years were not happy with their estimates.

The *New York Post* called the draft deal proposal "a major break-through," but not everyone agreed. "This is far from fair," said John Feal, speaking on behalf of the FealGood Foundation. "I just don't believe it's enough money."

Mayor Bloomberg felt otherwise. "It's a good settlement for every-body," he asserted on his weekly radio show. "I think it's fair and reasonable given the circumstances."

The *New York Daily News* did not look favorably on the settlement. A scorching editorial on March 13, called "Insult to 9/11 Injury," said of the victims:

> They are owed far better. The thousands of men and women who sacrificed their health in service at Ground Zero deserve incalcu-lably more than they stand to gain in the proposed settlement of their court cases. . . . Those who accept the terms will do so know-ing they never got a fair shake. And all will have grounds to damn a government—the U.S. government—that inflicted terrible injus-tice upon the [first responders]. Because Washington refused, in a disgraceful betrayal, to reopen the 9/11 Victim's Compensation Fund, 10,000 rescue and recovery workers have suffered through six years of litigation, only to be presented with a pig-in-a-poke deal and saddled with obscene legal bills.
>
> These Forgotten Victims of 9/11 will get far less than those who suffered similar illnesses and injuries and managed to file with the compensation fund before it closed. . . . The circumstances are tragic and were all too predictable. Because, despite long and continuing efforts by New Yorkers like Reps. Carolyn Maloney and Jerry Nadler, Washington turned its back on Americans who ral-lied to the country's service in time of war. The disgrace endures. [The September 11 Victim Compensation Fund applied only to the victims of terrorism on 9/11 and not those who were harmed by

their subsequent service on the rescue and recovery missions or the cleanup at Ground Zero and the Fresh Kills Landfill.]

James Nolan, the union carpenter whose claim inspired Jimmy Nolan's Law, was quoted by the Associated Press as saying, "We've had to fight for what we deserve," but he admitted he was happy the case was ending. Kenny Specht, a firefighter who developed thyroid cancer, told the *New York Times*, "If this settlement allows me to move on with my life, if it allows me to protect my family's future, I guess I don't have anything to fight about." But he sounded a note of regret regarding the nine years that had passed since 9/11 that resounded with all: "Why didn't they handle this in a timely manner?"

On March 12, the day after the settlement was announced, Judge Hellerstein asked the attorneys to meet in Court. Worby, Groner, Papain, and Carboy sat at one long table along with Napoli and Bern on the left, closest to the center of the room, while Tyrrell and DiMuro sat at a table directly behind them. Sitting in the front row were Warner and LaSala.

Warner stood before Hellerstein as the Captive's counsel and on behalf of all the stakeholders there. She presented the outline of the settlement, with its $575 million disbursement based on an agreed-upon point system of matching injuries to awards. She was efficient and professional, and her manner spoke to the seriousness with which the Captive managers believed they had approached the task. She was compelled, however, to reveal that, of the $1 billion initially in the Captive fund, more than $200 million had already been spent defending the case. LaSala then explained that this was due to the enormously complex legal and medical issues.

Hellerstein was clearly not happy that so much of the Captive fund had gone to the defense rather than the victims. Nonetheless he appreciated that the parties had arrived at a settlement and that doing so benefited the victims, which was preferable to spending more time litigating to an uncertain result.

The judge announced that he would take a week to consider the settlement. He also announced that he was going to convene a "fairness hearing" at which interested parties, including victims, would be allowed to speak; he too would share his thoughts on the settlement at that time. He set March 19 as the date.

Special Master Aaron Twerski believed the attorneys had made a tactical mistake in keeping their negotiations secret from Judge Hellerstein, and then presenting it to him as a fait accompli. Hellerstein wanted, some might say needed, to be part of any final settlement decision, and if the attorneys did not offer to involve him, then they should not be surprised that he chose to insert himself into the process.

The lawyers, by contrast, felt strongly that any settlement was by definition an agreement arrived at between parties outside of the court. Although in class action cases, judges typically are involved in the details of the settlements and fees, Hellerstein had refused to certify this as a class action. At this point there was no legal precedent for a judge's having the power to approve a mass tort settlement. Further, for Hellerstein to sit in judgment on what they had spent seven years litigating and more than two and a half years on painstaking and drawn-out negotiations was, to them, clearly overstepping his authority.

What Hellerstein claimed as transparency seemed to many to be grandstanding. How could a few individual plaintiffs at a fairness hearing speak to the complexity of this agreement, with its myriad calculations and its extensively and exhaustively researched and negotiated point system and severity classification? The fear was that Hellerstein could sink the settlement and send them all back on the path to litigation, a course that would consume more years, more costs, and more psychological pain to all those who craved closure.

"This will not be a giveaway," Hellerstein told the *New York Post* after meeting with the attorneys. The fairness hearing, he promised, would "be as fair and as just as we can make it."

The morning of March 19, 2010, was spring-like, sunny and warm, with temperatures in the 70s, a cause for optimism. As the attorneys walked up the steps of the federal courthouse at 500 Pearl Street, they were filled with nervous excitement; most were relieved for the victims, the city and the contractors, and themselves, relieved that they had finally arrived at a settlement and anxious about what Judge Hellerstein might do.

Hellerstein had commandeered Judge Harold Baer's large and ceremonial courtroom on the fourteenth floor, which was filled to standing-room capacity with responders, family, friends, and press. (Some seven hundred press outlets would eventually carry stories on the hearing.) A second courtroom next door, which had been reserved so the overflow crowd could listen to the proceedings via speakers, was also filled to capacity. It felt like the eyes of the whole world were upon them.

It was a public hearing, but, for both attorneys and clients alike, it was personal, the culmination of so many years of waiting, hard work, and, for the victims, finally, an acknowledgment of all their suffering. Families were seated throughout the courtroom. In the front row was Groner's wife (and litigation widow these long years), Sue, who had brought their children, Victoria, age twelve, and Hudson, age ten, to witness the singular legal event and see justice in action.

There was a lot riding on this hearing. Neither side wanted to even attempt to try a hundred cases, much less over ten thousand. There was a sense among lawyers and clients alike that it was time for closure—for the lawsuit to end, for responders to get compensation and validation.

One of the problems with litigation arising out of personal injuries is that, rather than giving the clients time to psychologically heal, the process keeps the trauma alive and fresh in everyone's mind. This was all the more true for injuries arising out of 9/11 service. The trauma continued to be replayed in the press, not only for the victims but for all who witnessed what had occurred at Ground Zero.

Napoli, Bern, Groner, and Worby, as well as Papain and Carboy, felt they had done the best they could to arrive at a fair settlement for their clients. WGENB had taken on cases no other lawyers wanted and, at their own expense, pursued them for more than seven years. Unlike a victim compensation fund, their settlement was a legal outcome of injuries proven and unproven. They had managed to get an offer of compensation for many victims who were ill, many of whom would have had great difficulty proving their case at trial. For most of the plaintiffs' attorneys the bottom line was: This was the best we could arrive at with no reasonable alternative in sight. Many of their clients wanted this settlement, and even more wanted the years of uncertainty, of waiting, to come to an end. It was hard to believe that, after all these years, Hellerstein wouldn't want a resolution, even an imperfect one.

The atmosphere in the room was incredibly tense. No one knew what was going to happen. It was more of a circus than was usual in the calm marble and dark wood rooms of 500 Pearl Street. There was a sense of foreboding among the attorneys, of catastrophe looming in the possibility that the settlement was imperiled.

Despite the weight of the responsibility before Judge Hellerstein, there was a brief comic moment when he first took his seat, sinking deep into the chair that was clearly set for a taller person. Still, the judge would make sure everyone heard him.

Candiace Baker had received a letter telling her about the hearing and explaining that if she wanted to speak, she needed to RSVP. Baker did, submitting whatever was requested. She hadn't heard anything further, so she presumed her name would be on a list of speakers. But when she arrived at the courthouse, one of the police officers told her she could watch from the overflow room on the fourteenth floor.

"No," Baker insisted, "I requested to speak at the hearing." When the officer told her that she couldn't, Baker recalled, "Basically, from that first person all the way until I got up to the room, I told every single person my story. I said that between respiratory conditions, gastro conditions, a bilateral mastectomy, a host of other conditions, side effects from this, side effects from that, I've had more needles, poked, prodded. I deserve it. I've earned the right to speak."

At the door to the courtroom, another security officer barred her entrance, telling her the room was full. She told him, "There may be people who may have been sicker than I was. . . . There was one girl, her name was Sandra Adrian, and she died from brain cancer. And she never had an opportunity to be heard. And I was with her at the landfill. And she was sitting side by side with me when I was nauseous and couldn't breathe. So, with all the time, work, effort, the emotion we put in, I believe that I deserve to be heard." The officer stood aside and let Baker in.

Before she could even find a place to sit down, one of the attorneys approached her. Baker explained that she was there to address the court, but after the attorney checked the list of speakers, he told her that her name wasn't on it. "I'm not going anywhere," she announced. "You are not going to shush me." Judge Hellerstein, seeing the confrontation, signaled to allow Baker to approach: "Bring her up here, bring her, bring her up here."

Baker told the judge that she deserved to be heard. The judge agreed that her name would be added to the list of speakers and asked that she take a seat nearby. Baker would get her day in court.

Keith Delmar, thirty-five, a New York City fireman stationed in the Bronx who lived on Long Island with his wife and their two children, was the first speaker. Delmar was handsome, if somewhat ashen-faced, dressed in his FDNY navy blue dress suit. His sleeves carried patches: on the right side, one for Firehouse Engine 273 on Union Street in downtown Flushing (Queens) and below it an "FDNY + MIA 09-11-01 Never Forgotten" patch; on the left, a Fire Department patch. He wore his decoration and name plate on the front of his suit, along with departmental pins on his lapels.

Delmar stood tall, his suit a little big on him, as though he'd recently lost weight, and his close-cropped dark hair was turning gray. He told the court that he had graduated high school in 1993, having been on the track team as well as being an all-county baseball player. He spent four years in the U.S. Marines, and then worked for a crane company before returning to New York, becoming a fireman in February 2001. Back then, he was in great physical shape.

On September 11 he lost ten friends who were firemen. Beginning on September 12 until December 10 he worked at the WTC site, doing search-and-rescue as well as removing debris. In January 2002 he was assigned to the Fresh Kills Landfill, where he worked for six weeks. "Despite the terrible smoke and dust, I never was provided a respirator by the FDNY or any of the contractors," he stated, suddenly becoming choked up. "I was never trained in any proper use and any maintenance of any respirators there."

He had his first ever asthma attack on September 17, 2002, a little over a year after the World Trade Center disaster. By October he had begun to suffer uncontrollable coughing fits. He went to doctors, who didn't know what was wrong with him. They prescribed various medications, but his coughing persisted. He was then given a methacholine challenge (a breathing test), and he failed it. As a result, he was put on permanent disability. "I was thirty-three . . . and my lifelong dream job of being a firefighter was taken from me."

Unable to work, he now collected $72,000 a year, three-quarters of the salary he had previously made. "It will never increase, and it will die with me."

"In addition to my physical problems, the dramatic change in my life, and the inability to work have been very difficult for me to accept. My wife and kids are constantly nervous and think something [worse] is going to happen to me."

The courtroom lapsed into a heavy silence as Delmar spoke. Everyone felt the weight of his testimony. Just seeing him in his dress blues so defeated by an invisible ailment was deeply affecting.

Nonetheless, Delmar stated, he supported the settlement as a way for the city to settle its claims and as a process that would offer closure to him and his family. He thanked the court for letting him speak and returned to his seat. Judge Hellerstein thanked him for his testimony.

Joseph Greco, a retired New York City detective, spoke next. He had a dark, receding hairline, swarthy complexion, and hangdog face, with a permanent five o'clock shadow. He spoke quietly, telling the court that he was in favor of the settlement because it was a big weight off his shoulders. "Not a day goes by that I don't think about what's going to happen to my wife and kids after I'm gone." It was a fear shared by virtually every Ground Zero responder in the room.

Greco was realistic about the settlement, saying, "No amount of money is going to bring back my health." But at least he could have peace of mind that his family would be able to remain in their home. He commended his lawyers to the judge, saying, "The compassion, friendship, and hard work they have shown is priceless."

The judge interrupted Greco to ask if he knew how much he would receive in the settlement. He did not. The judge then asked the same of Delmar. "I couldn't tell you, sir," Delmar answered. Hellerstein filed that information away for later.

John Walcott, the New York City detective who had been Worby and Groner's first Ground Zero responder client, spoke next. Walcott told Hellerstein that he'd been diagnosed with leukemia at age thirty-eight. He too had been an athlete in high school. He'd become a detective and had been involved in over two thousand arrests. He had been at the World Trade Center when it was bombed in 1993, so the minute he heard the news reports on 9/11 he knew it must be another terrorist attack. Although he wasn't scheduled to work that night, he headed to the site.

"I felt it was my obligation to go there," Walcott said. When it came to working at the WTC site cleanup, "I didn't hesitate. I went down there, ran down there on days off, like everybody else. Because we went down there to get you and your loved ones out of there. It is disheartening to me that it would take nine years for even the minute chance of a settlement. . . . There are so many people involved in 9/11 who made millions and millions of dollars, from the former mayor to everybody. Every election, every Democrat and Republican talks about 9/11, [but] not too many people mention the men and women who went down there [afterward]." The responders in the room nodded and murmured in agreement.

Still, Walcott was unsure about the settlement: "I don't know if I agree with the settlement. I have major questions about it." He pointed out that the September 11 Victim Compensation Fund, administered by Ken Feinberg, had distributed $7 billion dollars, and that had been shared by the families of some three thousand victims, whereas in this settlement over ten thousand were being asked to share some $600 million. That didn't seem fair to him. He also wondered how accepting a settlement might impact the possibility of recovering money under the Zadroga Act, if that were to be passed. (The much lobbied-for Zadroga Act was a Ground Zero responders' compensation and health bill that had not yet been passed by Congress.) The judge acknowledged that he had similar questions.

Several union representatives stood to speak. Francisco Paco Vega, from the Asbestos Workers Union, said that his members working at the WTC site, Spanish speaking or Russian or Polish, had followed all safety rules their superiors told them about. Yet those safeguards were not sufficient, and many were now sick and suffering and had been diagnosed with cancer.

John Delgado, representing the workers from Laborers Local 79 who did general labor, demolition work, and cleanup at the site, said that many of his members were now sick from working at Ground Zero and were in need. "Their families are suffering," he told the court. "There is a lot of stress out there. Their intentions were and still are, if we had to do it all over again, your Honor, with all due respect, we would do it all over again, regardless of whatever consequences would face us. We are here to serve and we are proud laborers. We are honored to serve, especially in New York City. We built New York City; we built it with pride. But our members have suffered significantly, together with Local 1280, together with Local 78, who have done tremendous work [in] lathing, asbestos, cleaning. . . . Our members are suffering today."

Michael Damato, a member of Local 79, testified that he had never been sick before working at the WTC site. Now he was at the doctor's weekly, and he'd gone from a good living to almost losing his house. While he didn't know the amount of the settlement, he believed that a settlement now was worthwhile.

"Thank you, sir," Judge Hellerstein said. "The next speaker is Candiace Baker. Good afternoon, Ms. Baker."

Nervous, Baker composed herself and began to speak. A New York City police officer assigned to Internal Affairs, she had been sitting at her desk on the morning of 9/11, typing, when she heard a "boom."

"It was just a noise in New York City. I did not know its importance. . . . I did not know what it meant." She recalled watching with other detectives as the second plane flew into the South Tower. She recalled that they were all teary at the sight.

She was first dispatched to different hospitals to wait for victims and survivors. When it became clear there would be none, she was tasked with manning a missing persons hotline. She took hundreds of calls, and to this day, the desperation, the panic, and the fear in those voices haunted her.

She was then dispatched to the Staten Island landfill. "I was there for over four hundred hours on overtime. I couldn't tell you how many hours on straight time and how many days. I remember having Thanksgiving dinner there, provided by the Red Cross. . . . When we got there, the respirators, they had them in a box. They weren't fitted to us, they weren't adjusted for us. . . . They gave us a filter, we put them on. Did we change filters? I know a group of us didn't because we were never told that we needed to."

It didn't take long for Baker to develop a cough. "Initially, I started coughing and coughing and coughing and coughing. When my throat started hurting and I had an ear infection, I decided to go to the doctor."

A note of resignation in her voice, she said, "The hardest thing I had to do was tell my oldest son that I had cancer. To this date I have undergone a total of five surgeries."

Judge Hellerstein asked an oddly personal question: "What kind of cancer do you have?"

Despite there being hundreds of people in the courtroom, it was completely silent as Baker answered. "I had breast cancer, and now they are checking me for throat cancer. I had chemotherapy for a year and three months. I had an allergic reaction to one of the treatments and I went into shock. I had my doctor sitting on the floor between my legs, hysterical, crying, telling me she was so sorry."

"I developed blood clots, causing necessary daily injections, countless medications, examinations, and tests; early menopause, causing hot flashes and night sweats. I was told that I would not be able to have any more children; they would not suggest it due to all of the medications in my system. Hair loss, lost toenails, no one ever told me that was going to happen. Mouth sores, daily nausea, pain in my limbs and my joints. I get lymphatic therapy in both arms due to the fact that they removed so many lymph nodes during my [double mastectomy]. I have gone to occupational therapy to regain my range of motion and sensitivity, lymphatic therapy to offer minimal relief for pain in my arms."

After taking a deep breath, she spoke directly to the judge: "As we protect the city, the presumption is that there is something in place to protect us in instances like mine and [for] others who have also randomly fallen ill. I participated in the World Trade Center cleanup and recovery, both voluntarily and assigned, and would not hesitate to do it again. But I did not ask for these illnesses and I did not ask for this disease.

"It's not about blame, but it is about accountability. Initially I could not cry; I felt that I did not have the right to. I felt that so many lives were lost, and I still had a chance of recovery [from my illnesses], so how could I complain? As days passed, however, I looked at myself in the mirror and I did not recognize the person before me. [That's when] I secretly cried in my bed and in the shower. . . . All of the random illnesses and conditions, such as pulmonary breathing problems, shortness of breath, and cancer, are not a coincidence."

The room was silent. While Detective Baker held back her tears, many in the room could not hold back theirs, overwhelmed by her selfless behavior, determination, and dignity. After all the years of filings, medical reports, doctor's visits, she reminded everyone present that the lawsuit boiled down to this: Human lives were at stake—they had served the city and its people, and for doing so they had become sick.

"My injuries sustained were not by choice," she said.

"Lastly, I ask you to have compassion for [all those who have] illnesses derived from the terrorist attack on September 11, 2001, and the understanding that the aftermath will still be unfolding for years to come. As you look at the settlement put before us, please take into consideration the cost of medications, the cost of doctors' bills, the cost of co-pays."

The judge turned to Baker and asked a naked question: "What do you think my ruling should be?"

Baker was caught off guard: "Your ruling?"

"Yes, ma'am."

The lawyers were surprised and somewhat taken aback. Rarely, if ever, had they heard federal judges ask a plaintiff how they should rule. This was an astonishing moment in the proceeding and in the litigation itself.

Baker considered for a few moments. When she spoke, she did not ask the city to pay a monumental sum for her pain and suffering. She did not ask the city to admit that it did not exercise the duty of care it owed her and every person whose work at the WTC began on September 12 and lasted until the last day of the cleanup. Instead she said simply, "I honestly can't say. . . . Looking from this day forward, I would like taken into consideration what we have endured, what our families have endured.

"What your role can be, sir, I honestly don't know. Just be as empathetic and compassionate as possible. That's all that I can possibly ask."

Baker had one final request. She had brought some photographs that she wanted to show the judge. There was a picture of the first responders at Ground Zero and photographs showing what Hellerstein referred to as "a picture of how her breasts look: injured, scarred" after surgery and reconstruction.

Defense attorneys had argued for years that solid tumors such as those found in breast cancer could not be proven to have been caused by working at the WTC site or the Fresh Kills Landfill. There were many other reasons, including genetics, they argued, that could explain an incidence of breast cancer. As the probability of proving cancer causation at that time was small, the defense agreed in the settlement to pay only a small amount of compensation for such solid tumor cancers.

Judge Hellerstein took it all in, saying the pictures showed "very vividly" what she had described. Whatever he had thought about such injuries before, whatever he was going to say about the settlement, there was no question to anyone in the room that day that Detective Baker's testimony had a deep impact on him.

Many in the audience, Groner included, had tears in their eyes. "I was blown away by her dignity, her courage and selflessness. And how well she represented what our heroic clients have had to endure. That moment is forever with me."

Judge Hellerstein spoke for the entire courtroom when he said, "Ms. Baker, thank you for insisting on speaking."

The day was not over. As emotionally draining as Baker's testimony had been, several other Ground Zero responders had signed up to speak.

Patrick O'Flaherty worked for four weeks at Ground Zero. He testified that he had developed strange rashes that would not go away, excessive sweating, and a persistent cough that developed into a throat-clearing sound that his family found disturbing. He was constantly in great pain, for which his doctors had no explanation.

Scott Chernoff, who had been an NYPD officer for nine years and was a 9/11 first responder, told the court that he was forced to retire for psychological reasons. He had endured numerous hospitalizations and electric convulsive therapy. He wanted to know why the plaintiffs were not going to be compensated for psychological trauma and PTSD. "I don't think this is fair at all."

Hellerstein asked Chernoff the same surprising question he had asked Baker: "What do you think my role should be as a judge?"

"I have no idea," Chernoff answered. "The law is the way it is. People like me will probably be swept under the rug, dismissed, like the city did. They fought very vigorously to have my case dismissed. They fought very vigorously to deny my claims, not even admitting that I had posttraumatic stress. I had to hire my own expert to diagnose my 9/11 posttraumatic stress."

The consequences for Chernoff had been great: "My career is over, my family gone, my house gone. I moved off Long Island. I no longer live in New York State." Before returning to his seat, Chernoff said that his overriding feeling was one of anger.

Thomas Maguire had founded the company Public Server Limited after the 1993 WTC attack to provide secure digital records of transactions and was put out of business by 9/11. He remained working at the site for the cleanup despite being aware, as an engineer, that he was putting himself at risk for toxic exposure. Maguire was appalled by the lengths the city and its officials had gone in order to deny basic medical care and compensation to "people from the NYPD, the FDNY, EMS, and the other emergency services that were down there as paid employees of the city." The very fact that they all had to sue to recover anything for their injuries was morally bankrupt. "The idea that Rudolph Giuliani and Michael Bloomberg have stood shepherd upon this battle is unconscionable." He was particularly offended by the city's rejection of Zadroga's claim. "The idea that you would pick apart a police detective's body and employ the chief medical examiner to find any possible way to deny this man a line-of-duty death benefit, to deny his family a line-of-duty death benefit, is outrageous."

He too suffered great consequences due to his disability: "My wife threw me out. She sold the house and blew through most of the money. She sold the second house to pay the taxes on the first house. If you were to take the entire settlement being offered today and distribute it [among the] claimants evenly, I could not buy back the personal possessions and real property I have lost as a direct and consequential result of 9/11, of my volunteer service in 9/11."

After the Ground Zero responders had finished speaking, Judge Hellerstein read from some of the letters he had received. A Red Cross worker urged him to bring the case to a close but questioned the amount of compensation and the lawyer fees. The judge said this sentiment was shared by many of the other correspondents. One called the city's delaying the case over nine years "an inhumane act."

The judge then asked his law clerk, Michael Cabot, to report some of the phone calls they'd received. Cabot said that most of the callers lived outside of New York and could not make the hearing. They spoke about their illnesses and their uncertainty as to whether their injuries would be covered. There was great confusion about what, in fact, they might receive. Not knowing the size of their individual award prevented them from making an informed decision about the settlement.

Then Hellerstein seemed to gather his thoughts for a moment, before standing up to address the room. Although many expected him to share his thoughts in the ensuing days, his doing so right then, so soon after the responders' testimonies, came as a surprise.

"I have no formal notes," he began. "I speak, as it were, from the heart." For the next twenty-five minutes, he spoke to an audience of attorneys and Ground Zero responders and their families, as they and the members of the press sat silently, trying to divine his intentions.

"I have been the judge on these cases since they began. The first cases were wrongful death actions that came in. The cases involving the responders grew out of that. . . . It has been the greatest burden in my life. It's been the greatest challenge in my life. I feel enormously grateful that I have been able to stay with these cases."

He noted that issues in the case had twice gone to the U.S. Court of Appeals for review, delaying the overall case for a total of some four years of the eight he had been hearing cases arising from Ground Zero.

"From the beginning, I felt that these are special, that the people who responded on 9/11 were our heroes. They did their jobs. They put themselves at risk. They were in the first line. They cushioned the blow that was inflicted on our city and our state and our nation, and on each of us as individuals. And they brought us back from that blow still a strong and vital city in a strong and vital nation."

In presiding over these cases he understood the passions expressed in court, both what the plaintiffs' attorneys were fighting for, as well as the defense's concerns. These were not run-of-the-mill personal injury cases against a well-funded insurance company or wealthy defendant. "These are ten thousand cases which . . . have been filed because people have said 'I've been injured.' . . . These are cases that have been defended with such vigor and aggressiveness as to put a metaphor in my mind of leaving no bridge unburned and no field unravaged." Hellerstein asked those in the courtroom to appreciate why it had taken so long to produce a settlement agreement.

Arriving at this settlement was an accomplishment, Hellerstein said. He appreciated that many of the victims were suffering and were anxious for resolution. He was compelled to make the following determination: "In my judgment, this settlement is not enough."

Some in the courtroom broke into applause, which Hellerstein immediately shut down, saying, "I don't want that. I'm a judge." He explained that although most settlements were a private matter between plaintiff and defendant in which the judge has no part, this was different: "This is 9/11. This is a special law of commons. This is a case that's dominated my docket, and because of that, I have the power of review. If I don't think it is fair, I'm going to tell you that, and you will make the judgment how to deal with it.

"Why do I say it's not enough? . . . Every plaintiff here, according to this agreement, is burdened by a lawyer's fee that's hard to gauge and will take a very large bite out of his recovery. That wasn't the case with the [September 11] Victim Compensation Fund. People did not have to wait eight years. People could get on with their lives immediately. People were given the money to deal with their ailments quickly. Where there were deaths, people were given the money to move on if they wanted to. This is eight years later and with very large legal fees."

Hellerstein wasn't opposed to legal fees. "Legal fees are earned." WGENB and the plaintiffs' attorneys "took on the cause. They financed this cause at great, great expense. And although I have various criticisms of their work . . . they brought us to this point in time. They deserve . . . a reasonable and perhaps even generous fee. [Nonetheless,] in my judgment, they are not entitled to their contract rights of a third. . . . So, I will fix the reasonableness of the fee."

As to the amount of the settlement, Hellerstein wanted the victims to receive more, and he promised to find ways to increase the funds available. He also believed that the amount allocated for each injury was, in some respects, subjective. Certain conditions, such as cancer, should be given a greater award, he believed, than what was allocated in the present scheme.

"Who can really say how a cancer is caused? I think there has to be additional negotiations to come up with what is a better and fair settlement. I don't think this is fair."

Finally, Hellerstein felt the settlement needed greater transparency: each plaintiff needed to know how much he or she stood to receive and needed to know how the attorneys arrived at that number, in order to make an informed decision about accepting the settlement. "I will not preside over a settlement that is based on fear or ignorance, or request opt-outs or opt-ins without people fairly being aware of what's at stake for what may be the most important decision of their lives. I think people are entitled to a neutral presentation, so they can decide what's in their best interest. I will make myself available, in union halls, in fire department houses, in police precincts, in schools. I'll come and I'll talk to you just as you have talked to me. And let's decide, is it good or is it not good?

"But it will be your decision. No one is going to twist your arms . . . and no one's going to make you feel afraid to exercise the right choice."

Hellerstein laid down his ground rules for a fair process whereby the victims understood their awards and their options. "I want an integrated data bank [of victims' injuries and awards]. I want transparency. I want accountability. I want judicial control over this process, because that's what's fair. If I'm the judge, I can be reversed. If the parties appoint someone, he's the dictator. We don't have dictators." Hellerstein promised that as judge he would oversee those experts chosen by the parties to determine the awards and the challenges and appeals of those award determinations.

Hellerstein wanted it understood that he was not doing this for his own greater glory. "This is no ego trip for me. This is work. . . . This is what's fair, and I will preside over a process that's fair . . . so we can all be proud of the results that we achieve . . . that will make us all proud and will do justice."

And so, with those thoughts, Hellerstein brought the day's hearing to a close. It was near 4:00 p.m. The plaintiffs' lawyers, who had feared that Hellerstein would interpose himself on the process and imagined he would try to cap attorneys' fees, were stunned that he had thrown out the entire settlement. Andrew Carboy said, "He just nuked that deal." Marc Bern was outraged and took Hellerstein's determination as an unfair blow. Paul Napoli was concerned that the case would never settle now, leading to years upon years of trial.

Bill Groner was greatly disappointed by Hellerstein's rejection of the settlement, believing it threatened to imperil any immediate resolution for the victims. However, he saw as positive that Hellerstein's pronouncements would translate into more money for their clients and more money awarded for cancers, something Groner had fought for. Hellerstein's ordering the plaintiffs' attorneys to lower their fees did not come as a surprise. However, Groner objected to Hellerstein's determining the amount as well as his implication that the plaintiffs' attorneys were being greedy for expecting the fees their clients had agreed in writing to pay them. The judge should have discussed this in his chambers with them before announcing it.

Immediately following the hearing, Christine LaSala told the *Washington Post*, "[Hellerstein] has now made it more difficult, if not impossible, for the people bringing these claims to obtain compensation and a settlement." Michael Cardozo, the city's corporation counsel, echoed her sentiments, saying "[Hellerstein's] reaction to the settlement will make it extremely difficult to resolve these cases." But to much of the outside world, the judge was a hero.

"The speakers got inside his heart," Baker told the *New York Times*. The *Daily News* proclaimed, "9/11 responders are lucky to have Judge Alvin Hellerstein." The *New York Post* took a harsher tone, with the headline "Zero Tolerance: 9/11 Deal Nixed by Judge, $575M 'Unfair' to Workers."

A few days later other opinions emerged. The *New York Law Journal* questioned Hellerstein's power of review in the case, quoting Howard Erichson, a Fordham University Law School professor who taught complex litigation: "I simply don't understand what gives the judge authority here." In a March 24 editorial, the *Post* called Hellerstein's action "judicial malpractice," concluding that he "was wrong to blow up the settlement." It would take the *New York Times* until May 3 to weigh in with an article titled "Empathetic Judge in 9/11 Suits Seen by Some as Interfering."

These criticisms of the judge provided small comfort. WGENB was deluged with panicked phone calls from victims wondering what would happen. There were plenty of responders concerned that this case would now never settle, and the attorneys were concerned that trying ten thousand cases could easily take several decades. In many ways, Hellerstein's rejection of the settlement was their worst-case scenario.

What they told their clients, though, was what they had to tell themselves: that they were going to craft a new settlement acceptable to the defense, the Captive, and Judge Hellerstein—in as little time as possible.

PART TEN

Aaron Twerski thought the attorneys were wrong to bring Hellerstein a settled agreement rather than taking him into their confidence as to how they reached it. "They literally dumped this settlement on his desk and thought that that would be over with," he said at a later date. "I think that was a tactical mistake. . . . They misread him. . . . [Hellerstein] has a very strong moral compass. This is a very, very substantial man."

At Patton Boggs, Hopkins was of the opinion that Hellerstein had no right to convene a fairness hearing, that his views on the settlement were irrelevant. However, he agreed with Dean Twerski that it was a mistake to just put something in front of Hellerstein and expect him to rubber-stamp it—with his ego, Hellerstein needed to be part of the process. "You need to give him a role to play."

DiMuro thought Hellerstein's fairness hearing was nothing short of a debacle. "It was not something a judge should do. It made no sense to me." The judge could have asked the attorneys to his chambers to explain how they arrived at their numbers. "But to do it publicly and basically embarrass everybody made no sense."

"We were stunned," DiMuro said. He claimed both LaSala and Warner were also upset and that both the defense and the Captive were entertaining submitting motions for Hellerstein to recuse himself: "He was no longer being a judge. He was not making any legal rulings. We had never heard of a judge doing what he did."

DiMuro was particularly taken aback by Hellerstein's saying "I don't think it's enough for the cancer cases." As DiMuro saw it, "when you have two private parties who have agreed to a settlement in which you had special masters appointed by the judge who signed off on the settlement . . . it's unheard of. There's no case law that we could find that allows a judge to do what he did. And we felt that's where he had crossed the line." DiMuro believed that Hellerstein had sent them back to the negotiating table so he would get the publicity for getting the plaintiffs a larger payout. DiMuro was tempted to have T-shirts made up with Hellerstein's quote that the defense had left "no bridge unburned, no field unravaged." However, he conceded Hellerstein's meddling might well benefit the Ground Zero responders.

For Judge Hellerstein to understand WGENB's fees, particularly in light of his demand to reduce them in the next iteration of the settlement, Denise Rubin was tasked with writing a memo that explained and quantified the extent of their efforts on behalf of the Ground Zero responders.

Her memo, which came to be known as "the fee brief," revealed the mind-boggling amounts of paperwork and hours devoted by WGENB. By the start of 2010, WGENB personnel had reviewed, analyzed, digested, and coded millions of pages of documents and analyzed hundreds of thousands of pages of medical, prescription, and insurance records for the plaintiffs' diagnoses and treatment received from medical professionals, hospitals, laboratories, and radiologists. Each of the more than ten thousand claims in the mass tort involved the time, effort, and expense of reaching out to those clients many times over for the entire seven years. With each potential client there was the initial intake and investigation of claims that required phone calls, interviews, and a review of the claimed illness and medical records, and then a determination of whether or not to accept the case. If the case was accepted, often the attorneys had to meet with the client to help him or her fill out an intake questionnaire and retrieve medical records.

WGENB did not accept every case. There were 811 claimants rejected upon initial telephone interview, 5,623 whose claims were investigated by the firm's staff and resulted in declining representation, and 437 who were rejected after review of their medical records and further investigation—a total of 6,871 rejected claimants for whom WGENB spent time but received no compensation.

Part of what made these mass torts possible and allowed WGENB to compete with law firms such as Patton Boggs was the joint venture's ability to create, manage and deploy databases. WGENB logs revealed that based on login from February 12, 2004, through March 8, 2010, staff spent just over 50,801 hours working in the Discovery Database, 46,457 hours in the Medical Database, and 221,207 hours in the Legal Database—a total of 318,465 hours of logged-in work on individual files. This did not include phone calls, in-person interviews, or legal work done in another program or without database involvement. Most of the legal work did not require logging in. The hours logged also didn't include tens of thousands of hours getting medical records, inputting symptoms, complaints, medical visits, tests and test results, diagnoses, treatments, and medications.

WGENB had to file a Notice of Claims against the city, and for those hundreds of clients who did not seek legal representation within the ninety-day period required to proceed they had to file motions for a Late Notice of Claim. They represented some 619 plaintiffs at hearings. In total, WGENB filed 5,551 Notices of Claim against the City of New York; 9,535 against the EPA; 8,304 against the Port Authority; 9,060 against FEMA; and 9,469 against OSHA. As a result of Jimmy Nolan's Law, WGENB filed 9,129 claims against New York City and 8,764 against the Port Authority.

There were vast amounts of data: by the end of 2009 WTC litigation documents, images, and transcripts accounted for 3.42 terabytes, or 40,256,810 files in 255,963 folders. The clients' individual files contained 64.6 gigabytes, or 402,427 files in 17,867 folders. As of January 29, 2010, the firm had uploaded approximately 139,269 medical records for plaintiffs (representing 4.771 million pages) and had uploaded 235,835 nonmedical documents (2.459 million pages). From these, WGENB produced 122,816 medical records.

WGENB maintained two websites: a publicly accessible site that was regularly updated with news and info about the litigation, and a private password-protected web portal, for which each client had a password to obtain discovery and facts on their case.

WGENB needed to research, interview, and hire litigation experts, and they needed to scour discovery reports and hire experts to refute the information that defense experts provided. Repeatedly staff combed through discovery and other information sources to refute the defendants' factual claims. Virtually every claim made by the defense's engineering clients was refuted by the evidence obtained during discovery. As of March 5, 2010, WGENB had received 7,603,294 documents (19.6 million pages) in discovery from defendants.

On top of all that, WGENB early on handled a significant number of press matters and devoted a substantial amount of time to lobbying and political efforts, meeting with Senators Clinton, Schumer, and Kirsten Gillibrand, Representatives Nadler and Maloney, and dozens of other representatives many times over the years. WGENB also hired Brett Heimov, senior partner of lobbying firm Winning Strategies, and Mark Childress, the former Clinton official who was at Foley Hoag. Bern and WGENB played a large role in lobbying for Jimmy Nolan's Law and for the Zadroga Act. On Zadroga, Bern lobbied to rewrite the bill and drafted updated language to the bill, which was ultimately accepted by the U.S. House Judiciary Committee. According to Rubin's calculations, Bern spent over three years and at least five hundred hours on his lobbying efforts.

Rubin made the argument that even a cursory reading of the settlement agreement reveals the enormity and complexity of the issues discussed and ultimately agreed upon. The WGENB settlement team—which was different from but overlapped with the litigation team—involved as many as thirty persons at any one time, including medical experts, attorneys, IT personnel, paralegals, nurses, and clerks. While there were many issues, none was more critical than the negotiation of the aggregate sum of money to be paid. This involved presentations and articulations of virtually every issue present in the litigation: the relative strengths and weaknesses of the immunity defenses, the labor law issues, and all the other defense asserted by the city and contractors; issues of duty, location, amount, and dates of dust exposure; causation and comparative fault. All of it took time and cost money and meant resources spent there rather than on other cases or new litigation.

While WGENB accepted the judge's direction to reduce their fees, it was important to them to quantify for him the time, effort, and expense they had expended in their prosecution of the plaintiffs' case so that when they did, Hellerstein would then approve it.

In the days after Hellerstein's fairness hearing, attorneys and staff at WGENB were still feeling shock, disbelief, and occasionally resignation. However, once the lawyers had time to digest his comments, they realized that a possible settlement was closer than his rejection might indicate. Over the next several weeks, the plaintiffs and defendants and the Captive negotiated and drafted amendments. The injury matrix and the severity index were adjusted to allow greater compensation for nonrespiratory solid tumor cancers (such as Baker's) as well as respiratory solid tumor cancers.

Victims' counsel agreed to reduce their fees from 33 percent to 25 percent, increasing the pool of money available for the victims by more than $50 million. New York City agreed to allow victims to keep any workers compensation money they may have received without deducting it from their settlement payout. Groner negotiated the same releases from various other workers compensation carriers, valued at more than $20 million. The Captive agreed to place an additional $55 million in cash into the agreement. (By contrast, the defense attorneys and the Captive's attorneys had already been paid their full fees.)

In order to bolster the integrity of the settlement awards, and with Hellerstein's approval, the parties had recruited the preeminent mass tort settlement award specialist, Matt Garretson, to administer and manage the awards. In an era of increasing legal specialization, Garretson, a graduate of Yale University and Kentucky's Salmon P. Chase College of Law, had found a niche in mass tort settlements. He was often the court-appointed "neutral" chosen to be an impartial party reviewing tort settlement awards.[1]

Ken Feinberg agreed to review award appeals and objections (a further check on Garretson—adding two layers of protection to the integrity of the awards). Also, at Judge Hellerstein's direction, WGENB engaged Roy D. Simon, a leading legal ethics scholar, to make sure the attorneys acted properly in advising and communicating with their clients about the settlement, neither coercing nor influencing them to accept what they did not understand or want.

Whether all these changes would be good enough for Hellerstein to approve, and 95 percent of the victims to agree to, remained to be seen.

Almost three months had passed since Judge Hellerstein rejected the proposed settlement. He had been clear about what he wanted, and WGENB, the defense, and the Captive had all worked hard to address his recommendations. And this time Hellerstein was able to have input into the settlement, which they now realized was critical to its adoption.

So it was with a certain amount of confidence that Warner rose once again in front of a packed courtroom at 500 Pearl Street to speak to Judge Hellerstein on June 10, 2010. She explained that after leaving the March 19 fairness hearing her client, the City of New York, had given her a clear instruction: find a way to hold the settlement together. Every day and most nights since March 19 they had worked very hard to present an amended settlement to the court.

Warner then gave a summary of the new settlement, a 104-page document with eighteen exhibits. Solid tumors were increased from 650 points to 10,000; respiratory cancers from 650 points to 2,500. Warner explained that these injuries would be very hard to prove in a trial as having been definitively caused by Ground Zero exposure—which, she argued, was another reason for the claimants to opt in to the settlement.

The settlement had been increased from a minimum of $575 million to a minimum of $625 million, which, if certain thresholds and conditions were met, could rise to $712.5 million.

Michael Cardozo, representing the City of New York, then spoke, saying that the city believed this settlement was very fair to all concerned and brought to an end a very, very difficult litigation. He added that Mayor Bloomberg shared that view.

Napoli stood to say, "For over the seven years since we first began this litigation, when no other firms would, our commitments to our clients have never wavered." He characterized the new agreement as the product of a long, hard-fought negotiation that produced a "bigger and better" settlement than had been arrived at three months before. He pledged that WGENB, in consultation with the court and special masters, would ensure that this complex settlement was understood by their clients so they could make informed decisions and that WGENB would do so in ways that were fully transparent.

Papain confirmed that as part of the settlement, health monitoring would continue. As to victims not opting into the settlement because of the potential awards they might receive as a result of the Zadroga bill, he pointed out that at this moment, there was no guarantee that it would pass and, if it did, what its final form would be. So this settlement represented the best possibility at present for victims to receive some compensation for their injuries and suffering.

At a hearing on June 23, Hellerstein again allowed the victims to speak. There was anger in the room that the settlement did not cover psychological ailments such as PTSD, nor was there coverage for children with birth defects born to Ground Zero responders. Some railed that after all this time, the amount of their compensation was insulting or not sufficient or not just. To these victims, the settlement did not adequately compensate them for their pain and suffering.

Hellerstein acknowledged that the settlement would not satisfy everyone, and that it would not adequately compensate everyone. Unlike the September 11 Victim Compensation Fund, they were discussing the settlement of legal claims that, given the nature of proof and evidence, were never going to receive as large an award. However, each side had addressed his concerns and the result was a good resolution of the nearly decade-long litigation and "the best possible terms for the plaintiffs." He defended his interference in the earlier proposed settlement, asserting that such a complex mass tort handled by so few lawyers, involving so many victims and such large sums, called for judicial supervision in order to arrive at a result that was fair and just. And he would continue to provide that supervision. He announced that he was supporting the revised settlement and suggested that the victims had reason to be satisfied with the outcome: "Mr. Matthew Garretson, who has more experience with mass tort settlements than anybody in America, has told me the protocol for this settlement is the fairest and fastest and the best he has seen."

"It is time this lawsuit ended," he added, "and settlements are a good way to end it."

Ken Feinberg, whom President Obama had just appointed administrator of a $20 billion fund for the BP Gulf Oil Spill, then spoke via a video hookup from Washington DC. He too supported the settlement and announced that he would take the next few weeks "to visit firehouses, to conduct town hall meetings, to explain to any claimants . . . who want to understand why I am a proponent of this settlement, why I think it is fair and reasonable . . . and why I think every single claimant should take advantage of this settlement." He told the victims they should accept the settlement not because it was perfect. "Perfect is the enemy of good," Feinberg quoted. This settlement was good, in his opinion, and that, as Hellerstein had noted, was the best result that could be achieved in the circumstances.

The lawyers who had been engaged for years in a relentless quest to reach a settlement now had to gather their strength for yet another push: they would have three months to meet the required 95 percent opt-in requirement for the settlement to take effect.

At the end of June, Napoli made a presentation to WGENB's Ground Zero clients on the amended settlement agreement, explaining how it had been restructured and its enhanced benefits. It was a solid presentation, and Napoli was at his best, moving through the various slides and charts to show how the settlement was improved on several fronts.

It was in everyone's interest—the judge's, the attorneys' on both sides—to have as many plaintiffs understand the amended settlement as soon as possible (and once they did, sign up for it). The clock was now ticking. There was a ninety-day deadline to get the required 95 percent opt-in for the most serious tiers of injuries (the least serious injuries had a lesser requirement). (They could, however, request an extension of time, which, if all parties agreed to it, the Captive could grant and Judge Hellerstein could, in his discretion, approve.)

The reason for the 95 percent opt-in requirement was that the Captive wanted the case (essentially) fully settled, not partially. To put it another way: the Captive wanted to avoid having to spend tons of money on trial expenses and lawyers and open themselves up to large awards that would embolden nonsettling plaintiffs to want to go to trial. Napoli and Groner didn't want such a high opt-in percentage for practical reasons: it would be hard to achieve. The injuries had been grouped into various levels of severity, and for all but the least severe, the threshold was 95 percent, the lowest number the Captive would agree to; for the least severe the opt-in was 90 percent.

Public meetings to present the amended settlement and answer questions were set for July 26, 2010, at the Michael J. Petrides School on Staten Island and on August 3 at the Queens County Supreme Court, Criminal Division, in Kew Gardens. Court-appointed administrators, such as Ken Feinberg, would be at the meetings as well as Judge Hellerstein and both plaintiffs' and defendants' attorneys.

Although many plaintiffs had expressed interest in opting in to the settlement, as August ended, few had actually signed the required papers to do so.

Just eight days after the announcement of the Hellerstein-approved amended settlement, on June 18, 2010, Representative Carolyn Maloney held a press conference to say that momentum was building to introduce and gain passage for the Zadroga Act.

WGENB was supportive of the Zadroga bill for all it could do to add to victims' recovery. If the bill passed, it would offer health coverage and medical monitoring, particularly for conditions not covered by the settlement, such as PTSD, and possibly more funds as compensation. However, WGENB were concerned their clients would opt out of the settlement in hopes they would receive more money under Zadroga. Adding to the confusion, Richard J. Alles, a deputy chief of the Uniformed Fire Officers Association, had been critical of the new settlement, writing, "Only the lawyers stand to make a windfall on the backs of their sick and injured clients." He was concerned that by signing on to the settlement the victims were waiving their chance to receive Zadroga benefits. He called on public support to allow the victims to collect from both sources rather than having to choose. The plaintiffs' counsel agreed with that approach. Groner asked Heimov to help him reach out to Senator Kirsten Gillibrand of New York to encourage the Senate to work in concert with the settlement attorneys to amend the Zadroga bill so victims could offset their settlement awards against future Zadroga payments.

The *Wall Street Journal* announced that the bill would come up for a vote in the next two weeks. Although Senator Gillibrand could not meet with Groner, Heimov reported to WGENB that the Office of the Speaker of the House, Nancy Pelosi, was open to their suggested amendment of the Zadroga bill. According to Heimov, if the bill went to the House floor in the next week—and that was a maybe—Pelosi would offer the set-off amendment; otherwise they would have to wait until the House was back in session in September.

The FealGood Foundation had become one of the most recognized organizations advocating for Ground Zero responders. John Feal and his members communicated with a large and diverse group of workers who, like Feal himself, were battling to get recognition for their service, greater health benefits, medical monitoring, and greater compensation from the government for their injuries.

Feal was heroic in attending to his fellow responders' issues. He was witness to their medical and health challenges, and he understood their traumas, their PTSD and emotional problems. He was able to get them involved in the cause of helping themselves and their fellow responders. He would organize vans to carry responders to lobby local, state, and federal officials. They told members of Congress of their grievances and asked for their help. They attended and spoke at hearings. When the media wanted to speak with responders, Feal would recommend his members.

In his zealous support of his members' needs, Feal sometimes found himself at odds with WGENB's efforts. It was hard for some Ground Zero responders to accept that the World Trade Center litigation was about inhaled dust-related injuries—and only those that were agreed to by the defense and the Captive. The negotiated settlement did not cover many of the conditions that many responders, including Feal himself, suffered from, as those conditions were not directly caused by the main legal claim in the suit: that the defendants failed to provide proper respiratory protection.

Beyond that, even for the injuries the Captive was willing to cover, Feal believed the awards should be greater. Napoli and Groner had been fighting for years for greater awards, but Feal, like the rest of the responders, wasn't privy to the complex negotiations and discussions between the various parties. All he knew was that a lot of money had been left on the table—money left to the Captive in reserve or paid out to the lawyers on all sides—money that should have gone to victims. Feal was also keenly aware that, even so, the $1 billion FEMA-funded Captive insurance itself was a pittance compared to the $7 billion VCF that was shared by the families of the three thousand victims murdered on 9/11.

For all these reasons, Feal's organization was mobilizing all his supporters and other Ground Zero responder groups to support the House vote on Zadroga. And they called on their members to reject the settlement agreement, which they believed asked them to sign away their rights.

Vincent Briganti, one of the Ground Zero responders support-ing the settlement, was leaving his doctor's office in Piscataway NJ (the Rutgers location) when a group of men wearing red T-shirts approached him outside. They asked him to sign a petition agreeing not to sign the settlement agreement. Briganti did not get their full names, but one, named Charlie, told him that he should sign their petition because the Victim Compensation Fund was going to be reopened, and they'd rather collect from that than "give all the money to Worby's firm because that's all [Worby, Groner, and Napoli] want."

Briganti didn't say anything to the man or sign the petition. He just got in his car and left. But he told WGENB so they would know this was going on. This dismayed Groner who regretted that the attorneys hadn't made the kind of personal connection with their clients that would have let them know WGENB was on their side.

On July 26 Heimov reported that the Zadroga bill was coming up for a vote and that the suggested amendment would be included. Heimov had attained a copy of the bill, HR 847—a Bill to Amend the Public Health Service Act to Extend and Improve Protections and Services to Individuals Directly Impacted by the Terrorist Attack in New York City on September 11, 2001, and for Other Purposes, also called the James Zadroga 9/11 Health and Compensation Act of 2010.

The Republicans thought the bill too expensive as drafted and wanted to debate it to make changes. The House Democrats were not confident they had enough votes for passage. Representative Peter King, a Republican from New York, concerned that Democrats would pass Zadroga without debate or negotiation, went so far as to call them "immoral cowards" if they tried to pass the bill without debate.

The *Daily News* claimed that the Obama administration had been reluctant to back the Zadroga bill because it mandated spending rather than leaving it up to the annual appropriations process. And while the White House had already increased spending for ailing 9/11 responders to $150 million, Zadroga would commit the government to spending many more times its current commitment.

At the city level, Mayor Bloomberg's top political advisers, including Deputy Mayor Howard Wolfson, had been furiously calling the New York delegation for help. "Our position is simple," a City Hall official was quoted as saying. "We want to put a bill on the floor that is going to pass."

Despite all these efforts, late Monday evening the news came that the House had failed to pass the James Zadroga 9/11 Health Care and Compensation Act. Only in September, after the summer recess, could the House try to revive the bill. Heimov cautioned that even if revived in the House, the bill had not yet even been considered in the Senate. That did not bode well for the bill's passage in 2010. WGENB again urged Ground Zero responders to opt in to the settlement, which was a sure thing, and keep alive their hope for Zadroga in the future.

Following the announcement of the amended settlement, a line of people came in to WGENB to ask questions about it and, in most cases, sign their opt-in documents.

As part of the amended settlement, both sides had agreed to weight certain injuries as more serious and severe than before. Although this was a matter of the computers recalculating the information they already had, in several cases this task was made more arduous by ascertaining that some clients had not submitted recent medical records (prior to March 2010), which could be the basis for a more accurate recalculation. WGENB already had a team of people busy doing recalculations of the most severe injuries. One of the criticisms that Hellerstein had leveled at the first proposed settlement was that individuals did not know how much money they were receiving. This time around a greater effort was made to communicate with individual plaintiffs concerning their potential award amounts, so they could make an informed decision on whether to opt in.

Although WGENB was able to calculate the great majority of cases based on the point matrix the Captive had agreed to, there were hundreds of other cases that required personal attention, whether because of circumstances that needed to be explained or changes in condition. There were clients who felt their injuries were more severe than the points awarded. Some clients indicated that they had more medical records than WGENB had for them. Some said they had new or worse injuries than what their records showed. There were also a number of "false negatives," where the client's condition was actually far worse than shown in the points they were given, and that required a manual review of their entire medical history by WGENB's medical legal team.

Doing these manual reviews could be very gratifying and an opportunity to know individual clients better. In the end, however, some yielded greater results, some not. And some would be referred to the appeals mechanism provided by the settlement, which Matt Garretson was leading.

Worby reached out to Groner with concern regarding Sister Cindy's case, which was now in the hands of her estate. She had had many health issues, including asthma, sleep apnea, and GERD, that she had believed were related to exposure to Ground Zero dust. At the time of her death she was on a respirator. Although both the South Carolina medical examiner who had autopsied her at Worby's request and Dr. Michael Baden, the former New York State medical examiner Worby had contacted on her behalf, believed she had died as a result of exposure to toxins at Ground Zero, Baden found the autopsy inconclusive as to whether there was dust in her lungs. Once again the science just wasn't there to validate the injuries in what seemed to clearly be a death caused by exposure to Ground Zero dust. All they could do was submit the case for consideration to the allocation neutral, who would have some very limited discretion to make awards based on medical records.

Gary and Alison Acker stopped by the Worby Groner office because Gary was concerned about his estimated settlement numbers. They met with WGENB attorney Chris LoPalo, who explained how the payout figures were calculated. Gary was sure that his medical tests did not reveal the extent of his breathing issues, which had become so severe that he could no longer tolerate a methacholine challenge breathing test. Such a test could have validated the severity of his respiratory condition and made him eligible for greater compensation under the settlement.

Gina Barrese asked Groner, "Would it be possible for you to review Gary's medical file and call him to discuss his case? Is there anything Gary's doctor can submit that would raise his secondary injury category above c_1, the lowest level of asthma?" Groner promised to look into it.

Gina also called WGENB's lead medical legal nurse, Barbara Krohmer, to say, "I know you're really busy, but I called you right after I hung up the phone with Gary. He got really bad news today from his oncologist. His numbers are up and the chemo's not working. I'm the first person he called—he has to figure out a way to tell Alison, his wife. I don't think there's much else they can do for him. He's so concerned about his wife and family, and with this bad news, he wants to settle his numbers on his case ASAP. I know Bill said he was going to speak to him later this week or early next, but is there anything you can do to hurry this along? Gary's really in a bad way—you know, he never complains and tries to laugh stuff off, but his voice started getting shaky when he was speaking, and so did mine. Help!"

Groner dove into Gary's medical documentation and was able to justify a recalculation that got Gary a somewhat greater award. Although it would make no difference in treating Gary's illness, it did give him greater peace of mind that his family would be able to afford to stay in their home. And that meant a lot to Groner, Gina, and everyone at WGENB who had come to know the Ackers over the years.

On Wednesday, September 29, 2010, Heimov alerted Napoli and Groner that the Zadroga bill was going to be introduced on the floor of the House within the hour. Asked about the bill's chances, Heimov was not optimistic. And even if the bill passed the House, it still had to make its way through the Senate, where the party numbers could change after the November elections, and not for the better: "[If Zadroga] is not signed by the President by December, then this thing is dead."

Despite Heimov's concern, that afternoon the House of Representatives passed the Zadroga bill by more than fifty votes: Democrats, 233 yeas, 14 nays, 7 not voting; Republicans, 1 yea, 169 nays, 8 not voting.

WGENB was eager to share the good news with their clients. And they needed to explain to them that they could be eligible to receive funds from *both* the settlement *and* Zadroga if they opted in to the settlement *first* and completed all paperwork before the president signed the bill into law (if indeed the law passed and President Obama signed it, as they hoped he would). However, it was also true that they could receive Zadroga funds even if they did not opt in to the settlement, but then they were limited to whatever the act awarded. And passage by the Senate was no sure thing.

The original deadline set for WGENB to have 95 percent of their plaintiffs opt in was September 2010. There had been near constant meetings in hotels and union halls to discuss the settlement and answer questions. However, as that first deadline approached, it was clear that they were not close to the 95 percent, so the parties and the court agreed to extend the deadline to November 8. By a little more than a month before the new deadline, on October 1, about seven thousand persons (71 percent) had opted in. It was a significant amount of support, but they were still some two thousand persons shy of putting the settlement into effect.

Napoli emailed WGENB staff, calling on them to go door to door that weekend to meet with clients, answer their questions, and hopefully get their approval: "I know you are in high gear, but we need to step it up."

John Feal had spent many years advocating for himself and for others to receive redress for the very real injuries they suffered and the debilitating psychological aftereffects of their trauma. His efforts and attention and those of his followers were on passage of the Zadroga bill to reopen the September 11 Victim Compensation Fund. Nonetheless, before the latest vote on Zadroga, Feal settled his own lawsuit against the city and its contractors, which was also covered by the Captive. He was one of several dozen individual orthopedic cases the Captive settled.

Napoli loved what he perceived as the irony of the fact that Feal, who was against WGENB's settlement with the Captive, had himself settled with the Captive. That they were different lawsuits didn't matter. To Napoli, who had a devilish side, it was too good an opportunity to pass up. He sent out a letter to all their clients advising that if Feal settled, they should settle too.

Feal was none too pleased about this. In a *New York Post* article, dated October 3, 2010, Susan Edelman reported, "A prominent 9/11 responder is furious that lawyers for nearly 10,000 other Ground Zero workers are using him—without permission—as a poster boy for the proposed settlement with the city." Edelman quoted Napoli calling Feal's complaints "ridiculous." Napoli insisted that the point of his email to clients was to show that Feal had settled his case before possible passage of the Zadroga bill, which would allow injured or sick WTC workers without pending lawsuits to file claims for compensation.

Emotions ran high. Feal and his foundation and individual Ground Zero responders launched their own press offensive. They continued to reach out to responders and to politicians through their own network of members, supporters, and sympathetic press and entertainment personalities, recommending that responders not sign the settlement. Sometimes this backfired. One woman responded to Feal at length:

Are you out on 3/4's pay plus life time benefits? Comes out to a nice penny every month huh? My husband was down at ground zero from minute one! He has gotten nothing but sicker every day. We understand why YOU can continue to fight and not NEED to settle because you are financially set. THIS SETTLEMENT MEANS NOTHING TO YOU. But to the other 9999 this is a fortune that may help our families finally start to [recoup] from all the lost pay & extensive medical bills, and also start to heal from ALL that we have been thru. . . . YOU are the one scaring people off who need it the most. . . . We want this behind us. Please explain to me what reasoning you have for prolonging this pain.

Hellerstein had promised there would be public meetings to explain the settlement and answer any questions responders might have. Groner was very much in favor of these meetings; the settlement agreement was complex, and it would have been unfair not to provide responders with extensive opportunities to have all their questions answered. He saw the meetings as his chance to sit with the clients and let them ask questions, voice concerns, or just vent. To develop trust where there was doubt. Regardless of whether or not they opted in, Groner wanted each of them to finally feel they had someone to whom they could ask the tough questions and get straight answers.

At a deeper level, Groner understood, his integrity and that of his partners was on the line. They had poured years of their lives into these cases to arrive at what they personally knew to be the best deal they could get, and they wanted their clients to know that.

On October 12, 2010, Groner, working with Kenny Specht, a firefighter who had developed thyroid cancer, held a luncheon meeting at Connolly's Corner restaurant in Queens for Ground Zero responders (many of whom were with the FealGood Foundation) to answer any questions they had. At first there was anger, upset, even yelling. The questions were blunt and honest, but they needed to be asked. And Groner tried to answer them all.

"Why isn't PTSD covered?"

"Because this isn't a fund where all injuries are covered—awards are based upon the failure to give proper respiratory equipment and the toxic inhalation illnesses that caused."

"Why isn't more money being awarded for cancer?"

"Because medical science hasn't caught up to the reality, and it is really hard to prove causation, even though we know in our hearts the dust causes cancer. We don't have enough scientific evidence for most cancers that a court would accept."

"Why did it take so long to arrive at a settlement?"

"Simply because the Captive refused to settle for all these years."

"Why didn't you meet with us earlier and more often?"

"Because we were overwhelmed by the task at hand. But you are right, we should have found a way."

"If you had to do it again, would you take on so many cases?"

To this one Groner answered, "Yes and no. No, because it overwhelmed us. But yes, because it gave us the leverage and power to be the lawyers in the room who negotiated the best settlement we could."

As the Ground Zero responders heard each of their questions answered honestly, understanding grew. Groner was under no illusion that they were happy with the settlement or the time it took or the way they had been treated, but it was some comfort to him that the responders had a chance to have their questions answered so they could make an informed decision.

Afterward Kenny Specht sent Napoli an email saying, "Billy came today ready to mend fences, speak of the facts and discuss the merits of the case with tired & frustrated 1st responders. He did not rush anybody and gave more than ample time to each person who attended and spoke today. . . . I think todays participation by Billy and his crew went a long way to addressing many concerns." Specht then wrote a letter to his fellow responders citing his positive interactions with the plaintiffs' attorneys and telling them that he was going to opt in.

Specht also wrote an op-ed for the *Daily News* edition of October 24, 2010, in which he said, "I can almost guarantee that this offer is the best it is ever going to get. To be very honest with you, I am not sure that holding out makes good sense. I'm not sure that a better offer will ever be something that is attainable. Is trial a better alternative? Possibly, but not probably. The possibility of years of litigation must be considered."

Still, time was running out. The *Chief Leader* (New York City's newspaper for civil servants) ran an editorial saying, "The settlement is in danger of falling apart, to be sure. The original Sept. 30 deadline has already passed, and the city confirms that 75 percent have opted in. Lawyers have until Nov. 8 to convince enough of the remaining workers to meet the new deadline." Ken Feinberg repeated his simple statement: "No settlement is perfect. But here, perfect is the enemy of good."

While WGENB was rushing to effectuate the settlement, there were simultaneous negotiations occurring with some of the other, related defendants who weren't covered by the Captive FEMA policy, such as Tishman Construction, Survivair, and several Fresh Kills contractors, including Evans Environmental & Geosciences, Phillips & Jordan, and Taylor Recycling Facility. The most significant of these supplemental defendants was, without question, the Port Authority.

On October 14 Napoli and Groner revealed that the Port Authority had agreed to pay $47.5 million to settle claims by 9,055 plaintiffs for injuries they alleged they had sustained during the rescue, recovery, and debris removal operations following the terrorist attacks of 9/11. These funds would be added to the total settlement but would be directed to those plaintiffs who had also sued the Port Authority.

"The most noteworthy and historical mass tort in the nation's history" is what attorney Paul Scrudato of Schiff Hardin, who represented the Port Authority, called the Ground Zero responder litigation. "It was the most egregious act of terrorism ever anywhere. It was brought right to the United States of America in New York City. Nothing but innocents were killed and it intersected with all elements of American society—not just the judicial system but public opinion and political figures in New York and D.C." Scrudato said of the case, "Everybody knew that they were being watched by history."

"This was no usual mass tort," he explained, "where you are representing a company who allegedly sold asbestos or other products years ago, and there are injured parties." After 9/11, when they established the original VCF, the American Trial Lawyers Association picked lead lawyers to volunteer pro bono for the first twenty cases. Scrudato was one of the few defense lawyers who volunteered. In that process he learned a great deal regarding 9/11 and Ground Zero. When firms were being interviewed to defend the Port Authority in the mass tort litigation, Scrudato's firm, Schiff Hardin, applied: "They liked our experience and liked the fact that we had the resources in New York to do it and—this is important—I think they felt like we had the right touch for it. That was important at every level because the litigation was only going to resolve if the participants had the right touch, meaning they weren't burn-the-forest lawyers. Lawyers who understood what was going on and had sensitivity to the interests of their clients in particular but also the litigation itself." Scrudato believed that in such litigations, how you conduct yourself is important because "settlements of these types of cases are really built on relationships and trust."

Scrudato never believed the Port Authority had any liability in a purely legal sense, because it had no control of the site. However, this was no ordinary case. At the start of the litigation they were mostly involved in the "nuts and bolts": interviewing experts, taking depositions. It quickly became clear that Judge Hellerstein would drive this to a settlement, and that the Port Authority would wait for the Captive to settle before they did.

"I thought Bill Groner was a straight shooter," Scrudato said. "He was a serious advocate for his clients. He understood the limitations in his case [as to the dispute over whether cancers that were showing up could be tied to exposure at the site], and he also understood that he represented ten thousand people who had injuries at every end of the spectrum.

"We had a number of meetings, but it became clear to me, as it probably became clear to Bill, that if we were going to get a deal done, it was going to be the two of us in the corner of a room talking to each other and being direct with each other about where we thought it should end up."

As Scrudato recalled, WGENB started their negotiation with him by asking for big numbers from the Port Authority, like $600 million, and then $300 million. He was candid in his refusals, and over time Groner got the sense that he was an honest broker.

At a mediation scheduled to discuss a possible Port Authority settlement, Groner and Scrudato stepped away to a corner to talk privately. Groner asked if the two of them could resolve the case right there and then. Both lawyers knew Port Authority's theoretical legal and financial exposure was large, given the number of cases, but Groner was keenly aware that because the Port Authority wasn't involved in the cleanup the chances of holding them accountable were close to zero. He suggested a number, and Scrudato countered. In a matter of minutes, they agreed on a figure just shy of $50 million. They still had to get the consent of their clients and create the appropriate paperwork, but they were confident about their ability to do so.

Judge Hellerstein had wanted the lawyers to find ways to put more money in the pot, and the Port Authority's contribution of almost $50 million made a big difference. Scrudato later said, "It was a good deal for the Port Authority, and I think it was a fair deal for the first responders, bearing in mind what we thought the Port Authority's liability was."

In late October 2010, as the November 8 deadline loomed, Denise Rubin wrote Judge Hellerstein requesting extra time to reach the 95 percent opt-in required for the settlement to go into effect: "We ask that in the dual interests of justice for our clients and *rachmones* [compassion] for one very overworked appellate attorney, we might have until at least mid-December." Hellerstein did not answer immediately, leaving WGENB to continue its efforts.

Over the next few days, most of the major newspapers weighed in, grudgingly recommending that the responders opt in to the settlement, accepting what the *Daily News* in its lead editorial on October 25 called "the bird in the hand." Francis X. Clines in the *New York Times* wrote, "Rejection would mean years more of individual suits. The judge who fought hard for the plaintiffs has wisely counseled acceptance."

Napoli was rallying his troops to get the necessary opt-ins by the November deadline: "Only 13 days left. Each of you need to set ten appointments a day to get this done. If you are doing this—figure out how to do it—stay late, wake up early. If someone does not want to come in, ask the travel team in that county to go right away to their house. This is our last push, we all need to push extra hard this week."

Napoli's approach was necessary, as failure to meet the clients, answer questions, and get their consent would doom the settlement. In the first week of November, a team of plaintiffs' attorneys held meetings at the Brooklyn Marriott on Adams Street, the Hilton Garden on South Avenue on Staten Island, the Hilton in Melville, Long Island, the Marriott on Grand Central Parkway in Elmhurst, and the Hyatt Regency in New Brunswick, New Jersey.

Even so, a very small fraction of plaintiffs, perhaps fifty out of ten thousand, decided against opting in to the settlement. Napoli, Bern, Worby, and Groner all put in a disproportionate amount of time talking to these responders, some of whom included their earliest clients in the case. Some had been fighting for so long, they didn't know how to stop. They were sick, and sometimes their treatments affected their memory or made them overly emotional. These clients wanted what WGENB could not give them: guarantees of exactly what their awards would be—and in some cases, a greater payment than what WGENB calculated as their estimated settlement. It was very difficult for all involved. Those clients were the exceptions, but that made their decisions no less painful.

And there was still work to be done. Groner and Napoli committed to spending the last weekend before the time limit expired in the office, setting aside a conference room to make themselves available for any remaining clients who had questions about the settlement.

On November 8, 2010, as the midnight deadline was fast approaching, WGENB was closing in on reaching the settlement thresholds—but they were not there yet. Then, at the last moment, Judge Hellerstein intervened, finally responding to WGENB's extension request by issuing an order to extend the deadline to midnight on November 16.

As they were trying to reach the 95 percent threshold for the most serious injuries, word came from Heimov that the Senate intended to hold a vote on Zadroga the week after Thanksgiving. The Democrats needed one more Republican vote to end the filibuster and bring the bill to a vote. At the moment, they were begging Senator Lisa Murkowski of Alaska for that vote.

With the November 16 deadline almost upon them, there was a mad scramble to get the remaining settlement forms signed, which included releases of their claims against the city and its contractors. Groner had taken it upon himself to meet with the most serious cases (which were often the ones due to receive the greatest awards). He was made deeply aware of the human cost of the victims' injuries. "It's really tearing me apart, going to next meeting now," he emailed Napoli. "Last one was fire chief who lost his son in towers and he is seriously injured." Some were in such poor health that the physical act of signing was itself a challenge.

Groner felt it was not just his job but his responsibility to meet with these clients in person. It was his obligation to present them with the settlement, explain it to them, and help them make a cost-benefit decision about whether to accept it. The risk of going to trial was that the jury could award the responders less than what was now being offered, or nothing at all; the benefit was that they might get more. Going to trial would also have a psychological cost, having to relive the experiences and being called upon to testify and be cross-examined. On top of that, a jury decision often gets appealed.

And the years it would take to try the cases—how much longer could responders afford to wait?

The attorney's job is not to force clients to either settle or go to trial, but rather to give them all the information they need to make an informed decision. These were often frank and difficult conversations with individuals suffering from multiple illnesses, including cancer, or their surviving spouses. What made these conversations all the more difficult was that Groner was often the bearer of bad news: a lower payout, the difficulty of proving causation. He wrote in an email, "Trying to convince widows of death by cancer to opt in is the worst experience of my life."

Throughout the day on November 16, 2010, Groner kept checking the tallies of opt-ins to see if they had met the required minimum numbers for the Captive to accept the settlement before the midnight deadline. The most serious injuries reached the 95 percent threshold, while the lesser injuries were lagging. Groner, to quell his concerns, reread the settlement agreement to confirm his memory of the numbers. He was delighted to see that the 95 percent requirement was for only the fourteen most severe categories. They needed to reach only 90 percent on the rest. Accordingly, at 5:50 p.m. they passed the mandated minimums. The settlement agreement would be deemed accepted.

In WGENB's office, there were no shouts of joy, no champagne uncorked. They were all too stunned. So they continued to watch the numbers rise.

By 10:00 p.m., of those Ground Zero responders suffering from the most severe injuries, more than 98 percent had opted in; in the next most severe tier of injuries, more than 97 percent had opted in; the next level (the second least severe) had more than 96 percent opt in; and the lowest tier comprising the least severe injuries passed 90 percent (which was beyond the requirement). This was gratifying evidence that the Ground Zero responders wanted an end to the litigation and to settle their claims.

Throughout the years of litigation, the responders had always had one foot rooted in the past. They deserved to have the cost of their heroism acknowledged. And it was time to move on.

The lawyers, however, were well aware of all the work that lay ahead and that was sure to take up the next many months, if not years, of claim submissions, reconsiderations, appeals, and adjustments.

On November 18 the WTC Captive Insurance Company sent out an official press release confirming that the participation threshold of eligible plaintiffs had been reached. The allocation neutral, appointed under the agreement, reported the opt-in numbers to Judge Hellerstein, who had previously declared the amended settlement "fair and reasonable" in the face of "potent defenses" by the city and its contractors under the law. Attorneys for the plaintiffs noted that 98 percent of their clients in Tier 4, claiming the most severe injuries that could possibly be tied to work at the site, agreed to the settlement.

Christine LaSala: "It has been my personal and professional mission to ensure that we negotiate a settlement that is fair and reasonable to all sides and I am extremely heartened that the overwhelming majority of plaintiffs have decided that is exactly what we achieved."

Margaret Warner: "This process has been intense for all sides, but the numbers of people opting in show that the settlement we developed and the process to obtain compensation has been judged fair and transparent by those plaintiffs."

Paul Napoli: "We negotiated for over two years to achieve this settlement for our clients, which we truly believe is the best result, given the uncertainty of protracted litigation."

Mayor Michael Bloomberg: "This settlement is a fair and just resolution of these claims, protecting those who came to the aid of this City when we needed it most." Aware that the Senate had not yet voted on or passed Zadroga, Bloomberg added, "We will continue our commitment to treatment and monitoring of those who were present at Ground Zero. This settlement can also help encourage the Senate to follow the lead of their colleagues in the House of Representatives and pass the James Zadroga 9/11 Health and Compensation Act, which will now be a less expensive proposition due to the payments made under this settlement agreement."

Judge Hellerstein was concerned about those plaintiffs who had not opted in and those who had withdrawn from the settlement and those who, although eligible for the settlement, could not be located by WGENB or the other attorneys. He announced that, on their behalf, he was appointing a special counsel, Michael Hoenig, to represent them and determine if they wanted to opt in to the settlement and what options were available to them if they did or if they did not. Hoenig would work closely with WGENB to make sure the remaining Ground Zero responders made informed decisions concerning the settlement.

Arriving at a settlement was a tremendous achievement, but for most of the Ground Zero responders, it was too little, too late. They deserved better.

For more than seven years, lawyers on all sides had worked very hard, mastering complex medical issues and navigating an ocean of documents. The hurdles faced by WGENB and Sullivan Papain had been enormous: the city had spent almost a quarter of a billion dollars to oppose them and took the position that they need not pay even a dollar to the responders. The defense took every opportunity to try to dismiss the case, swamped them in discovery, and negotiated very vigorously against them—all the while being well-paid for doing so. WGENB took the cases on contingency, and their finances were strained to the limit—and beyond—as they borrowed funds to pay overhead and expenses for the litigation, often at exorbitant interest rates.

It was never going to be an easy case to prove because medical causation of the toxic nature of Ground Zero dust was slow to document. The science remained behind the reality of what they and the Ground Zero responders knew to be true. And it would be logistically impossible to try ten thousand cases. So arriving at a settlement was a good result.

Yet Groner was well aware of the hard truth that the Ground Zero responders got a raw deal. The responders were, for the most part, healthy young men and women in the prime of their lives, working as police officers, firefighters, emergency rescue personnel, or city, utility, or construction workers. Many were working at dream jobs and had imagined they would have long careers doing so. They had sacrificed, without hesitation or question, as a matter of course, for the benefit of others, for their city and the nation.

Now they were sick and could no longer do the jobs they loved, and were not going to get better. They had to endure being questioned and doubted about their injuries and illnesses. And while they would receive some compensation, it was for only some injuries and illnesses, but not all. No amount of money would ever make them healthy again.

Groner also had great remorse that he all too rarely had the kind of one-on-one relationship with the clients that he most enjoyed in his personal injury practice. That feeling of trust that is critical to a healthy attorney-client relationship was impossible in a mass tort situation—and Groner deeply regretted that, believing it added insult to injury for many of his Ground Zero responder clients. But the reality was he was never going to be able to offer that to ten thousand clients (or even one thousand).

In the end, Groner felt that WGENB was able to deliver to the Ground Zero responders the best possible result that the system, with its limitations, allowed. It gave some measure of validation to these selfless heroes, some compensation, and the opportunity for closure. In this way, Groner hoped they were allowing the responders to move beyond what was surely the most difficult time of their lives and, last but not least, have the opportunity to live in the present and not the past.

PART ELEVEN

In the days leading up to a renewed Zadroga vote in the Senate, New York lawmakers announced they had secured the needed Republican vote from Senator Olympia Snowe (from Maine), but "not before we deal with the tax bill," referring to the tentative accord with the White House to extend the Bush-era income tax cuts. However, according to Senator Gillibrand's office, they did not have the sixty votes needed (fifty Democrats plus at least ten Republicans) for cloture to end debate and proceed to a vote. The cost of the James Zadroga 9/11 Health and Compensation Act was pegged at $7.4 billion, an amount many Republicans still objected to.

John Feal and his FealGood Foundation members launched a superhuman effort to contact every legislator and every media contact they had to lobby for the bill's passage.

On December 8, 2010, WGENB's lobbyist Brett Heimov announced, "The vote will take place around 5:00 p.m. today." He continued to send status reports on the legislation every few minutes. It was a roller coaster, and hard not to get swept up in the emotion. The waiting carried over to the next day, when Heimov emailed, "Coming up now." And then a short while later: "Zadroga lost." In the end they did not have enough Republican support, and the bill stalled along party lines, with a vote of 57 to 42.

To which Napoli replied, "Now what?"

Heimov answered, "Nothing. . . . It is dead."

Senate Majority Leader Harry Reid of Nevada was the sole Democrat who voted against his own party and against cloture. This was mystifying, until Heimov explained that it was a tactical move by Reid to save Zadroga for another vote. Reid knew full well that under Senate rules anyone who votes against cloture can bring the bill back up in the future. And that was exactly what he was planning to do.

They did not have the sixty votes *yet* to overcome Republican resistance to Zadroga. But at least they had a fighting chance.

It was amazing how something unforeseen could come out of left field just when WGENB needed it to change the tenor of the conversation, to add new facts or urgency, to weight the conversation in favor of the Ground Zero responders. Was it merely because their cause was just? Was there some greater force at work?

On *The Daily Show* on December 13, 2010, Jon Stewart led with the failure of the Senate to pass the Zadroga bill. Stewart went ballistic, calling the senators "WTC cowards" and "9/11 NON-responders" and branding them the "Lame-as-F@#K Congress."

It seemed as if every media person in New York had seen the program. The next day other networks started to cover the story. On Fox News, Shepard Smith called the Republican obstruction "shameful." Rachel Maddow featured an extensive excerpt from *The Daily Show*, letting her listeners know Stewart had done a "great service."

But Stewart wasn't quite done yet. On December 16 *The Daily Show*'s last show of the season and its last for 2010, Stewart opened by saying, "Before we go, I want to talk, one last time, about something called the Zadroga bill." He explained that the bill was named after a police officer who was thought to have died of respiratory illnesses incurred as a result of his Ground Zero heroism. He described the compensation act as a "Win, Win, Win," and he urged the senators to "just fucking do it." Calling the senators "worst responders," Stewart said there were more than enough votes to pass the bill, more than the fifty necessary, but the Republicans were blocking the vote with a filibuster. Stewart was quick to point out that the Senate had no problem passing an extension of the Bush tax cuts that primarily benefited the rich. He also called out network news stations for not covering the issue in more than two and half months (while covering the "news" that Beatles songs were now available on iTunes). "This is an outrageous abdication of our responsibility to those who were most heroic on 9/11." He pointed out that the only network that had covered the failure to pass the Zadroga law was Al Jazeera, which had scooped all U.S. networks. That was the network, Stewart joked, "that Osama bin Laden sends his mixtapes to."

"I would like to see one of these senators," Stewart railed, "have the balls to explain why somehow getting a tax cut extension for wealthy Americans is more important than suffering Ground Zero workers."

For his next segment on the program, Stewart had invited four Ground Zero responders to discuss the Senate filibuster: Kenny Specht, FDNY; Chris Baumann, NYPD; Ken George, Department of Transportation; and John Devlin, heavy equipment operating engineer. "We're disgusted and we're disappointed," Specht said. "And, unfortunately, we are hurt."

"We went down [to work at Ground Zero] for the love of this country, for the love of our city. We didn't turn our back on anybody," said Devlin, adding that it was wrong that nine years later they were still fighting for health benefits. Devlin was suffering from stage four inoperable throat cancer; George suffered from heart and lung disease; and Baumann from brain injury and cancer.

Stewart played a clip showing Senator Mitch McConnell getting choked up because Senator Judd Gregg, whom McConnell often lunched with, was leaving the Senate—then Stewart accused McConnell of having no such emotion for the plight of Ground Zero responders. "Where is his human feeling?" Devlin asked.

Another of Stewart's guests that evening, former presidential candidate Mike Huckabee, said, "Every Republican senator should vote for this."

The following day, Stewart's show was all anyone could talk about. And thanks to the internet, there was a way for people to watch clips of the program there and then. The sense of outrage, the shame of the senators, was all over the media.

Perhaps it was because Christmas was just a week away. Perhaps it was because it was the end of the year and work was winding down and Christmas time is when most people make their charitable donations. Whatever the reason, the show went viral, and the Republican senators, shamed by Stewart, were now shamed by millions of Americans.

John Feal and his FealGood Foundation members redoubled their efforts. Their determination helped turn the tide and made passage of Zadroga unstoppable. By the weekend the *New York Times* was reporting that Senator Gillibrand had Republican support for the bill. "We have the votes we need," she said. "We have indications from several Republicans that they very much want to vote for this bill." Senator Reid, the majority leader, said that he was open to allowing another vote on the health plan before Congress adjourned.

By the middle of the next week, the Senate had cut the bill's spending to $4.3 billion over five years. The funds for the bill were to come from a 2 percent fee on government procurement from certain foreign countries (rather than taxing American corporations' foreign earnings, as originally suggested). The revised Zadroga bill was brought to the floor of the Senate by Reid and passed overwhelmingly. The House passed their version soon after.

The James Zadroga 9/11 Health and Compensation Act expressly provides health care for those exposed to toxins released by the collapse of the World Trade Center towers. The bill also reopened the VCF. Sponsored in the House by New York Democratic representatives Carolyn Maloney and Jerrold Nadler and Republican Peter King, the bill had the support of the entire New York congressional delegation. In announcing its passage, Maloney said:

> To 9/11 responders and survivors who have suffered for so long, help is finally here. With this vote, Congress repaid a long-overdue debt and answered the emergency calls of thousands of ailing 9/11 first responders and survivors. This bipartisan compromise is a strong program that will save lives. I thank Speaker [Nancy] Pelosi and Leader [Steny] Hoyer for their dedication to those who are sick or injured because of 9/11. I applaud Senators Gillibrand and Schumer for brokering the compromise reached today, and I

remain eternally grateful to my friends and co-authors, Jerry Nadler and Peter King, and all our colleagues in the New York delegation.

Nadler also spoke:

Today's victory is without a doubt the proudest moment of my thirty-four-year career in government. Along with Carolyn Maloney, my staff and I have worked on this legislation for literally nine years. We have stood with first responders and community survivors through the numerous lows and battles over the course of years. We have grieved at the many losses—losses due to 9/11-related illnesses and due to cold political odds and seemingly insurmountable hurdles. But, today, thanks to the work and patience of so many responders, survivors, elected officials, and our allies in disparate corners, we have achieved the sweetest of victories. And it comes not a moment too soon. The plight of 9/11 responders and survivors is very serious and immediate. Thousands are sick and, until now, justice has seemed so far away. I am so proud that our government has done precisely what it is here for—to take responsibility for its citizens after the ugliest of attacks against our nation. Thanks goes out in particular to Congresswoman Maloney, Congressman King, Senators Gillibrand and Schumer, John Feal, Manhattan's Community Board 1, my entire staff, and so many others who have done so much.

Senator Gillibrand, in her memoir *Off the Sidelines: Speak Up, Be Fearless, and Change Your World*, recalls speaking in the Senate for passage of the Zadroga bill: "To be clear: I did nothing brilliant. I didn't deliver my address with great oratorical style. I didn't even speak in my own words. I just read a letter [from a Ground Zero responder] and allowed myself to feel the pain contained in it and show that pain to the world."

After the Senate and House had passed the Zadroga bill, it was sent to President Obama for his signature. By law, the president had ten days—that is, until January 3, 2011—to sign the bill, or it would be considered vetoed. Because the president was leaving for a much-anticipated family vacation in Hawaii, the bill was taken aboard Air Force One for signing.

Meanwhile, over at WGENB, despite the excellent news, after reading the final text of the Zadroga bill, the attorneys realized they had a crisis on their hands. Under the language of the new bill, only those victims who had signed their settlement paperwork with the Captive and the non-Captive defendants *before* the president signed the bill could also apply for additional Zadroga funds. (If they had not, then they could receive either settlement funds or Zadroga funds, but not both.) The shocking reality was that settlements of up to $100 million with the non-Captive defendants, such as the Port Authority, weren't even close to the stage where the responders could sign off on them. And it could easily take months to get the papers for these complicated settlements signed and processed. Beyond that, there were almost a thousand agreements for the Captive settlement that plaintiffs had filled out improperly and that needed to be revised, corrected, and resubmitted.

Napoli, Groner, and Bern were all trying to arrive at possible solutions. On December 23 Groner called Heimov to ask the president, via his chief of staff, to hold off signing the bill. Heimov emailed back, "I have given the situation to the White House and Gillibrand's office and am waiting for a response."

Groner reached out to Worby as well as to Ken Feinberg for creative suggestions. Feinberg offered: "Simply have Judge Hellerstein declare that the effective date of any paperwork that will be signed by your clients will be declared *nunc pro tunc*—back to the date of enactment of the legislation. The Judge is in no way perverting the statute; he is merely declaring that the release itself will be deemed valid as of the enactment date so as to preserve the right of the plaintiff to participate in Zadroga."

Worby's idea was to have WGENB sign their clients' paperwork, and have that held in escrow by the court, pursuant to an order by Judge Hellerstein. Groner and Napoli both liked the idea of involving Hellerstein. So Rubin drafted an order for the judge, saying that any claimants who by December 31, 2010, have expressed their intent to sign the settlement releases will be deemed by the court to have signed those releases for purposes of being eligible to apply for Zadroga Act benefits.

The next day, December 24, Groner was relieved to learn that Obama had not yet signed the bill. He sent the proposed order to Special Master Twerski, who approved and then submitted it to Hellerstein for his signature. The waiting was tough, and the tension among the attorneys was acute.

In the spirit of the Holiday season, and in recognition of what Feal had accomplished, he and Groner had the following email exchange:

John

I wanted to wish you, the members of your organization and everyone who worked with you congratulations on a Herculean effort with almost impossible odds. As a result of your selfless and tireless efforts thousands of deserving people will benefit.

I look forward to trying to convince the [settlement administrator for Zadroga funds] that the settlement monies from the litigation were only a down payment on the true compensation that my clients deserve.

But critically I also want to ensure that my clients' health conditions are closely monitored particularly the health patterns I have seen which clearly have a medical footprint and I will ensure my voice is heard, particularly [regarding] cancer, interstitial lung disease and auto immune issues.

Thank you John and have happy holidays.

Sir,

Thank you and have a blessed Holiday. I am humbled and floored by the support shown for this historic bill passing. But make no mistake it was a group effort of everyone from individuals, organizations, elected officials and the resolve of the American people that got this done. What I can tell you sir is that, I will advocate to the fullest to ensure cancers and all illnesses are added under this bill. We are far from done and will continue to do what is right for the 9/11 community.

Happy Holiday's!!!!!!!!!!!!!!!!!!!!!!

"Any Nation that does not honor its heroes will not long endure"

Abraham Lincoln

Peace & Love

John Feal

Christmas came and went without President Obama's signing Zadroga into law, but also, ominously, without Hellerstein's signing the order that would have rectified the situation with the unsigned settlements. So Groner pursued Plan B: as extra protection, WGENB started discussions with all the supplemental defendants involved (such as the Port Authority) to amend their settlement agreements. This covered about $75 million in the settlement.

On December 26, Hellerstein had still not signed the order. On December 27, a blizzard closed the courthouse, and again there was no signed order from Hellerstein. Obama continued to hold off on signing Zadroga into law, but less than a week remained for him to do so.

Despite their efforts, on December 28 Judge Hellerstein announced that he would not sign the order, declaring that he didn't have the authority to backdate an agreement.

In the midst of all this high-stakes tension, Susan Edelman at *the New York Post* emailed Napoli:

Hi Paul,

For an article due at 4 p.m. today, have the settlements with the Port Authority, barge and landfill been approved by the responders yet?

Have they received and signed the releases? . . .

It appears that responders cannot apply for compensation under the reopened VCF if they sign the releases for the PA and other civil actions after Obama signs Zadroga.

Does this mean the settlements are dead?

Please explain for the story.

Thank you, Sue

She emailed Groner the same questions. Napoli and Groner decided it was best just to avoid her, but they thought they should counter her suggestion that the settlements were going to fail. In keeping with Napoli's devilish sense of humor, WGENB issued a press release with the headline "Don't Go to the *New York Post* for Legal Advice, Say 9/11 Attorneys."

On December 29, Obama was still waiting to sign the Zadroga bill. WGENB was pursuing their Plan B, as all of the supplemental defendants signed amended settlement agreements, indicating that the paperwork the responders would sign in the future would be deemed backdated.

Groner was greatly concerned that the Department of Justice, which would administer Zadroga payments, would not accept this. The WGENB partners discussed whether, if actual releases needed to be signed immediately, WGENB as attorneys could sign on behalf of their ten thousand clients. But WGENB's retainer agreements with their clients didn't give them that authority, and without power of attorney no one can sign for another person.

Groner phoned Roy D. Simon, their well-regarded ethics counsel, previously hired at Judge Hellerstein's direction, and brought him up to speed on the crisis they were facing. Did they, in these circumstances, have the right to sign for their clients, even though power of attorney was not given in their retainer agreement?

Simon's reply: "Under the rules of ethics, you not only have the implied authority, but you have the responsibility to sign on their behalf since it is in the best interests of your client."

Groner responded, "Professor, please put that in writing and send it to me immediately."

Groner then emailed Heimov, "Tell the White House we need one more day, URGENT."

After they received Professor Simon's letter, they signed one release, along with a rider containing all their clients' names; once completed and signed, these were sent and received by defense counsel.

Two day later, on December 31, Groner gave the all clear to Heimov, who had been in constant contact with the White House throughout the process.

On January 2, 2011, President Obama signed the Zadroga bill into law. The Ground Zero responders would now have not only their long-awaited and hard-fought settlement from the City of New York, but health care, health monitoring, and the possibility of additional funds from the federal government.

It was a rare WIN-WIN-WIN.

In the end, 99 percent of the plaintiffs accepted the settlement. New York City paid $712 million, the Port Authority and several others paid $100 million, for a total settlement of $812 million to more than ten thousand Ground Zero responders. Some responders received more than $500,000; a few, more than $1 million. Most received between $50,000 and $150,000. Those with lesser injuries received anywhere from $3,000 to $50,000. In addition, the Zadroga Act would reopen the VCF and would further help thousands of responders.

By the time final payments were made, it was some nine years since Groner and Worby had been asked to consider taking on a lawsuit by a Ground Zero responder against the City of New York. It had overtaken their legal practice and their professional lives and seeped into every corner of their lives for days, nights, and years. They and their partners had become experts in arcane areas of medical expertise and science, sometimes besting the experts themselves, because unlike the experts, they had ten thousand cases they could call upon to see the effects of Ground Zero dust.

Napoli and Bern had kept their initial promises to Worby and Groner to create and fund an infrastructure to handle this massive enterprise and to use their prior mass tort experience to enable the partnership to take on and successfully prosecute these cases—cases they litigated for nine years, through a complex set of medical, scientific, and legal challenges that few would have been able to persevere through all the way to settlement.

What had occurred at Ground Zero and on 9/12 and the days that followed during the cleanup were never seen before, an impossible-to-imagine set of circumstances and an unbelievable and heroic response. The litigation that arose out of it was unlike anything any lawyer had ever experienced, and has since been called by Judge Hellerstein and the special masters, "the most complex case in the history of American mass tort litigation."[1]

Nothing was as it appeared or as expected. The Ground Zero responders' illnesses were not consistent; throughout the course of the litigation, many of them remained unexplained by science or medical studies. The defense attorneys DiMuro and Hopkins would tell you that science and medicine had not proved that most of these illnesses were the result of exposure to Ground Zero dust. They would say that, in this, the law was on their side.

Hopkins would say the Second Court of Appeals disregarded the law in rejecting the immunity defense. Most every lawyer would tell you that Judge Hellerstein exceeded his authority in rejecting the first settlement agreement and in holding a fairness hearing.

Both sides would tell you that this was a case where what happened outside the courtroom, in the press and in the halls of Congress—even on late-night television—had as much influence in the case as, if not more than, what occurred in the courtroom.

Yet, in the end, they would all say this was the best result that could be arrived at. At moments DiMuro, Hopkins, LaSala, and Warner thought the settlement should have been less; the victims' lawyers and the responders themselves thought it should be more, and that more conditions should have been covered. But they could all say with no small amount of pride that they had arrived at a settlement as well as validation and closure for the Ground Zero responders.

On 9/12 and the days that followed, the city and its contractors made many decisions that the attorneys were now, some nine years later, second-guessing. One could reasonably ask: Should the federal government have allowed the city to be in charge of what was an environmental disaster of catastrophic proportions? If the city had exercised more caution, and treated Ground Zero and its debris as a toxic site and required all workers to wear full head and body hazmat suits with breathing gear, there would certainly have been far fewer injuries (if any). However, doing so would certainly have taken longer—and if the area had been closed off for a longer period, of, say, one to three years, would that have had a catastrophic result on New York City and its economy—and therefore on the U.S. economy? This was a cost-benefit analysis that was difficult to make.

As to the litigation itself: Should the city have spent more than $200 million in legal and administration costs to fight the responders' lawsuits? Should the contractors, who undeniably did their best to clean up Ground Zero in record time under the worst of circumstances, be subject to litigation to find them at fault for having done so? Did Judge Hellerstein impose himself unnecessarily on the process? Was litigation even the best way to compensate heroes who came to the city's and nation's aid at great peril to themselves? Did the legal process take far too long? Was the compensation as much as the responders deserved, or needed?

The plaintiffs' attorneys had several misgivings, but in the end, WGENB had taken a great challenge against logic-defying odds that almost no one else was willing to carry for as long and as hard as they did. And they saw it through to the best possible conclusion. And that was no small thing.

The Ground Zero responders were heroes who took on the task of the cleanup, willingly, without hesitation, for many long hours, days, weeks, and months at great personal risk. In the months and years that followed, many became ill, and many have died. Many were able to manage their illnesses, but there were few cures. Medicine could not erase the health problems they suffered. Science could not yet prove the cause of many of their injuries. In the final analysis, it was the legal system, imperfect as it is, that brought the parties together in Judge Hellerstein's courtroom that turned out to be the strongest vehicle to help the greatest number of Ground Zero responders. And Groner could live with that.

EPILOGUE

After the settlement was approved and signed, Dean Aaron Twerski reflected on the accomplishment: "We were very proud. We worked very, very hard. . . . We brought order out of chaos. Did people get enough? Hard to tell. It had to settle well within the $1 billion figure. My own feeling is that the city knew that the cleanup could not be done in ten months. They had to know. . . . They wanted to get the city back to work again. That was goal number one. Whether people would be endangered by that? I don't think it's that they didn't care, but they simply didn't care enough.

"This was a job that, had it been done over two and a half years, three years, we probably would not have had the same number of people that were seriously injured. In that sense, I think there was plenty of fault. . . . They had to know that people were working ten hours every day of the week, week after week. . . . You couldn't work that many hours with inadequate equipment. This was not a case of no fault. . . . I think there was real fault here."

Thomas Ryan filed for a disability pension in 2009, and at first he was denied. The NYPD then sent him to their own doctors; when three of their pulmonologists found him to be suffering from a variety of respiratory ailments, he reapplied and was awarded the disability pension. Ryan retired from the NYPD in 2010. Today he says, "I'm not going to be vindictive. I'm not going to be angry at what happened down there. If it was to happen again and they told me the air was bad . . . I would still go, because that was my job. I don't hold any grudges or anything. . . . I'm more disappointed that I had to retire. . . . If I would have stayed, I would have had a really good career. My last few years there, I was doing dignitary duty, protecting heads of state, working in Manhattan, working at the UN as a detective. . . . I probably would have stayed another thirty, thirty-five years. But, hey. Everything happens for a reason, right?"

Ryan is grateful that he did not become more seriously ill. "Some guys got sicker. Some guys are sick and never documented it, never reported it. And they've long since retired and now they're having issues. And these are guys that are generally healthy and nonsmokers, and they're having breathing issues. . . . Lots of guys have stomach, digestive issues. That's one thing I don't have. Mine's just the lungs, so, I mean, I feel fortunate. I mean, yes, I'm on medicine and everything and I'm retired young, but look at it this way, I'm home, I got three kids, I'm able to put them on the bus, take them off the bus, it's kind of a blessing in disguise. That's kind of the way I have to look at it."

As a mass tort defense attorney, Paul Scrudato saw Judge Hellerstein's role as crucial. Hellerstein clearly believed that "it would not be good for anybody if these cases of these men and women went to trial." From the very first, Hellerstein was focused on the end game without ever getting into the cases' details. "Which," Scrudato said, "is what a good judge does."

In Scrudato's opinion, the defense lawyers in the case were "a good group of lawyers, very professional, tough, worked hard for their clients." On the other side, "a lot of the big plaintiffs' firms in New York rejected these cases because (a) they were too politically charged, and (b) they thought they were largely just a bunch of guys with runny noses." Napoli and Groner "took a real risk in bringing these cases on and invested a lot of money in them. Had some serious debt to finance this thing. . . . And there was no guarantee of an outcome." It requires a special DNA to be willing to take that risk, which "Napoli had and . . . Bill had that enabled them to be successful here."

Scrudato is of the opinion that to get a deal done you need warriors, and that in Tyrrell, Hopkins, DiMuro, Warner, Napoli, Groner, and Hellerstein you had just that. "You had all the stars aligning to get this thing to the point where the end result would be fair to all of the litigants. In mass torts, you rarely see that, because people have different interests and incentives, different motivations. In this litigation, you had that alignment, for which Hellerstein deserves a lot of the credit."

For a few Ground Zero responders, such as Gary Acker, the settlement came too late.

Gary and Alison, at home in New Jersey, were supposed to leave for Florida the next day. Gary, a bull of a man, couldn't stand. He had told Alison to go out—he would be fine. But she hovered, and then he said, "Call an ambulance," which he'd never done before. The next morning, at 6:00 a.m., age fifty-nine, he passed away at Robert Wood Johnson University Hospital in Hamilton, New Jersey, with Alison, his wife of thirty-nine years, at his side.

Before he died, he had one pressing concern: "After I'm gone, what will happen to my wife and kids? Will they able to stay in our house?" That his family would be taken care of meant the world to him.

Today Alison, who lives in Florida, says, "I wished he hadn't gone [to Ground Zero]. But I knew I couldn't stop him because when he saw someone needed help, he was the first one there. . . . That's who he was. He was there to help people always. . . . He lived the life that he was made for, that he loved."

Looking back on the case, James Tyrrell said philosophically, "Every major litigation ends in a rational compromise." He believed that the settlement, arrived at within the policy limits of the Captive, was something he could be proud of, and that in the end, the responders "were treated fairly."

For the next two years the WGENB joint venture was involved in the detail work attendant to the settlement, including the various payment schedules, verifications, appeals, and recalculations, in dialogue with the Garretson firm and Ken Feinberg.

In time, each of the lawyers, who had been in constant contact for some nine years, sometimes moment to moment, returned to their law practices, older if not necessarily wiser from the experience. Napoli and Bern eventually parted ways with Worby and Groner. Differences between the partners led to their estrangement, but in recent years some fences have been mended. Paul Napoli and Marc Bern also went their separate ways, not on the best of terms. Napoli, whose offices were so close to Ground Zero, would himself develop leukemia, one of the cancers caused by Ground Zero dust exposure. Although initially the odds were not good, he survived. He and Bern made a sizable contribution to the 9/11 Memorial & Museum in their names and the name of their law firm, which can be seen today on the museum's wall of donors.

David Worby and Bill Groner ended their legal partnership on amicable terms. Worby still occasionally practices law but continues to pursue his other interests, including songwriting. Groner has launched a mediation service that uses a more holistic approach to conflict resolution.

James Tyrrell, Joe Hopkins, and Chris DiMuro have all gone to different law firms, but each continues to practice environmental and toxic tort defense and corporate work.

Margaret Warner remains a senior partner at McDermott Will & Emery.

Judge Hellerstein remains on the federal bench, hearing cases.

Over the years, as more and more scientific studies of responders' illnesses were published, the link between those illnesses and Ground Zero dust that the victims' lawyers and the responders fought so hard to establish came to be more generally recognized and accepted.

In 2012 Dr. John Howard, the WTC Health Program administrator, along with NIOSH announced that cancers would be covered under Zadroga, and to date over seventy different cancers are now covered.

There is no official tally of how many persons who worked on the cleanup died as a result of illnesses related to Ground Zero dust. The *Guardian* (U.K.) recently estimated "at least 1,000 people—and probably many more."[1] The FDNY reports that, as of 2018, 111 firefighters have died of WTC-related illnesses, 44 of cancer.[2]

In May 2018 the 9/11 Memorial & Museum announced the dedication of a monument to the Ground Zero responders who worked on the rescue and recovery effort following the attacks. To be called Memorial Glade, according to the museum's press release, "the design includes a pathway . . . flanked by a series of large stone elements pointed skyward that are worn, but not beaten, symbolizing strength and determination through adversity." One of the major funders is Bloomberg Philanthropies, the foundation of the former mayor.[3]

John Feal and the FealGood Foundation continue to advocate and care for Ground Zero responders. Along with Jon Stewart, they were involved in raising public awareness to support the renewal of the Zadroga Act in 2015, when it was imperiled.

As for Candiace Baker, her spirit and determination remain strong. After she retired from the NYPD, she continued to deal with her health challenges. Her chemo treatments had made her joints ache, and as time went on, she decided she could no longer handle the cold in New York. She was getting depressed. Knowing that her life expectancy was already diminished because of her illness, she decided that she didn't want to spend her remaining years as someone who stayed inside all winter, avoiding the damp, the snow, and the cold, looking out the window at the passersby. She moved to Florida and has been living near West Palm Beach in a well-appointed home she's decorated, with an enclosed pool in the backyard. She still travels to New York to see her oldest son and his wife.

She remains angry about the way the city behaved to those who, like her, served at Ground Zero and the Fresh Kills Landfill on 9/12 and all the days that followed. The city, in her opinion, should have taken some responsibility for their illnesses. "We took an oath to protect the city, and the city should have protected us."

Baker describes her life today this way: "For the most part, what you see is what you get. I'm pretty laid back, I'm pretty relaxed. I'm not wound too tight. I go to doctor's appointments. I go to the lab, get my lab work done, and I go to a therapist." She still has a host of physical ailments, including bilateral lymphedema, from which she has a lot of pain in her arms.

It is worth repeating what Baker told Judge Hellerstein at the fairness hearing: "I participated in the World Trade Center cleanup and recovery, both voluntarily and assigned, and would not hesitate to do it again. But I did not ask for these illnesses and I did not ask for this disease." This is true of every responder who suffered injuries as a result of their exposure to Ground Zero dust.

"I don't know what the future holds," Baker said recently. "But I try to keep it moving because a body in motion stays in motion, and a body at rest will go to rest. But, for the most part, you can't hit a moving target, and I try to keep moving."

A NOTE ON SOURCES

Litigation, for better and sometimes for worse, amasses a tremendous amount of information that proved invaluable to this book, including depositions, medical research, motions, briefs, court orders, hearing transcripts, letters, and emails—to name just a few of the byproducts. Although this amounts to millions of pages of documents, they are, for the most part, digitized and accessible. Having litigated the case, Groner had digested, debated, processed, and lived the great majority of the material and knew where to find the most relevant documents. The Centers for Disease Control (CDC) collected and catalogued hundreds of medical articles and studies related to Ground Zero dust and its detrimental effects. In addition, all the press related to the litigation was collected and archived, in particular the coverage in the *New York Post*, the *New York Daily News*, and the *New York Times*.

We are grateful for our interviews with (in alphabetical order) Alison Acker, Candiace Baker, Gina and Paul Barrese, Marc Bern, Andrew Carboy, Chris DiMuro, John Feal, Kenneth Feinberg, Dr. Greg Fried, Lyndon Harris, Brett Heimov, Mindy Hersh, Joseph Hopkins, Dr. John Howard, Dr. Philip Landrigan, Raul Martinez, Suzanne Mattei, Tom McHale, Dr. David Prezant, Thomas Ryan, Denise Rubin, Kevin Russell, Paul Scrudato, Aaron Twerski, James Tyrell, and David Worby. Whatever intelligence the book imparts is because of them. Any mistakes, errors, or omissions that occur anywhere in the book are entirely our fault.

In addition, we want to acknowledge the work of Dr. Benjamin Luft, the Edmund Pellegrino Professor of Medicine at Stony Brook University School of Medicine and director of the Stony Brook WTC Wellness Program, whom we also interviewed and whose Remembering 9/11 Oral History Project recorded more than two hundred oral histories from Ground Zero responders. Originally housed at Stony Brook University on Long Island, the collection is now at the Library of Congress in Washington DC as part of the American Folklife Center. This is a permanent and invaluable resource.

As part of our research, the following books were consulted and were very helpful:

DePalma, Anthony. *City of Dust: Illness, Arrogance, and 9/11.* New York: Financial Times, Prentice Hall, 2015.

Gonzalez, Juan. *Fallout: The Environmental Consequences of the World Trade Center Collapse.* New York: New Press, 2002.

Lioy, Paul J., and Thomas H. Kean. *Dust: The Inside Story of Its Role in the September 11th Aftermath.* Lanham MD: Rowman & Littlefield, 2011.

Luft, Benjamin J. *We're Not Leaving: 9/11 Responders Tell Their Stories of Courage, Sacrifice, and Renewal.* New York: Greenpoint, 2011.

Marra, Frank, and Maria Bella Abbate. *From Landfill to Hallowed Ground: The Largest Crime Scene in America.* Dallas TX: Brown, 2015.

There is also a tremendous amount of video material available, much of it accessible on YouTube or online, from 9/11 itself to the present, from news stories to documentaries, including pivotal episodes of *60 Minutes*, Arnold Diaz's *Shame on You*, and *The Daily Show with Jon Stewart*, all of which contributed to making the narrative more expansive and more compelling. Unless otherwise specified, all quotations and personal stories are from our interviews and associated research.

NOTES

PART ONE

1. Over the course of its history, there have been several mass graves for indigent citizens buried in New York. A million people are buried in a mass grave on Hart Island. Thousands are buried in potter's fields beneath Washington Square Park, Union Square, Bryant Park, and Madison Square Park.

2. Tom Templeton and Tom Lumley, "9/11 in Numbers," *Guardian*, August 17, 2002.

3. Louisa Dalton, "Chemical Analysis of a Disaster," *Chemical and Engineering News*, October 20, 2003. Dalton quotes Gregory Meeker of the U.S. Geological Survey, a participant in the early dust collection and analyses: "Six million ft2 of masonry, 5 million ft2 of painted surfaces, 7 million ft2 of flooring, 600,000 ft2 of window glass, 200 elevators, and everything inside came down as dust when the towers collapsed."

4. "New York's Governor and Mayor of New York City Address Concerns of the Damage," CNN *Transcripts*, September 11, 2001, http://transcripts.cnn.com/TRANSCRIPTS/0109/11/bn.42.html.

5. Lisa Guernsey, "Keeping the Lifelines Open," *New York Times*, September 20, 2001, https://www.nytimes.com/2001/09/20/technology/keeping-the-lifelines-open.html.

6. William C. Thompson Jr. (comptroller of the City of New York), "One Year Later: The Fiscal Impact of 9/11 on New York City," September 4, 2002.

7. U.S. Department of Labor, OSHA, "A Dangerous Worksite," n.d., https://www.osha.gov/Publications/WTC/dangerous_worksite.html.

8. See U.S. Department of Commerce, National Institute of Standards and Technology, "NIST WTC 7 Investigation Finds Building Fires Caused Collapse," April 21, 2008, https://www.nist.gov/news-events/news/2008/08/nist-wtc-7-investigation-finds-building-fires-caused-collapse.

9. Jimeno and Loughlin were discovered on September 11; Jimeno was rescued at 11:00 p.m. and McLoughlin at 7:00 a.m. on September 12. It was only once they were safe that their rescues were reported.

10. David B. Caruso, "Mystery 9/11 Rescuer Reveals Himself," *Washington Post*, August 14, 2006, http://www.washingtonpost.com/wp-dyn/content/article/2006/08/14/AR2006081400860.html; Rebecca

Liss, "An Unlikely Hero: The Marine Who Found Two WTC Survivors,"
Slate, September 11, 2015, https://slate.com/news-and-politics/2015
/09/the-marine-who-found-two-wtc-survivors.html.

11. See Hellerstein, Opinion Denying and Granting Motions for Judgment on the Pleadings and for Summary Judgment, 21 MC 100, 03 Civ.
00007 et al.

12. "Ceremony Closes Ground Zero Cleanup," CNN, May 30, 2002, http://
edition.cnn.com/2002/US/05/30/rec.wtc.cleanup/.

13. See Anthony DePalma, "What Happened to That Cloud of Dust?," *New
York Times*, November 2, 2005, https://www.nytimes.com/2005/11/02
/nyregion/what-happened-to-that-cloud-of-dust.html?module=inline.

14. Comments made to *Asbury Park (NJ) Press* in 2011, according to Dr.
Lioy's obituary in the *New York Times*, July, 11, 2015.

15. Thomas Ryan's testimony to the Luft Archive, now part of the Library
of Congress, is quoted throughout this section.

16. U.S. Department of Labor, OSHA, "A Dangerous Worksite."

17. The exact number of persons who worked on the Ground Zero rescue
and recovery is not known. Estimates range from forty thousand to
ninety thousand. Ninety thousand is the estimate given by Dr. Benjamin Luft of Stony Brook. Luft served as chairman of the Department
of Medicine at Stony Brook from 1994 to 2006 and is now the director
and principal investigator of the Stony Brook WTC Wellness Program.

18. In 2003 Walcott would find a match from Olaf Gierszewski, a thirty-
eight-year-old German Navy petty officer who had signed up at a German bone marrow donor center. The cells were flown to America and
transfused into Walcott following chemotherapy. Walcott has been in
remission since.

PART TWO

1. A. J. Loftin with W. Dyer Halpern, "Whatever Suits Him," *Westchester
Magazine*, September 23, 2008, http://www.westchestermagazine.com
/Westchester-Magazine/October-2008/Whatever-Suits-Him/.

2. Persons injured as a result of the 9/11 attacks had to have been injured
(or died) in the first twelve hours following the crashes and as a direct
result of the attacks. If injured, they had to have been treated within the
first twenty-four hours after being injured. In the event they didn't realize at first that they were injured, they had to have been treated within
the first seventy-two hours. Ground Zero responders and rescue workers who were injured within ninety-six hours after the attacks could

also submit claims to the VCF. However, their injuries had to be verified by medical records made at the time by the appropriate medical professions. And all claims needed to be filed by December 22, 2003.

3. At a later date, families of 9/11 victims and Ground Zero responders would sue Saudi Arabia as being complicit in the crimes.

4. Under General Municipal Law, Section 205A.

PART THREE

1. A study from September 2004 came to the opposite conclusion: "9/11 Search-and-Rescue Dogs Exhibit Few Effects from Exposure to Disaster Sites," *Science Daily*, September 15, 2004, https://www.sciencedaily .com/releases/2004/09/040915112139.htm. Two years later studies seemed to confirm that dogs didn't get sick nearly as much as humans: Amy Westfeldt, "Trade Center Search Canines Don't Show Signs of Ills at Rate of Humans," Associated Press, October 21, 2006.

2. Hickey was an employee of a company hired by the city and Port Authority. He worked at the World Trade Center site from September 13 through November 7, 2001.

3. Hellerstein established other Ground Zero–related master complaints, such as MC 102 (for workers or office cleaners inside buildings surrounding Ground Zero who were exposed to dust) and MC 103 (for those who qualified for MC 100 and MC 102 because they worked at both places).

4. The four contractors and many of the subcontractors did have their own coverage. Many had self-insured retentions whereby they would have to pay the first dollars up to a certain amount. Also, using their coverage would cause an increase in premiums, and that could hurt them financially. Many coverages weren't remotely enough to cover the task before them.

5. See Department of Homeland Security, Office of Inspector General, "A Review of the World Trade Center Captive Insurance Company," OIG-08-21, June 2008, https://www.oig.dhs.gov/assets/Mgmt/oig_08 -21_Jun08.pdf.

6. The city was not in exactly the same position as its contractors in terms of liability. A federal law capped the city's liability at some $350 million, which it did not do for its contractors.

7. See World Trade Center Health Panel, "Addressing the Health Impacts of 9-11: Report and Recommendations to Mayor Michael

R. Bloomberg," n.d., http://www.nyc.gov/html/om/pdf/911_health _impacts_report.pdf.

8. This was an anomaly. Judge Hellerstein wanted everything 9/11-related to be on the record and transparent. This meeting was more of an introductory session to see if Hellerstein could craft a road-map for this mass tort.

9. It would take until 2009 for her death to be considered a line-of-duty death, her brain cancer a result of her exposure to Ground Zero dust.

10. The Robert T. Stafford Disaster Relief and Emergency Assistance Act (Stafford Act) is the federal law by which declaration of an emergency or a presidential declaration of an emergency triggers financial and other assistance from FEMA.

11. In April 2006 the city released a Draft Master Plan that would trans-form the landfill into a park almost three times the size of Central Park, with no mention of a memorial, to be completed by 2036.

12. Judge Hellerstein's earlier decision had found ATSSSA applied only until September 29.

13. See Suzanne Mattei, "Pollution and Deception at Ground Zero," *Sierra Club*, 2004.

14. "Preliminary Listing of Established Human Toxicological Effects Associated with World Trade Center Toxic Emissions (Supported by Peer-Reviewed Human Studies)," September 29, 2004, draft.

PART FOUR

1. WGENB would need to demonstrate that the harm to the responders was caused by exposure to the dust and debris at Ground Zero. They would show the toxic nature of the dust's components (cadmium, silica, glass shards, and benzene) along with medical studies that showed such harmful components could cause the illnesses present in their clients. WGENB would then need to show that the city and its contractors had failed to provide adequate protection, that not every-one received the proper personal protective equipment, and that, if they did, it wasn't properly fit-tested and filters were not replaced when needed. Further, compliance was an issue: wearing respira-tors was not enforced. The responders' faces were protected only by hardhats and half-face respirators, which, as noted, were problematic in their use. Even when the responders were given protective suits (at Fresh Kills, for example), these were not full head and body suits with breathing apparatuses They would also show that the responders were

not protected from exposure as they traveled to the site and ate their meals there and that they often removed their protective equipment in order to communicate.

2. *Parker* is important because the case involved a plaintiff who claimed he had developed leukemia as a result of exposure to benzene while working for seventeen years as a gas station attendant. The plaintiffs wanted to call experts to prove causation, but they were not going to introduce evidence of the specific levels of benzene in the station's gasoline. And there was no other methodology introduced to prove the levels of exposure to benzene. The defendants claimed that this didn't meet the *Frye* standard and moved to exclude and end the case for lack of proof. The judge disagreed. But the defendants appealed, and New York's appellate court agreed with the defendants and dismissed the case. The appellate court recognized as scientifically reliable the three-step methodology established by the World Health Organization and the National Academy of Sciences: (1) proof of the plaintiff's level of exposure to the substance in question; (2) proof from a review of the scientific literature that the substance is capable of producing the illness (general causation) and the exposure level at which it will produce that illness (dose-response relationship or threshold); (3) proof that the plaintiff's exposure to the substance likely caused the illness, and elimination of other possible causes (specific causation).

PART FIVE

1. Fumento is also the author of *The Myth of Heterosexual AIDS*.
2. For example, the Port Authority admitted that on 9/11 "PAPD [Port Authority Police Department] officers begin participation in controlling site access; in so participating, PAPD officers are required (and do) follow access rules and procedures established by the City of New York." They also uncovered correspondence that as of 9/12 the Tully Construction Company was supplying services to New York City at the World Trade Center site on a time and material basis. Another important document uncovered by the plaintiffs' attorneys was the New York State Department of Environmental Conservation's User/Training Manual, which was given to all agencies and contractors. This confirmed that the city had its own Accident Prevention Plan for Post-Disaster Search, Rescue, Demolition and Cleanup, which stated that "each site supervisor shall accept the responsibility for seeking the safest most practical method to perform the task of search, res-

cue, demolition, cleanup and recovery." They found a whole host of documents affirming that New York City was in control of the Ground Zero site and its cleanup. On September 22, 2001, the FDNY held an Incident Command Post meeting, whose minutes revealed that the city's Department of Health (DOH) as well as the City's Department of Design and Construction (DDC) were in control of safety and health issues and logistics at the site. There were situation reports from Bechtel, which document that DDC and contractors were in control of the site; the minutes from a Turner project meeting reveal that OSHA was only in consultation mode and that DDC and contractors were controlling operations at the site. Documents from the various construction companies made clear that they were in control and subject to New York City regulations. But they also had their own city standards of safety to maintain, in particular with regard to exposure to hazardous or toxic materials. An October 5, 2001, letter from EPA's Bruce Sprague to Kelly McKinney at the city's DOH establishes that the EPA had no control over operations at the WTC site. Various other documents demonstrate that DDC assumed responsibility for the transportation and shipping of debris.

3. An OSHA Air Sampling Results Summary, dated October 24, 2001, and sent to Bovis Construction staff and subcontractors, stated that 53 of 410 asbestos samples exceeded OSHA's limits and that dioxin and PAH levels were elevated. Further, on November 19, 2001, Mike Ramsey, a senior industrial hygienist for Liberty Mutual, warned Bovis that quartz exposure levels were 1.5 times OSHA's permissible exposure limit.

4. A December 16, 2001, Warren & Panzer Engineers Daily Report noted that PAPD officers at the site were not wearing respirators. The minutes of a December 21, 2001, meeting of the PAPD, OSHA, and DDC stated, "Respirator and other [personal protective equipment] usage has been below compliance levels with the exception of hardhats." On December 31, DDC and FDNY found, "Respirator use has been declining." On January 11, 2002, Cate Jenkins at EPA wrote a memo that included a section titled "Why Cleanup of WTC Contamination Is Ineffective to Date." On January 13, 2002, Liberty Mutual again documented that workers were not using their respirators. A February 19, 2002, letter from Bruce Rottner, the DDC Environmental Health and Safety Services director, to Ray Master (the Bovis company's safety representative), found violations of health and safety regulations and ordered corrective action within twenty-four hours. Rottner

also warned of toxic airborne contaminants, oxygen displacers, and the need for atmospheric monitoring and the use of self-contained breathing apparatus for workers. Throughout the rest of February, March, and April, Rottner continued to find daily violations. On March 15, 2002, DDC acknowledged elevated levels on the site and considered requiring full-face respirators in Six World Trade Center. On March 27, 2002, Robert Martin, the national ombudsman for the EPA, wrote a memo to Jane Kenny at EPA describing all the hazards and the lack of responsible government intervention and the disregard of relevant laws at the site.

5. See "September 11 Attacks," posted by Brave New Films on June 7, 2006, https://www.youtube.com/watch?v=zWJsn_ea6_k.

6. Twerski and Henderson are much honored and well-regarded in the field of tort law, having served, most notably, as co-reporters of the American Law Institute's *Restatement of the Law (Third) Torts: Products Liability.*

7. Although Napoli overestimated by a factor of four how many claims would be filed, he may not have been wrong concerning how many responders would over time claim injury.

PART SIX

1. The $400 million figure first surfaced in a *New York Daily News* article of September 3, 2006.

2. Kenneth Feinberg is a Washington DC–based attorney who has frequently served as a court-appointed special settlement master, including in cases such as Agent Orange product liability litigation. He was appointed special master of the September 11 Victim Compensation Fund, working for thirty-three months pro bono to develop the regulations for and to administer the fund, calculating compensation and awards, and eventually distributing some $7 billion. He also administered the $20 billion BP *Deepwater Horizon* oil spill fund.

PART SEVEN

1. This was also a reference to Sir James Tyrrell (no relation), one of the evil enforcers in Shakespeare's *Richard III*.

2. See Benjamin J. Luft, *We're Not Leaving: 9/11 Responders Tell Their Stories of Courage, Sacrifice, and Renewal* (New York: Greenpoint Press, 2011).

3. In 2014 Jimmy Nolan's Law would be found unconstitutional, having applied to only one claimant. However, in 2018 Napoli, having

appealed the decision to the Second Circuit and prevailing there, had the law reinstated.

PART EIGHT

1. Lanny Davis served as special counsel to President Bill Clinton, and as an attorney has been affiliated at different times with both Patton Boggs and McDermott Will & Emery. He is a partner of the law firm of Davis, Goldberg & Galper PLCC, and a partner of the public relations firm Trident DMG.
2. Mireya Navarro, "Ground Zero Workers Reach Deal over Claims," *New York Times*, March 11, 2010. https://www.nytimes.com/2010/03/12/science/earth/12zero.html?emc=eta1.

PART TEN

1. In 2007 Garretson's firm was appointed the "neutral lien resolution administrator" in the VIOXX case's $4.85 billion settlement.

PART ELEVEN

1. Alvin K. Hellerstein, James A. Henderson Jr., and Aaron D. Twerski, "Managerial Judging: The 9/11 Responders' Tort Litigation," *Cornell Law Review* 98 (2012): 127.

EPILOGUE

1. Joanna Walters, "9/11 Health Crisis: Death Toll from Illness Nears Number Killed on Day of Attacks," *Guardian*, September 11, 2016, https://www.theguardian.com/us-news/2016/sep/11/9-11-illnesses-death-toll.
2. See Never Forget Project, "Statistics from 9/11 and 15 Years Later," n.d., http://neverforgetproject.com/statistics/.
3. See Dana Schulz, "New 9/11 Memorial Monument Honors First Responders Exposed to Ground Zero Toxins," *6sqft*, May 31, 2018, https://www.6sqft.com/new-911-memorial-monument-honors-first-responders-exposed-to-ground-zero-toxins/.